T0360775

How to Create a
Successful
Business Plan
For Entrepreneurs, Scientists,
Managers and Students

How to Create a
Successful
Business Plan

For Entrepreneurs, Scientists, Managers and Students

Dan Galai
The Hebrew University of Jerusalem, Israel

Lior Hillel
Independent Business Consultant, Switzerland

Daphna Wiener
Optimize Risk Management Ltd., Israel

World Scientific

NEW JERSEY · LONDON · SINGAPORE · BEIJING · SHANGHAI · HONG KONG · TAIPEI · CHENNAI · TOKYO

Published by

World Scientific Publishing Co. Pte. Ltd.
5 Toh Tuck Link, Singapore 596224
USA office: 27 Warren Street, Suite 401-402, Hackensack, NJ 07601
UK office: 57 Shelton Street, Covent Garden, London WC2H 9HE

Library of Congress Cataloging-in-Publication Data
Names: Galai, Dan, author. | Hillel, Lior, author. | Wiener, Daphna, author.
Title: How to create a successful business plan : for entrepreneurs, scientists,
    managers and students / Dan Galai (The Hebrew University of Jerusalem, Israel),
    Lior Hillel (Independent Business Consultant, Switzerland), Daphna Wiener
    (The Hebrew University of Jerusalem, Israel).
Description: New Jersey : World Scientific, [2016]
Identifiers: LCCN 2015047285| ISBN 9789814651288 | ISBN 9789814651516
Subjects: LCSH: Business planning.
Classification: LCC HD30.28 .G347 2016 | DDC 658.4/012--dc23
LC record available at http://lccn.loc.gov/2015047285

British Library Cataloguing-in-Publication Data
A catalogue record for this book is available from the British Library.

In-house Editor: Shreya Gopi

Typeset by Stallion Press
Email: enquiries@stallionpress.com

Printed in Singapore

Contents

Part 4: Getting the Most Out of Your Business Plan

List of Figures

List of Abbreviations and Acronyms

AMA	American Marketing Association
B2B	Business to Business
B2C	Business to Consumer
CAD	Computer Aided Design
CAGR	Compound Annual Growth Rate
CB	Chairman of the Board
CEO	Chief Executive Officer
CFO	Chief Financial Officer
CLV	Customer Lifetime Value
CMO	Chief Marketing Officer
COGS	Cost of Goods Sold
COO	Chief Operating Officer
CRM	Customer Relationship Managemen
CTO	Chief Technology Officer
EBIT	Earnings Before Interest and Taxes
EBITDA	Earnings Before Interest, Taxes, Depreciation and Amortization
EDI	Electronic Data Interchange
EPS	Earnings Per Share
ERP	Enterprise Resources Planning

ESOP	Employee Stock Option Plans
EU	European Union
EVP	Executive Vice President
FDA	United States Food and Drug Administration
FIFO	First In First Out
G&A	General and Administration
GAAP	General Accepted Accounting Principles
GDP	Gross Domestic Product
ICT	Information and Communications Technology
IFRS	International Financial Accounting Rules
IPO	Initial Public Offering
IRR	Internal Rate of Return
ISO	International Organization for Standardization
ISV	Independent Software Vendor
JOBS act	Jumpstart Our Business Startups Act
LIFO	Last In First Out
LLC	Limited Liability Company
LOI	Letter of Intent
LP	Limited Partnership
MIL	United States Military Standard
NASDAQ	National Association of Securities Dealers Automated Quotations (an American stock exchange)
NDA	Non-Disclosure Agreement
NPV	Net Present Value
OEM	Original Equipment Manufacturer
OTC	Over the Counter
P&L	Profit and Loss
POS	Point of Sale

QA	Quality Assurance
QC	Quality Control
R&D	Research and Development
RFP	Request for Proposal
ROI	Return on Investment
ROS	Return on Sales
SAAS	Software As A Service
SEC	US Securities Exchange Commission
SH	Shareholder
SOX act	Sarbanes-Oxley act
STA	Short-Term Assets
STL	Short-Term Liabilities
TüV	Technischer Überwachungsverein (English: Technical Inspection Association)
UL	Underwriters Laboratories (USA)
VAT	Value Added Taxes
VCF	Venture Capital Fund
WACC	Weighted Average Cost of Capital

Image Credits

The authors gratefully acknowledge the following internet sources for the data published by them. Most of these sources have been widely referenced and appear in many websites on the internet. We have cited the original source where possible.

1. Figure 3.3 on page 41 appeared in the article "Fastest Growing Demographic on Facebook: Women Over 55" in February 2009 with the source cited as InsideFacebook. com, which is now part of Adweek. The author is not cited at the source. See more at: http://www.adweek.com/socialtimes/fastest-growing-demographic-on-facebook-women-over-55/217037
2. Figure 3.6 on page 53 appeared in the article "The First Mobile Phone Call was Made 40 years Ago Today" from April 3, 2013 by Zachary M. Seward, published on the Quartz website. The image is credited to David Yanofsky. See more at: http://qz.com/70309/the-first-mobile-phone-call-was-made-40-years-ago-today/
3. Figure 3.9 on page 56 appeared in the article "2 Billion Consumers Worldwide to Get Smart(phones) by 2016", published on the emarketer website. The author is not cited at the source. See more at: http://www.emarketer.com/Article/2-Billion-Consumers-Worldwide-Smartphones-by-2016/1011694#sthash.Tuvt5eM9.dpuf

4. Figure 4.3 on page 93 appeared in the article "Don't buy the Galaxy S5 when it launches next month" by Zach Epstein, published on the BGR website. See more at: http://bgr.com/2014/02/12/galaxy-s5-price-details-sale/

5. Figure 4.4 on page 93 appeared in the presentation "Internet Trends" by Mary Meeker, Kleiner Perkins Caufield Byers published by KPCB on May 28, 2014. See more at: http://www.kpcb.com/internet-trends

6. Figure 4.7 on page 96 appeared in the article "The Penny Gap" by Josh Kopelman on the First Round Capital website on March 10, 2007. See more at: http://redeye.firstround.com/2007/03/the_first_penny.html

7. Figure 4.8 on page 105 appeared on the World Robotics website in 2014. See more at: http://www.worldrobotics.org/

8. Figure 4.12 on page 138 appeared at Source: PricewaterhouseCoopers/National Venture Capital Association MoneyTree™ Report, Data: Thomson Reuters. See more at: https://www.pwcmoneytree.com/

9. Figure 4.13 on page 140 appeared at Source: PricewaterhouseCoopers/National Venture Capital Association MoneyTree™ Report, Data: Thomson Reuters. See more at: https://www.pwcmoneytree.com/

10. Figure 4.14 on page 142 appeared at Source: PricewaterhouseCoopers/National Venture Capital Association MoneyTree™ Report, Data: Thomson Reuters. See more at: https://www.pwcmoneytree.com/

11. Figure 4.15 on page 145 was published by Ernst and Young in their periodic publication: Global IPO Trends, Ernst & Young.

12. Figure 4.16 on page 147 was published by Ernst and Young in their periodic publication: Global IPO Trends, Ernst & Young.

13. Figure 5.5 on page 196 appeared in a graphic presentation of the U.S. Beverage Business Results for 2014, Liquid Refreshment Beverage Market Share. See more at http://www.beverage-digest.com

Preface

Only a small fraction of entrepreneurs successfully navigate their way to a stable, profitable and viable enterprise. The majority of entrepreneurs — and their financial backers — have learned the hard way that even with a great original concept, technological ingenuity, an "assured" market and an exceptional team, the establishment and sustainment of a successful project is no sure thing. In fact, many projects possessing all of those important qualities have experienced failure shortly after their inception or within less than five years.

There are numerous causes for failure. Three major categories include:

1. **Poor market analysis**
2. **Insufficient business planning**
3. **Weak presentation**

How to Create a Successful Business Plan addresses all of these areas and helps the entrepreneur leap over these hurdles. One of the first and most critical benefits is that it addresses the business's **internal needs** by making a professional and truthful analysis of the project's status unavoidable. And when the manager reaches the stage of **external presentation** a thorough planning process will ensure a complete and comprehensive presentation well suited to the audience. The goal of this book is to help remove many of the initial obstacles standing in the way of an entrepreneurial project, providing a realistic and convincing business case and as importantly — providing a roadmap for the work at hand. This may not guarantee success but it is certain to increase its likelihood and facilitate cooperation with investors or with potential strategic partners. Inadequate planning, resulting in an unprofessional business plan, may cause irreversible damage to a project's image and may ultimately threaten its very existence. A successful experience will help the business team open doors again in the future.

Some entrepreneurs are "serial entrepreneurs", who have been through the planning process many times and have developed expertise in this area. However, many more entrepreneurs are starting their first venture, and they could be scientists, engineers, from the medical profession or from a variety of other professional backgrounds, with little or no business training. This book was written with those entrepreneurs in mind, providing the knowledge required to plan and launch their project or company and navigate the business world successfully. New project leaders within established companies, and managers planning and implementing innovations or major shifts in policy, have those same needs and can also benefit greatly from this book. We also provide a detailed methodology to guide executives responsible for attaining important business goals such as raising capital, locating marketing channels, or searching for potential joint-venture partners. Businesses who wish to raise capital or get financial aid or benefits from financial institutions and the government or non-government organizations will be prepared for these steps. In addition, the book is targeted towards sophisticated investors and service providers who would like to have a more critical view of the business plans and ventures presented to them. Because entrepreneurs and other readers come from widely varied backgrounds, many may be unfamiliar with some business terms. This book is presented in a concise and focused format with examples throughout to guide any entrepreneur through the preparation of most or all of the work behind the business plan, in-house.

This book is based on MBA-level course material and blends theoretic material with a very practical approach.

When it comes to writing a business plan, the entrepreneur faces a bewildering selection of options. There are countless experts who will provide tips, formats, structures and even automated software for business planning. But just as each entrepreneur is different, each business is different, particularly those breaking ground on new frontiers — whether in medicine, energy, IT, telecom, entertainment, consumer products or countless other areas evolving worldwide. For these entrepreneurs there is no one "cookbook" with a recipe that will do the job for them when the ingredients are so varied.

This book presents a **structured approach** for the professional preparation of the business plan. We address questions, problems and concepts to which the entrepreneur and project manager do not always pay adequate attention, but which are of fundamental importance to the business and its future partners. The emphasis is on the *dynamic process* of the preparation of a business plan — before and after the business plan document is written.

Part 1: An Introduction to the Business Plan

Chapter 1

What is a Business Plan?

1.1 Defining the Business Plan

The business plan is a crucial component in planning a new enterprise or in evaluating an existing one. It serves as an essential tool when contemplating major strategic changes or introducing new innovations in a business. Based on a comprehensive review of a business's various elements, including the technology, production, marketing and management of the proposed product or service, a good business plan presents a course of action and the forecasted financial results. Above all, a business plan should clarify the business's prime focus and targets, and propose the means for achieving them.

A successful business plan must be a concise document, generally ranging from 20 to 50 pages, which can convince the reader that the plan is realistic and feasible. The document should analyze the business's strengths and weaknesses and unique capabilities, and demonstrate convincingly that this is a viable business that can thrive over time in the designated business environment.

Initially, a business plan should be written as an **internal document** that is used as a work tool by the entrepreneurs and management in charge of the business. Once it has been revised and reworked it can serve as an **external document** to introduce the business to outsiders for creating strategic business ties, raising capital and promoting the business in numerous other ways.

The business plan's scope must be broad and it must discuss long-term goals, highlighting the **business strategy** at the core of the business. Over the course of its lifetime, a company will generate many other plans and documents, including periodic plans and reports to the management and board of directors. All of these relate to specific tasks, goals and accomplishments within a given time frame, such as on a quarterly or annual basis. Ideally they will be evaluated against the milestones determined in the business plan, and these milestones in turn will be adjusted as the company progresses and new opportunities arise. However, the business plan is often the only document that presents the company's long-term strategy along with a detailed roadmap towards its essential business goals. And that is precisely what makes a business plan unique and invaluable.

While a business plan presents a long-term view, it still requires constant revision, as the company is certain to experience many changes, internal and external, throughout its lifetime. Using the business plan as a **dynamic document** and updating it periodically will ensure that it stays relevant. Changes in the company's capabilities, operating environment, competitive environment or legal environment, as well as new opportunities that will arise, will all necessitate reassessments and revisions of the business plan. It is especially important to provide potential investors, even those who have been fully updated verbally, with an amended, up-to-date business plan. An outdated business plan can potentially harm the company by steering it off course and undermining the company's position.

The business is ultimately evaluated on a financial basis, and the bottom line will be the **economic justification** for the new enterprise. Even when an enterprise's goals are social or philanthropic rather than a return on capital invested (eg. in the case of non-governmental organizations — NGOs), investors and interested parties should be able to evaluate the business plan and compare it with other options using economic parameters. This will ensure that the valuable time and money invested are put to the best possible use.

This book is entitled *How to Create a Successful Business Plan* and it will walk you through all of the phases of planning and decision-making required for preparing the written document called "The Business Plan." The process, which this book will unravel in detail, is important in its entirety. Shortcuts taken on the way to a written business plan often result in a plan that may sound great, but which lacks a solid, well-thought-out foundation.

1.2   Who Needs a Business Plan?

The business plan is an important tool for any type of enterprise in every possible field, whether it is a bricks and mortar plant, an Internet startup or a social venture. Business plans are essential for completely new innovations as well as for well-established enterprises.

Business plans are advantageous to any business that evolves and changes, and particularly to:

1. New business entrepreneurs.
2. Entrepreneurs and managers innovating within an existing company or organization, also referred to as **Intrapreneurs.**
3. Managers who are evaluating major strategic changes within a company or organization.

To simplify the terminology, we will use the following terms in a broad sense throughout the book:

- The term "entrepreneurs" will refer to business managers planning new ventures or changes within their companies, as detailed above.
- The terms "enterprise," "firm," "business," "project" or "company" will be used to refer to the business that is being planned, whatever its field and regardless of whether it is a

completely new company or a new project within an existing company.

- The term "product" will describe the product or service that the enterprise plans to offer, whatever it may be: a medical device, a web site account, a media application (app), a social event, a cause, a service or a myriad of products and services, many of which we may not even be able to imagine today.

We provide various examples throughout the book. Many are technology based, but the same methodology applies to products which are not necessarily technologically complex.

Chapter 2

The Goals of the Business Plan Process

What is the primary objective of the business plan process? Entrepreneurs may often be under the impression that the business plan is basically a presentation tool for attracting outside investors and partners or developing marketing channels. As we stated in Chapter 1, these are certainly primary functions of a business plan, and a business plan will contribute tremendously to developing ties with investors, banks and business partners.

However, any seasoned investor or business partner will be able to identify an unrealistic or superficial business plan, and a poorly written document will hinder rather than promote potential cooperation. Therefore, the very essence of the business planning process is the gathering of information and its comprehensive analysis by the entrepreneur and the business team. This ensures that they become familiar with the product or service, the real capabilities of the enterprise, its potential customers, the market, the competitors, the economic factors and the business potential. Through the business plan process, the firm can focus on objectives that may be ambitious but are also feasible, and will be able to prepare a realistic plan to achieve these goals. At the completion of this process, the entrepreneur will have become knowledgeable enough and the business plan itself mature enough to stand up to the most meticulous scrutiny of investors and other outside parties seeking to evaluate, and hopefully justify, their participation in the business.

2.1   Internal Goals

There are five primary internal goals in the business plan process. Achieving these goals will significantly improve any entrepreneur's ability to set up and manage the enterprise and make the right decisions along the way.

These goals are:

1) **Establishing Order and Structure**

In the early days of the dot-com era, startups were renowned for being unstructured, and were characterized by young and inexperienced teams at the helm pursuing many directions simultaneously. This unconventional and flexible environment was thought to enhance creativity and lead to innovation. Venture capital was more easily accessible then. Business plans were often more about the idea and less about the manner of realizing them or about their financial and other implications. This chaotic period ended with the burst of the Internet bubble.

The business plan process that we describe here requires a structured team effort and a methodical approach. This should not curb or conflict with creativity, but rather, should channel the team's creative efforts in directions that will optimize the business potential.

In an established company, the business plan will serve as a platform for planning strategic changes, revising organizational goals, getting everyone on the same page and working together to fulfill these goals.

2) **Objectivity**

New companies often begin with an idea, a vision, optimism and a lot of enthusiasm. These are indispensable and valuable assets, especially in light of the risky and rocky road ahead for most new enterprises. On the way to success, the company will have to overcome numerous obstacles and face criticism and doubt, not to mention competitors and initial failures. Without faith and enthusiasm as a positive driving force, most companies would never make it.

However, it is important to be aware that this very enthusiasm may also compromise objectivity, which is very much needed for channeling these positive energies most effectively. An impartial view of the company's potential will ensure that the entrepreneur neither imparts an overly rosy view of the situation, nor ignores real risks which must be addressed. These risks might be internal or external:

— Internal risks include lack of resources and skills within the company.
— External risks include existing competing products and technologies, potential reactions of competitors and external economic factors.

The business plan process compels the entrepreneur to cope with the objective facts earlier, rather than later in the venture's development. In many cases, this process may lead the entrepreneurs to revise their original ideas and modify their business outlooks, with the resulting changes ranging from minor to very significant. A good hard look at the objective factors will generate a more descriptive, coherent and less biased view of the business. The resulting decisions will be more rational and resources will be better allocated. As a result, the entrepreneur will be better equipped to face future events, meet risks and seize opportunities.

3) **Team Integration**

A new enterprise's team will often include members with different professional backgrounds. The challenge is to work together on one common agenda in order to achieve shared goals, with a clear understanding of the hierarchy and breakdown of responsibilities, as well as of timetables and resource allocation. Numerous issues can arise. What is the division of responsibilities? What is the time-frame for each task? How much will go to development at the expense of other areas such as marketing, and vice-versa? The business plan will serve as an important unifying document guiding these decisions.

Even a seasoned team that has been working together for years experiences conflicting opinions and interests. A new team which has just begun collaborating has not yet established any common ground and may encounter major barriers in communicating differing visions and conflicting needs. Valuable time and resources can be saved by using a business plan to get the team to work together as quickly as possible.

A comprehensive business plan addressing all the aspects of the enterprise will reduce friction and create a stronger team that works together towards shared goals. A business plan demands a clear definition of the business's scope, with a single, unambiguous perspective. It documents the business's plans, goals and specific milestones, which are understood and accepted by all team members. The economic value and cost of each element of the business is explicit. This common set of goals will have a decisive impact on the company's long-term success. We will explain this process step-by-step in this book.

A team approach does not end with the first draft of the written plan, but must become an established and permanent working mode within the company, with team members learning from the business plan process. There must be constant ongoing communication among the different team members so that decisions are made based on the most current information, with periodic reviews and corresponding updates of the business plan. The basis for cooperation is the common goal towards which everyone is working.

4) **Identifying and Bridging Gaps**

Each member of a dynamic and multi-disciplinary team of entrepreneurs will have a specific skill set. Some members will be novices, and others acclaimed professionals in their respective fields. While some team members in a company may have outstanding skills, others will often lack skills. This shouldn't come as a surprise; even an expert scientist who has spent years in a particular area of specialization may not have acquired the skills needed to run a complex project over a long period of time. Countless new startups suffer from poor management and from an unrealistic assessment of the skills required. This may not be apparent at first, but will become more problematic as the company faces new challenges, such as investors becoming involved or the company entering new markets.

One of the benefits of the business plan process is that it will map out the tasks and skills required, and employ objective business indicators which have to stand up to the test of time. Even if you are completely new to the business world, you will be compelled to create a complete, comprehensive picture and consider all the factors affecting the venture, and not only technical or scientific ones. The business plan process will help define your plans and goals in business terms appropriate to the specific environment in which you propose to do business, and will enable you to chart a roadmap with clear milestones and indicators for measuring progress. These milestones represent tasks to be performed, time frames to be maintained and specific goals to be reached.

The written business plan will serve as a reference document making it easier to supervise the progress of the project. It will help define under what conditions it is feasible to proceed and how progress can be evaluated at various milestones along the way. It will also help prepare you for establishing partnerships with other parties in order to complete the skill set you need, whether in marketing, development, production or other areas. Eventually, you will be better prepared to meet potential investors and business partners.

5) __Intrapreneurship__

The first of the internal goals of the business plan process is establishing order and structure as a balancing force in an environment also characterized by creativity and innovation. The business plan process does not conflict with innovation at all; in fact, it enhances it by encouraging new ideas and creating a feeling of partnership and ownership among the team members.

Involving employees in the business plan process can inspire **intrapreneurship** by increasing employee motivation and strengthening identification with company goals at all levels. There are often untapped resources within the organization, and no one knows more about each individual task than the worker performing it. Often, that very employee may have ideas on improving the product or service or making the process more efficient. In addition, managers and other workers working in concert increase everyone's sense of involvement across the board and strengthen identification with company goals at all levels. This process can be an exceptional catalyst for generating new ideas, enhancing processes or identifying new markets.

2.2   External Goals

Few and far between are the entrepreneurs with the resources to start up a company and fulfill its objectives without any external resources. Even businesses that are successful locally will usually need to partner with investors, distributors, manufacturers, consultants or others in order to branch out successfully at a wider level. The external goals that are achieved through the business plan process may be critical to ensuring the company's success.

A good part of the business plan process entails being as well-prepared as possible for potential obstacles along the way. The business plan should describe in a convincing and clear manner what lies on the road ahead, and how the business will confront both opportunities and risks. In this sense, the business plan will serve as a showcase for the company towards potential new partners. By keeping the business plan up-to-date, its content will remain as relevant and as accurate as possible.

First impressions are important. Often, because of time or geographic constraints, or other reasons, a new venture is first introduced to potential investors through its business plan, or the plan's executive summary. The business plan is frequently sent out to selected potential investors or partners at the very initial stages of introducing the business, before these parties can meet the entrepreneurs themselves, visit the lab or factory, or see a prototype. Clearly, the business plan will have a strong impact on how potential investors or partners react to the project. Venture capitalists are often sifting through piles of business plans, seeking the real winners. A poorly researched or presented business plan can result in a dead end, even if the project itself is excellent. On the other hand, a great business plan can open doors and improve the chances that a venture can obtain the support it needs.

If you have made it through the door, successfully establishing a relationship with an angel investor, venture capital fund, distributor or another third party, you can then use the business plan to determine the terms and price of a potential deal and ensure that this new contract, which creates an interconnected relationship between the parties, has a strong foundation and is based upon agreed goals.

There are three main external objectives, or goals involving parties outside of the new venture:

1. Raising Money through Capital Investment or Debt

A new venture may begin on a limited budget, involving just a few entrepreneurs working on their own time and with their own funds. But to get a good idea off the ground, you will eventually need to utilize expensive resources, including employees, offices, a lab, research, consultants, production facilities, marketing, travel — and the list goes on. The need to raise money is almost always inevitable, whether for the primary or ongoing financing of the new venture's needs, or as a temporary bridge on the path to financial independence. Even those few entrepreneurs lucky enough to be financially capable of funding the new venture on their own may not wish to do so. Raising capital is also a means of sharing the risk, which may be a desirable strategy, particularly with new ventures. When financing is required, there are two possibilities: raising capital in return for a share of the new venture, or raising debt. We describe the different options in detail in Section 4.5.

Many of us have become familiar with venture capital funds (VCFs) since the 1980s, when they enjoyed a phenomenal growth. However, VCFs actually date back to just after World War II. Other investment channels, such as institutional investors, stock exchanges and loan and credit institutions date back centuries. The various financial tools for evaluating investments or credit risk are well-established, and a business plan has long been one of the basic requirements of potential investors and lending institutions. The many government or other institutional incentive programs will also invariably have a business plan listed among the prerequisites for evaluation and consideration.

Not all potential investors or debt holders will examine the business plan in the same manner. A bank, for example, may require that a business plan ensures loan repayment, and are less interested in the business beyond that. On the other hand, other potential partners may be less concerned with different aspects of the business, depending on their particular areas of expertise. A potential marketing partner, for example, may be more focused on the characteristics of the product itself, and less on the marketing plan, as they themselves are able to provide the necessary marketing expertise. A VCF looking to participate actively in the management of the new venture may overlook certain planning flaws which can be overcome by new joint management, if the business plan is otherwise sound and there is a reliable team to work with.

2. Developing Marketing Channels

There are many great products that never made it in the market, while inferior products with similar functions were very successful. Your venture not only has to provide a great product or service, it also has to stand out over the course of time in a potentially brutally competitive market. This is true for new ventures as well as for existing businesses or products aspiring to improve their market penetration. So together with the financing solutions, you will need to seek and find the most effective marketing solutions, often by partnering with marketing channels and distributors that already enjoy a position in the target marketplace.

Because these market operators will also incur a certain share of the risk, they will need assurances that your product will enhance their product selection, market position and bottom line and will be worth risking their time, effort and reputation. They, too, will usually require a business plan, particularly when a significant investment in resources is required to get the product established in the market.

Having marketing channels already in place for your new product even before the final development is complete is a great advantage, and will increase the prospects of successful market penetration. There are two primary benefits. First, you will have detailed information on the market environment and existing competing products which will help you focus on the differentiating features that will make your product stand out. Second, the market operators will have sufficient time to prepare for the marketing of your new product.

A marketing partnership is also invaluable when your new product or service requires an aggressive marketing effort to educate a conservative market or to reach a widespread market within a short period of time. In such cases, the marketing section of the business plan will describe the marketing strategy, but the actual detailed work plan should be developed with your new partner, who brings the necessary expertise. It will be the sections on financial justification and technology which will give your marketing partner the assurances needed before investing time, effort and often financial resources in your product.

The business plan is the most significant tool in establishing a working relationship with potential marketing partners based on clear terms and expectations. Successfully convincing a high quality marketing partner will prove a significant first step in inspiring them to pitch your product to potential customers enthusiastically and effectively.

3. Establishing a Joint Venture

The term "joint venture" refers to the partnership of two or more parties with common interests in a business venture. Joint ventures often arise out of the specific interest of one party to work on an ad-hoc basis with other parties who have complementary skills that they might be otherwise lacking. In such a case, there may be a division of tasks based on each partner's expertise. For example, joint ventures could be formed for the purpose of research and development, production or marketing.

The partners share in the risk and costs, as well as in the rewards, based on the terms of the joint venture contract. The joint venture may be a jointly-held business entity, or include a pre-agreed division of benefits.

The business plan for a joint venture will often be very focused and specific, with a strong factual foundation, as each party will bring significant expertise to the process. The plan will serve as a tool for developing cooperation and for reaching a mutual understanding.

2.3 When to Prepare the Business Plan

We described the internal goals in Section 2.1, and demonstrated how, from the outset, the business plan process will significantly improve the prospects of the new venture. Initially, the business plan will create a framework for the new venture and identify different areas where more information is needed, or which require more careful planning. By preparing the business plan, you will have a clearer idea of when to approach outside parties, such as investors or potential partners. The decision of when to prepare the business plan will depend on several considerations:

- Some entrepreneurs will begin writing the business plan at the very inception of their new venture, in conjunction with the information gathering and strategic planning processes. Preparing the business plan at an early stage can prove very helpful in detecting incomplete areas which need more work.
- Other entrepreneurs will write the business plan only once they are comfortable with the maturity of their ideas and plans.

The earlier you begin, the more likely you are to make revisions and corrections. Over time, the environment will change, internally and externally, and all new developments and knowledge must be incorporated into the business plan. Nonetheless, there are many advantages to beginning to think in terms of a business plan from the start. Whenever you choose to begin, the business plan will only be complete after all of the necessary elements have been researched and planned.

After finalizing the business plan, be prepared to revise it periodically. It needs to be current at all times. There is nothing worse than sending an out-of-date business plan to investors. They will be alarmed if they suspect that you have either made no progress in your venture, have failed to keep up with current market information or that you have just not bothered to submit an up-to-date document. Revisions should be made from time to time, whether to reflect changes in the competitive landscape, to record your progress, to update the financial results or for all of the above reasons and more. Fortunately, with desktop publishing tools available, preparing a quarterly or semi-annual update is technically not that difficult, and will be well worthwhile, as it will ensure that you keep abreast of all developments inside and outside your business. Be sure to revise and update your business plan not only periodically, but also in the case of significant events, good or bad, which cannot and should not be ignored.

Sometimes the timing of writing or revising the business plan is determined by an external event, such as a particular trade show, a roadshow or an upcoming negotiation. Don't wait till the last moment. Plan ahead and be prepared.

Part 2: Planning the Business

Chapter 3

Gathering Information and Analyzing the Business Environment

The stage of gathering information and analyzing the business environment will give you the initial answers to the following questions:

- What is the scope of your business? In what areas is your business active?
- Who are your potential customers? How can you attract them (or more of them)?
- Is there a need for your proposed product or service, and if so, how pressing is that need?
- What is the total market potential for your product or service?
- What is the financial potential for your business?
- What different submarkets or segments can you identify?
- How competitive is your market, and how will your product or service be positioned to contend with competitors?
- How does the technology of your product or service compare to the existing technology and to future innovations that your competitors might introduce?
- What is the financial environment to be considered?
- What is the legal and/or patent environment to be considered?
- What is the environmental impact of your business?
- What is the social contribution of your business?

On the basis of the answers to these questions, you will have a better understanding of the opportunities and risks, and be able to make the critical Go or No-Go decision.

Because the initial stage of information gathering is costly, in terms of both time and money, some entrepreneurs may be deterred from gathering information altogether or from amassing sufficient information. However, opting to proceed with this stage of the preparation and executing it well actually saves more costly resources in the long run. If you decide to go ahead with your project, the knowledge you gained during the initial information gathering stage will help you plan, find the right partners and employees, raise funds, avoid obstacles, generally run a more efficient business or project, and, ultimately, increase your probability of success. As a result, your chances for long-term viability and profitability will increase. Even if you decide to abandon the idea and perhaps pursue some other goal, arriving at this decision at an early stage will save time and money and help you avoid a losing proposition. The information gathering stage will also serve as an important learning experience for your future as an entrepreneur.

3.1 Defining the Business Scope

The very first and most critical step to take is to carefully define the scope of your business, meaning that area in which most of your efforts will be focused. This determination, which will identify the marketing, technological, economic, social, geographic and legal environments in which you will be active, will have substantial implications for all of your ensuing decisions. Defining your business scope will enable you to establish precisely what your venture does, in what areas, and for which customers. These determinations represent the essence of your business, and will subsequently guide you in gathering information, analyzing data and planning further steps.

Although defining your scope of business may seem like a relatively straightforward task, it may prove to be rather complex and should be well thought out. The following examples demonstrate how dramatically the definitions of a venture's business scope may differ, even within the same area of business:

- "IT Development" is broader in scope than "Software Development for Education," which can be narrowed even further to "Educational Software for Teaching Language to Preschoolers" or to "Educational Software for Teaching Language to Preschoolers on Mobile Platforms."
- "Garment Manufacturer" can be narrowed down by the type of couture, the quality of fabrics used, the segment of the market targeted, the geographical target markets, whether local or international, the marketing channels to be used, etc.
- The scope of a company specializing in hybrid seed varieties could become:

  o A research and development (R&D) company selling its knowledge to manufacturers.
  o A hybrid seed manufacturer selling seeds.
  o An agricultural company selling produce grown from hybrid seeds.

- A company with expertise in the field of wind energy could become a consultant in sustainable energy, a wind turbine developer, a producer of wind turbines or an electricity generator selling its output to a utility company.
- The scope of a telecommunications company could be the "development, production and sales of telecommunications

> *Wide scope or narrow?*
>
> The extent of your business scope should be carefully considered. A wide scope may lead to a lack of focus at the planning stage and later on. A narrow scope may prevent pursuit of desirable areas of development, limiting the business' potential and thus increasing the risks for your venture.

equipment" or "telecommunications infrastructure project analysis and management" or the "implementation, operations and servicing of telecommunication services," among other options.

- An Internet service provider (ISP) could provide Internet access only, or could expand its scope to include related services such as homepage design and content editing, e-commerce solutions, cloud storage, etc.

In each of the examples above, the selection of one scope rather than another demands a different strategic approach, from the information gathering stage through the planning and execution stages.

As you amass more knowledge and experience over time, the scope of your business will naturally undergo changes, much like every other aspect of the business strategy and plan. Don't be discouraged if this is the case. The goal is not to adhere rigidly to the initially defined scope; rather, it is to undertake a continual and dynamic process that will lead you in the direction offering the best prospects and that will eventually steer the business towards achieving its maximal potential.

Amazon is a well-known example of a company which has redefined its business scope many times. Since its inception in 1994, Amazon has evolved from an Internet-based store specializing in selling books, to a comprehensive market place offering items as varied as toys, home gardening tools, digital products and art, to name but a few. Further advances included providing a B2B platform for Internet marketing to other businesses and developing additional products, such as the Kindle reader and cloud storage, and services, such as Amazon Publishing and Fulfillment. This process took several years and was heavily influenced by technological availability and changes in the market and competitive environment.

3.2   The Need for the Product or Service

Once the scope of the business has been defined, you will need to begin examining the business environment. The first essential step is determining whether there is a compelling need for your product or service. It is the entrepreneur's task to establish this, not only in order to be able to interest others in the business, but, first and foremost, in order to reassure the entrepreneur himself of the validity and viability of the business idea. Proving the need for your product or service is particularly important when the product or service is innovative, or when you are trying to interest investors and partners who are not familiar with the market environment in which you plan to operate.

In some cases, there is a need or vacuum in a sector which generates an environment seeking a solution. The solution may be a completely new category of products or an improvement of existing products and processes. Shortages of raw materials, cost efficiency and safety are all examples of concerns which drive innovative solutions. For example:

- The health industry's needs are endless. Enormous sums of money are invested by governments, research centers and businesses in seeking medical treatments for a host of diseases, including cancer, diabetes and many others. Consumers spend generously on healthy lifestyles (health foods, fitness clubs, etc.) as well as on products and techniques for weight loss, pain management, memory improvement and solutions for insomnia.
- Agriculture's vulnerability to climate changes and water supply, together with the growing global population, increasing urbanization and the movement of populations from rural areas to the cities, creates a perpetual need for improvements in crops and yields. This drives innovation in areas such as irrigation, fertilization and harvesting methods.

- Concerns for the global environment, together with the search for alternative renewable sources of energy, have led to intense research efforts and technological developments worldwide. Many governments have developed special incentive packages for both developers and consumers, with the goal of reducing dependence on fossil fuels and transitioning to renewable energy sources.
- Computing and media products such as computers, tablets and smartphones are continually being reinvented. Each generation of products creates new possibilities and new ways of working in areas such as security, content sharing, content recognition and endless other applications.
- In the automobile and aircraft industries, composite plastic materials have long been replacing traditional metal and other parts in order to lower costs and to strengthen vehicles while making them lighter and more fuel efficient. On-board computers, advanced sensors, telecommunications systems and other advanced systems for enhancing safety, performance and comfort are changing the automobile experience altogether.
- Varied and shifting fashion and beauty norms create a demand for products for weight loss, hair loss prevention or unwanted hair removal, among others. This gives rise to the development of numerous new methods and products.
- The food industry is also constantly changing. A notable trend is the introduction of healthier products, with lower fat content, fewer calories and/or fresher and improved quality of components.

No industry is immune to innovation and renewal. Even very traditional industries, which, because of their philosophy or way of life, maintain old methods or products, may need to adopt some innovations, even behind the scenes, such as in management methods, quality control or in their approach to the environment.

Merely identifying a compelling need for your product or service is only part of the justification for your business. You must also quantify that need and calculate how much money your potential customers will be willing to pay. This process will be explained in Sections 3.3 and 4.2 of this book.

In the examples that we provided above, the innovation seeks to solve existing compelling needs. However, in other cases, it is not the need which drives the solution, but rather the solution or new technology which generates the demand. If the solution is attractive enough, or even "revolutionary," it can create an entirely new, previously unimagined market.

- Thanks to the astounding advances in the semiconductor industry over the past 40 years, computer chips have become integrated into an immense array of smart products, from highly sophisticated complex systems to everyday, inexpensive consumer products. Products are being further enhanced with telecommunications and Internet connectivity, creating the new "Internet of things (IoT)" in which objects transfer data over a network without requiring human interaction.
- Many technologies originally developed for the military or aerospace industries have acquired civilian applications. These include developments in nuclear power, telecommunications (notably Wi-Fi), encryption devices and algorithms, security protocols, digital photography, GPS navigation systems and even plastic surgery.
- Research in DNA science has led to breakthroughs in medicine, forensics and other areas.
- Nanotechnologies, originally developed in university labs, are being integrated into new products such as sunscreen, cosmetics, food packaging and disinfectants and are being adapted for use in water desalination and disease prevention.

When you want to apply a technological solution in a new product, it is all the more important to ascertain that there will be a market for this product, and that the application of the technology for the market is feasible. The following questions must be answered:

- Does your product solve a problem for a significant number of potential customers?
  - o What kind of problem does it solve?
  - o Would your potential customers agree that this is a pressing problem? How eager are they for a solution?
  - o Is there a price for not solving this problem?
  - o Will your potential customers understand how you product solves their problem? Will they accept your solution?
  - o If your product does not clearly solve an existing problem, what is the justification for your product?

- What other characteristics affect the demand in the market?
  - o What competing or substitute solutions to your product are currently in the market?
  - o Are you offering improved effectiveness or efficiency? Whether at the manufacturing stage or at the end user level, there is always a demand for improved functionality, savings in time, energy or other valuable resources and for improvements in safety, comfort and convenience. Consider whether the added value is significant enough to create a substantial demand. For example, microwave ovens have become standard kitchen equipment because of the convenience they offer. Smartphones have replaced earlier generation mobile phones because of their increased functionality, ease of use and other benefits. Computer Aided Design (CAD) software has completely transformed engineering and planning, much as financial software has replaced long handwritten ledgers.
  - o Is the demand a result of a social trend? An ever-growing interest in healthy living has driven the market for health clubs, gyms, health food and wearable "digital

lifestyle monitors". Similarly, growing environmental concern has created a demand for green products and technologies.
  o Is there a change in legislation or regulations which has created a need for new products and services? Regulations and standards in the areas of safety, health, environment among others have been responsible for the standardization of many products and technologies, including safety systems in cars, disposable medical supplies and recycling technologies. As a result, many materials and methods have become non-compliant with the latest standards, and have been replaced. The issue of legislation or regulation is a dynamic one. Numerous service providers specialize in ensuring their customers' compliance with regulations in a variety of areas. This service can be costly, but being found non-compliant may be even more expensive.

• Who is the customer?
  o Is your customer the end user? The distributer? Or someone else? Make sure you understand the identity of your planned customer.
  o Who makes the decision in your customer's organization? Is it a manager, or a buyer, the accounting department or perhaps several different people within the organisation? If your customer is a household, will the decision be made by a parent, an adolescent or a younger child?

• How evident is the need for your product or service?
  o Are your customers already aware that there is a problem to be resolved, or is the problem going unnoticed? Will the need be created by advertising and PR?
  o How aware are your competitors of this problem?

If the need for your product or service is pressing, it will certainly be much easier to elicit interest from your potential customers. However, it will also attract competitors seeking to offer their own solutions to this problem or need.

The graph in Figure 3.1, "Perceptual Mapping," utilizes a helpful methodology for analyzing different aspects of existing needs and products. This type of graph is also often called a positioning map, with the x-axis representing the first parameter and the y-axis representing the second. The selected parameters can be as narrow or broad as you choose. For example, if evaluating a food product, the x-axis might illustrate the product's sweetness and the y-axis could display its caloric content. In this hypothetical case, products low in calories and not sweet would appear in the lower left quadrant, products low in calories but sweet would appear in the lower right quadrant, and so forth. By mapping different existing products along this graph, it will be easy to identify

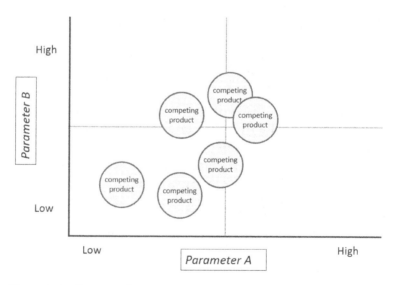

Figure 3.1: Perceptual Mapping

In Figure 3.1 above, the competing products are mapped based on the selected parameters. The spaces in which there are currently no competing products are bare areas.

which market areas have a greater density and variety of products competing with each other, and which areas are bare, with few or no products sharing the examined characteristics at a particular point in time. Opportunities may lay in the bare areas, but beware! Sometimes there are no products because there are no buyers. Research on the history of products which have been introduced in this market area will be helpful here. Find out if there were previous attempts to introduce a product into this area which failed.

If, ultimately, you are successful in introducing a product or service into a bare area, you will have developed a new market niche with few or no competitors. How long you can hold on to this niche depends on how unique your product or service is, how much time and resources a competitor would need to challenge your product or service, and other factors.

This type of graph is usually confined to two dimensions only, and many such graphs may be required in order to examine more than two parameters. When researching a food product, you might want to also consider price in relation to quality, or other considerations. A third dimension may be added to the two dimensional graph by using different colors, for example. In order to ensure that your graph reliably reflects market realities, conduct a thorough study of the market competition before its preparation.

The history of motorcycles presents an example of the potential use of the "perceptual mapping" graph. Until the 1950s, motorcycles in the United States had very powerful engines and were considered suitable mainly for stereotypical recreational motorcycle bikers rather than for mainstream working and family men, and they were completely off limits for most women. Many people could not imagine themselves using a motorcycle for day to day activity. Not only did they not need such powerful engines, but they also felt that these bikes had a negative social connotation. However, in the mid-1950s, Honda first introduced more refined, less macho models with smaller engines. These new motorcycles, which were strikingly different from previous bikes, created an instant demand exceeding all expectations. Figure 3.2 shows how Honda successfully filled a bare area which had not previously been targeted by competitors. Since then, other bare areas in the motorcycle sector have been filled, and today, motorcycles are available in all shapes and sizes to fit a wide range of needs and tastes.

Identifying a market need is very helpful, but scores of products and services have achieved success without any sort of objective need ever having been established. This is especially true of novel products, particularly different gimmicks or very trendy items, from the hula hoop to the Rubik's cube, Bratz dolls, saggy pants, Crocs shoes and countless other different items which became unbelievably popular in a way that many would argue was virtually impossible to predict.

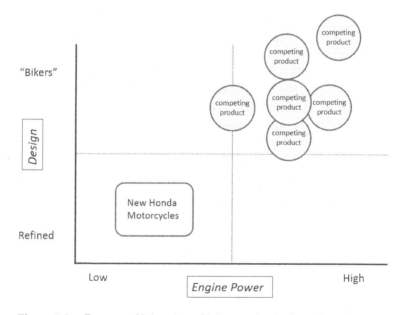

Figure 3.2:   Perceptual Mapping of Motorcycles in the 1950s

In Figure 3.2 above, Honda successfully introduced a new motorcycle model in a bare area on the perceptual map, creating a new market.

Building a business case for a product or service for which there is no established need is possible by comparing it to an analogous product or services. Many such products were introduced to consumer markets successfully through effective educational campaigns about the benefits of the new product or service, and/or by launching an outstanding marketing campaign. In many cases where there is no established market need, demo products, test markets and positive focus groups responses can prove very helpful.

3.3 The Market Potential

The market potential, whether current or in the future, is one of the most important factors influencing the success of your product or service. A deep understanding of the market potential is vital to the business in setting its objectives and priorities. Generally, a new business, or even an established one, cannot serve all potential markets simultaneously and priorities will have to be established.

> **Market potential** is defined as the estimated maximum sales income for all companies from the sale of a particular product during a given time period. This amount is measured in units sold and in revenue.

Initially, the market potential should be analyzed objectively, without considering how your business activities could influence the market. Following your initial analysis, you should determine how different strategies available to you could affect overall market potential as well as your share of the market.

There are three stages in the evaluation of market potential:

1. Market segmentation: Dividing the potential market into different subsets of consumers using specific criteria.
2. Understanding the characteristics of each market segment as well as the demand in each segment, both in terms of units and financial potential.

3. Estimating the market potential over a given time. The total market potential is the sum of the market demand of all the market segments.
The three stages are elaborated below:

1. Market Segmentation

Market segmentation identifies distinct groups of potential buyers within the market. Generally, three criteria can be used to identify different market segments:

- The segment's common needs.
- Specific segment characteristics.
- Expectations of how the segment will react, for example, to a marketing campaign.

The criteria used to segment the market will often be adjusted in response to changes over the lifespan of a product or service or to changes in the market itself. If a new version or model of a product or service is introduced, there may be a need to reevaluate the segmentation.

The market for medical diagnostic products can serve as an example for reviewing segmentation criteria. Typical criteria will include:

- The type of tests to be conducted with the proposed kit or machine.
- The volume of testing required, which can differ dramatically depending on the location. A small clinic will probably have a much smaller volume then a large hospital, for example.
- The professional level of the end users. For example, they may be doctors, nurses, professional lab technicians, nonprofessional assistants or the patients themselves engaged in home use.
- The conditions of the work environment. For example, sterility will vary widely in different venues, from sterile operating theaters to household use or field conditions.

- The regulatory environment.
- The level of standards and requirements.

Over time, the market segments will change. Some markets will shrink or disappear, as in the case of treatment of diseases which have become rare, such as polio or tuberculosis. Others will grow and eventually include the majority of the population. For example, testing for various medical indicators, such as blood sugar, blood pressure, ovulation and pregnancy were once performed only by medical professionals, but home testing products are now in widespread use.

Choosing the right segmentation method and understanding the various market segments are both important, as each segment's preferences and requirements will be different. Understanding these differences is invaluable in developing the product or service and marketing it.

Further discussion of market segmentation can be found in Section 3.4.

2. Understanding the Demand of Each Market Segment, both in terms of Units and Financial Potential

Market demand is tested over time and there are different stages in a product's life cycle, as we will describe in detail in Section 3.6.

Important stages include:

- Increase in demand: the product is in the growth stage
- Stable demand over time: the product is in the maturity stage
- A decrease in demand: the product is nearing the end of its life cycle
- Unstable demand: an unclear trend
- Changes in demand due to new competitors entering the market or due to competing or substitute products becoming more mature

- Seasonal changes in demand, due to weather and holidays. Major events such as elections, sports events or cultural events.
- Changes in demand due to economic factors, such as inflation, unemployment, general market sentiment or other indicators
- Changes in demand due to social trends
- Changes due to regulation (e.g., environmental regulations, trade barriers, etc.)

Understanding the demand is critical for two important reasons:

- First, demand will certainly be one of the deciding factors in choosing whether or not to proceed with a project. A small or shrinking market will not appeal to large companies that look for substantial and growing markets, but may still prove an opportunity for small companies.
- Second, trends in demand will be a major consideration in selecting the business strategy and in choosing an action plan. For example, a company introducing a product or service with a seasonal market trend, such as holiday gifts or swimwear, will need to prepare accordingly. This can entail preparing large storage facilities for stock, creating a suitable marketing campaign and organizing sufficient working capital to carry the business until the sales peak. Or, if the market is characterized by disloyal customers, the strategy might focus on customer retention, as we frequently see with airlines and telephone, cellular phone, cable and Internet providers.

3. Estimate the Market Potential Over a Given Time Period. The Total Market Potential Is the Sum of the Market Demand in All the Market Segments

To determine the market potential, a degree of forecasting is required. Forecasting the market potential as part of the company's sales outlook will be described in Chapter 5. Figure 5.3 is an example of a table of the total market potential.

Estimating the potential of each market segment will allow your company to prioritize and identify which market segments to serve initially, which ones to expand to at a later stage, and which market segments not to serve at all.

3.4   Customer Characteristics

Once you have a deeper understanding of the entire market, it will be time to analyze the sections of the market most relevant to your new product or service. A very strong familiarity with customer characteristics is essential for all areas of industry, products and services, especially if you are trying to succeed in a new market. Comprehensive market research and familiarity with your customers are critical factors when planning a successful marketing strategy.

Customer profiles must be analyzed separately in each targeted market segment. The most pressing questions include:

- What are the buying patterns of your potential customers?
  - o Is this a one-time purchase or will the purchase be recurrent? If the purchase pattern is repetitive, how often is a purchase likely to be made? Examples of purchases repeated periodically include various food items, cosmetics or recreational activities. The purchase of a new car is far less frequent, and a new home may be purchased once or twice in a lifetime, if at all.
  - o What is the quantity sold per sale? There is a big difference between sales to OEM's (Original Equipment Manufacturers), that can potentially buy large quantities of your product, or to distributors who also make large-scale purchases, and sales directly to end users. End users can be differentiated as institutional customers, such as schools, hospitals, etc., serving large numbers of people, or smaller end users, such as small businesses and households.

o Is there strong brand loyalty in this market? Brand loyalty will determine how open potential customers are to trying new brands and ultimately changing brands. Brand loyalty can be divided into four common categories:

- Buyers who stay loyal to one brand and are not open to changing it.
- Buyers with split loyalty, who choose from two or three brands on a regular basis, and stick to those select brands only.
- Buyers who regularly shift loyalty from one brand to another, depending on price, delivery time or other considerations.
- Disloyal buyers who are completely indifferent to brands. While it may be easier to induce such buyers to try your brand, they are less likely to remain loyal to it.

Strong brands include Coca Cola, with a fixed base of customers, many of whom would not consider changing brands. In fact, some real die-hard customers object to any changes at all, whether in the Coca Cola recipe or in the packaging. Another brand very well-known for a high level of customer loyalty is Apple.

o How open is the market to innovation?
Answering this question has proven to be absolutely crucial when introducing new products or services. When it comes to technological innovation, a young techie market often actively seeks and quickly adopts new innovations, but the majority of the market might be more reluctant to follow. In other markets, hard core loyal customers may resist change of any kind. Consider the two companies we mentioned in the previous paragraph, Apple and Coca Cola. Both have a strong base of extremely loyal customers, many of whom will not consider changing brands. However, while many Apple lovers eagerly await the very latest technological

advances from Apple, many Coca Cola customers oppose any change at all in their product.

o What opinion leaders and other influences exist in the market? Opinion leaders and endorsements have been smoothing the way into markets (and sometimes out of them) for decades:

- Top athletes, actors and other celebrities are in demand to promote a large variety of products. Michael Jordan, for example, has endorsed products ranging from Nike footwear and apparel through the Chevy Blazer and Hanes underwear. Other popular celebrity endorsements have been made by Tiger Woods, Leonardo DiCaprio and Nicole Kidman, to mention just a few.

- Clothing, jewelry and accessories are regularly gifted to movie stars and celebrities in the hope that their being seen with them will promote the product.

- Each field has its renowned critics and writers who review products in professional or popular publications. Their ratings can strongly influence consumers. A Zagat or Michelin review in the restaurant industry has a major impact on the restaurant's prospects, pricing and potential customers. Many consumers rely on leading reviewers for advice on software, computers, smartphones and other items. These reviews are often easily available on YouTube or on social media. Sometimes, consumers rely on peer reviews for advice, and customer ratings on sites such as Amazon.com, TripAdvisor, Airbnb and eBay can have a significant impact on potential orders.

- A reliable customer base that can provide references is invaluable when promoting products. An Enterprise Resources Planning system (ERP) used by leading corporations is more likely to be adopted by new customers who are inclined to rely on the research and product selection processes of their successful peers. With innovative products, it is vital to quickly gain the endorsement of an influential customer who can influence the rest of the segment to follow, as many customers do not want to be the first adopters, but prefer to wait to be sure that the bugs have been fixed on someone else's time.

- Having medical products approved and endorsed, and, optimally, used by influential research labs and medical centers will establish the brand as a reliable and tested one.

o Are there dominant homogenous segments in the market? Important population segments include gender, income level and life stage. For example, the needs of retired senior citizens are very different from the needs of other segments such as college students, young professionals or blue collar workers. These needs also vary from one geographic location to another. Another homogenous segment is a generational cohort, or a group of individuals bound together by having shared the experience of common historical events. Examples include:

- The Depression cohort
- The World War II cohort
- The post-war cohort
- The baby-boomer cohort, which is further sub-segmented into the leading edge and the trailing edge
- Generation X
- Generation Y

Each of these cohorts have different desires, needs and tastes, which must be understood to launch a successful marketing campaign targeted specifically at them. Marketing strategies may differ widely based on the characteristics of each segment. Segments include not only individuals, but also institutions and companies, such as high tech companies, various industry sectors, medical institutions, the financial sector, etc.

o What are the customers' product usage patterns?

Product usage may vary greatly from one customer to another. For example, in 2009 the statistics on Facebook users showed a great difference in the usage of 18 to 25 year olds and that of users over age 65 (Figure 3.3). Since then, the usage of older generations increased significantly.

Product usage patterns provide very valuable information for planning your marketing budget and campaign. Usage patterns will differ not only according to age group, but also according to other characteristics, including institutional usage (corporations, the public sector, etc.) and personal usage. Facebook, for example, is more widely used by individuals for personal communications, whereas other social networks, such as LinkedIn, are more typically used by individuals for business use.

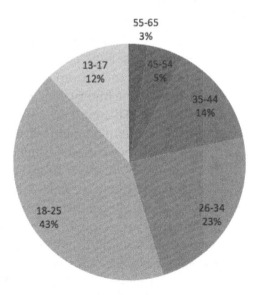

Figure 3.3:   US Facebook Users by Age Group in 2009

Source: *InsideFacebook.com*

o What are the customers' sensitivities?
Particular user sensitivities can be central factors in a consumer's decision-making process, and one brand might be selected over others for a variety of reasons. Some of the most common user sensitivities include:

- Price sensitivity
- Sensitivity to quality and reliability
- Sensitivity to design and appearance
- Sensitivity to brand reputation: preference for an established brand over a new one, or for a brand with a younger image over one with a more mature image
- Timing requirements, e.g., the need for specific delivery times or quick service
- Service and post-sales support demands
- Sensitivity to ecological parameters. This area of sensitivity has grown significantly over recent years, with many consumers preferring a "greener" product and environmental impact becoming an important priority. This is reflected in greener packaging and in the rise in sales of hybrid and electric cars, decomposable products and recycled products.
- Sensitivity to safety. This is a common sensitivity with many products, from baby products to automobiles, heavy machinery and construction. Safety is often promoted by regulators and legislators, through the enforcement of demanding standards and norms, regarding the product, its usage, its components and raw materials. Many certifications provide indicators of safety in different market sectors.
- Religious, patriotic or other more personal emotional sensitivities. For example, a consumer decision to buy or not to buy might be made in the context of supporting a particular cause or a local industry.
- Sensitivity to market opinion and the choices made by fellow consumers. This can be complex and express

itself in different ways. For example, with most new technological innovations, the majority of users will wait to see how it works for other users before trying it out themselves. Yet in other cases, particularly when the manufacturer has a proven track record and the product has a certain "buzz" to it, customers are driven to be among the first owners of a new innovation. Another example is a children's fad, which works on a must-have basis; if a few classroom opinion leaders have one, the rest of the children will want one too.

o What are the customers' demographic characteristics? The importance of using demographic data in marketing a product targeted for the general public has been proven in marketing research countless times. Some of the parameters are similar to those mentioned above in the section on homogenous segments. Among the main demographic factors are:

- Income level
- Age
- Sex
- Country of origin
- Ethnic background
- Current location or address
- Size of household
- Educational background
- Cultural background
- Recreational preferences
- Specific health needs

o What sort of decision-making process takes place before the purchase?

- Is the purchasing decision made by one individual, or are there more people involved in the process?
- Is the decision-making process structured in a formal and rigid manner, as in the case of government tenders, or is there a more flexible dynamic involved?

- Is the end user also the decision maker?
- Is the end user the individual who pays for the product or service?

For example, in the broad area of children's products, it is important to differentiate between the end user and the decision maker, who may or may not be the child, and to understand the dynamic over the purchasing decision which might take place between the child and the caretaker.

In many corporations, the decision-making process will involve many levels, from the engineers who prepared the specifications, through the executive, who may or may not have approved all of the specifications and will typically also have a limited budget, to the buyer who issues the order. In a sales effort targeted at an institutional customer, it is essential to identify and understand these different levels. A good sales team will not only strive to move beyond corporate buyers and make sure that the end users are familiar with their products, but will also pitch their product at the executive level whenever possible.

o Where are the customers located? Are they concentrated in one area, or dispersed over a large geographic area?

The importance of understanding where your customers are located is clear: many parameters change significantly in different geographic locations, including:

- Tastes and culture
- The local economy (influencing buying power)
- Distribution and advertising channels
- Safety and security
- Logistics
- Government regulation
- The tax environment
- Nature and climate

If shipping is a large component in your product's cost structure, you may need to consider where you locate your plant, or whether you can target customers beyond a certain radius. Climate is a major consideration with many products, such as solar-based systems, which require a minimal amount of sun and are most in demand in sunnier climates.

o What marketing channels are relevant for each group of consumers?

Different marketing channels include:

- Direct sales
- Manufacturer's representatives
- Distributors and resellers including:
  - Retailers — selling to end users
  - Wholesalers — selling to smaller retailers
- E-Commerce
- Telemarketing
- Sales through consumer groups
- Institutional sales
- Catalogue; Mail orders
- Door-to-Door sales
- Peer-to-Peer sales (such as on eBay, Airbnb and other platforms)

The list of ways to characterize customers is endless. No method of describing and characterizing different segments of the market is wrong, so long as it is relevant and helpful in promoting your understanding of the market.

E-commerce has presented an important challenge in customer characterization. It still has immense untapped potential, particularly in large segments which are not yet a part of this market. Many tools are available which allow precise segmentation by user group, interests, as well as localization, and are helpful in creating new challenges and opening up new opportunities for your product or service.

3.5   The Competitive Environment

One of the most important elements in the analysis of any target market is having a sound understanding of your competitors. Most markets around the world are highly competitive, and companies enjoying a long lasting dominating position or monopoly are the exception rather than the rule. In some countries, providers of electricity and other utilities enjoy a monopoly status, and some companies benefit from long-term government contracts. Unique products that are patent protected may benefit from that status for a period of time. However, for most products and services, the competition is looming right behind you and you need to be prepared.

> A *competitor* is anyone providing similar goods or services or substitute goods or services.
>
> Foresight is invaluable when analyzing competition. Be sure to consider the possible reactions of your potential competitors when you have introduced your product into the market.

* Types of competitors and level of competition in the market
  Your competitor may be providing the very same goods or products, or products similar to your product or good substitutions for it, as in the following examples:
  o In the frozen produce industry, competitors include other companies providing frozen produce, as well as companies in the fresh produce industry, and even in the canned produce industry.
  o Competitors for electronic books, such as Amazon's Kindle, include other brands of electronic books, in addition to e-book applications which can be used on a PC or iPhone. Hard copy books should also be considered as competitive product substitutions.
  You have to keep constant tabs on the market, becoming familiar with any newcomers or any other changes taking place, in order to be able to predict impending changes.

The main factors determining the magnitude of competition are:

o The number of market players, or the number of companies competing for the different market segments.
o The market share of the different market players. You may find that there is a fairly even distribution of the market and each player has a similar sized piece of the pie, or you may find that there is an unequal distribution, with one or more market leaders holding larger parts of the market. For example, the cellular phone industry has been very dynamic. Nokia once enjoyed a dominant market position, but declined rapidly from 2010, as Apple and Samsung have grown. Today, Chinese companies such as One Plus and Huawei are trying to challenge Apple and Samsung and grab a significant market share.
o The level of aggression and intensity of the market in general, and particularly of the market players who are your direct competitors and can potentially threaten your success.

- If your aim is to successfully penetrate a large part of the market, you are a "market challenger" and your direct competitors are the "market leaders."
- If your aim is to build up a specific niche in the market, you are a "market nicher" and your immediate direct competitors are the various companies working in similar niches. In the future, some of the bigger competitors, such as the market leaders, may also seek to take over your niche.
- If your aim is to follow the market and become one of several active companies while mitigating potentially costly mistakes, you are a "market follower."

Whatever your aim, it is important to become a market expert by studying the environment. This will enable you to plan how and when you approach the market, using up-to-date and validated information on the market's characteristics.

Once you are familiar with the layout of the market, the following indicators will help you assess your relative strengths and weaknesses against those of your competitors:

o Research and development abilities in unique and specialized areas.

o Level of innovation and technological advantages.

o Production facilities and skills or efficiency in logistics: For example, Amazon's warehouses and fulfilment capabilities are a core strength allowing the company not only to fill orders for its own customers, but also to provide fulfilment services to other businesses.

o Design capabilities: Apple Inc. is a company considered to have consistently beaten the competition with ingenious product designs.

o Skill in identifying new opportunities: Cisco is a company that has identified and acquired many innovative companies in the micro communications and telecommunications software and hardware sector. Corporations such as Google, Facebook and Yahoo have been actively acquiring companies in the Internet arena.

o Identification of market needs and trends and integration of existing technologies into new products to meet these needs.

o Quality level: quality standards and procedures, international quality certifications.

o Marketing skills: quality of marketing strategy, quality and quantity of marketing channels, including working relationships and geographic reach, market share and reputation.

o Financial means: available internal and external financial resources.

o Management capabilities: quality of management team, level of experience and prestige. The importance of high quality management can't be underestimated. Great managers will skillfully maximize the full potential of their resources.

- Collaboration with competitors
  When analyzing competitors, it is advisable to keep an open mind and consider which competitors may become allies. Many of the large corporations in the market actively seek to collaborate with younger, newer companies that are working on promising technologies. This can lead to a win-win situation; the large corporations have resources and are established in the markets, while the startups bring innovative ideas and technological skills. Corporations in all areas, from pharmaceuticals to web technologies, are actively seeking new opportunities to adopt and integrate new technologies by collaborating with smaller companies. Google, Apple, Amazon, Yahoo and Facebook, to name just a few examples, have each made dozens of investments and acquisitions over the past years in areas ranging from web services and mapping to voice over IP. Figure 3.4 presents a graphic representation of an internet

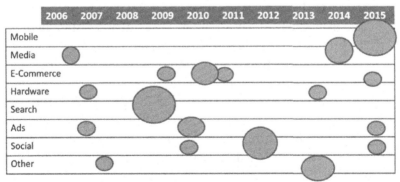

Figure 3.4: A Graphic Presentation of the Acquisitions of an Internet Company Over Ten Years.

company and the different technologies which it acquired from other companies during this period, in addition to its own research and development.

There is no clear formula for determining whether an acquisition, exit or collaboration is the optimal strategy for a new enterprise. In some cases, having a powerful partner provides the new company with competencies they could not otherwise attain and yields excellent results. However, such relationships also create dependence, and if your technology loses its status on the corporate agenda, you might find that the innovation in which you have invested years has been moved to a low priority or has even been permanently placed on hold.

Becoming deeply familiar with the competitive market is the best way to be fully prepared to evaluate collaboration opportunities. If you know your competitors well, you should have a better idea of their motives. You will also be in a far better negotiating position if and when you do decide to collaborate.

3.6   The Technological Environment

In order to compete in the technological environment, you need to acquire an excellent understanding of the existing technologies and technological capabilities. By becoming familiar with the technological environment, you can ascertain whether your technology has a significant advantage over that of your competitors. Analyzing your technology within this context enables you to assess what technological resources are available for your project, and what gaps need to be filled, whether in your team's skills, your facilities and equipment, or in other areas.

This evaluation is particularly important in companies where technological advantages can prove strong selling points. Having technological advantages which can be maintained over time is a key strategic asset in many high tech companies. But for any company providing goods or services which utilize technology to any degree, it is advantageous to understand the technological environment. For example, the furniture industry may not appear to rely on new technologies, but an entrepreneur in this area will often benefit more by becoming familiar with advanced design tools (such as 3D modeling software), production methodologies (such as CAD-CAM), new materials (such as innovative plastics and fabrics) and e-commerce, rather than relying on a narrower knowledge base.

In studying the technological environment, you should strive to answer the following questions:

- What are the technological means and capabilities required for initially developing your product and maintaining activity over the long term?
  - o Do you have these means and capabilities?
  - o If not, where can they be obtained? At what cost?
  - o What is the detailed work schedule for your technical team, up to the implementation and post-implementation stages?
  - o What parts of the technology have been patented (or are patent-pending)? Do any of these patents block your path into the market?
- What are the conventional technologies in your area?

  Research the existing processes for development, production and quality assurance in similar companies. In many instances, there is a lot to be learned from the experiences of others, whether good or bad, and you will be better positioned to make good decisions in planning your own processes.
- What is your product's life cycle?
  - o Most products have a limited lifespan and sales will rise and fall at different stages of the product's life cycle. The "classic" product life cycle is shown in Figure 3.5.
    - ▪ The earliest stage in a product's life is when it is first introduced and penetrates the market.

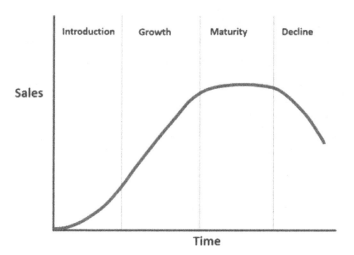

Figure 3.5:   Product Life Cycle

- Once the product penetrates the market successfully, it can enjoy a period of growth over time, as the customer base grows.
- At the stage of maturity, the product maintains a stable level of sales and profitability.
- Towards the end of the product's life, there will be a period of decline, which will generally result in terminating the sale of the product.

Product sales will usually decline when a newer replacement, or substitute, which is either of better quality or cheaper (or both), successfully penetrates the market. This new replacement product will usually have a similar product life cycle and will eventually be replaced by the next model, and this process continues. One of the most important factors determining the product's life cycle is technological innovation. Cellphone industry leaders, such as Samsung, Apple and Huawei try to gain market share from competitors by continually introducing new smartphone models.

Product sales also decline as a result of changes in cost structure and profitability, regulatory considerations, varying market trends and other factors.

- The length of the lifespan differs greatly from product to product.

  o Cellphones and computers are striking examples of products with short product life cycles per model; not many of us are walking around with the same type of cellphones we had just a few years ago (Figure 3.6). We might see several generations overlap in the market, as shown in the overlapping curves in Figure 3.7.

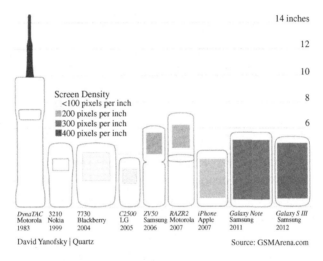

Figure 3.6:   The Evolution of the Cellphone

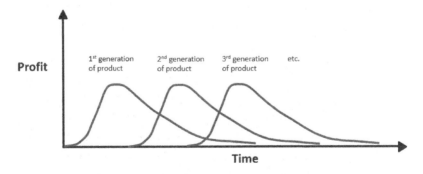

Figure 3.7:   Profits from Overlapping Product Generations

In order to compete in markets with short product life-cycles, companies have to plan the next generation of products early enough. They may even need to work on the next two or three generations at the same time they are trying to penetrate the market with a specific model. Examples of companies which failed to do so include the Japanese companies Sega and Nintendo, which lost large parts of their market share in computer games to Microsoft and Sony in the 1990s. Similarly, Nokia and Blackberry both lost their leadership positions in the cellphone market to the newer smartphone companies, with Apple and Samsung in the lead.

o In the fashion industry, the length of the product life cycle is very much dependent on the nature of the product. Popular items like classic jeans can have a very long life cycle (e.g. Levi's 501). Some high-end fashion items (like Burberry or Hermes) will remain fashionable for many years. Other items will have much shorter life spans, often as short as a single season.

o In the automobile industry, the length of the product life cycle was traditionally between three to five years. In recent years, due to the impact of constant innovation in other consumer markets and the abundance of innovation in the automotive market (e.g. on-board computing and connectivity, new materials, new designs), the life cycle has been shortened. Automobile makers now present new features in their models every year (and at every important trade show, such as the Detroit, Paris or Geneva auto shows).

o In industries which require substantial research and development and financial investment, such as the passenger airplane industry, the length of the product life cycle will be quite long, even several decades.

o There are examples of industries whose products have extremely long life cycles, such as the traditional wine and cheese industries in France. In these highly conservative industries, which are much less sensitive to the introduction of new products, the product life cycle length will be decades, and even centuries.

o The product life cycle for a fad will often have a single sharp rise, and will drop rapidly when consumer interest dies out, as shown in Figure 3.8.

Let's further examine product life cycles by identifying the different stages of the cycle as applied to specific product sectors. Our examples relate to modern economies, and the stages may differ in developing countries.

Product Life Cycle

Stage	Example
Introduction	Electric and hybrid automobiles, 3D printing, drones, nanotechnology, wearable technology.
Growth	Cloud computing, smartphones (see Figure 3.9), tablets, e-commerce, IT security.
Maturity	Personal computers, GPS navigation, cellular phones, microwave ovens.
Decline	DVDs, CDs, fax machines.
Obsolete	Floppy discs, film cameras, video cassette players, typewriters, black and white television, phonographs.

Understanding your product's life cycle will clarify some very important points, including:

• What is the length of your product's life cycle?
• At what stage of the life cycle is your product currently situated? The introduction stage? Growth? Maturity? Or decline?
• Is your technology well suited to current and future market demands and expectations?
• What type of technological innovation might generate market demand?

Not all technological innovations will sell products. You need to determine whether your proposed innovation

Figure 3.8:   Typical Fad Product Life Cycle

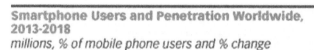

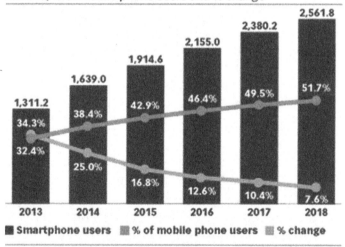

Figure 3.9:   Smartphone Users and Penetration

improves any of the parameters that your customer values, which often include quality, availability, user-friendliness, safety, ecological impact and cost. If your product offers a significant enhancement of features that are important to your customer, it may generate market demand. However, not every innovation sells well. Google Glass, for example, was initially praised for being an innovative new device with a wide range of uses, but it was not adopted when first launched, and Google eventually suspended sales of this product in January 2015 and is redeveloping the product.

Other innovations may have a potentially interested customer base, but not for paid features. For example, users are often reluctant to pay for services and information on the Internet, particularly as they are accustomed to having free access to an abundance of services.

With many technological innovations, the majority of users will wait for the market to really adopt the product, before purchasing and using it themselves. They do not want to buy the product at premium prices, or to be the "guinea pigs" using the products before all of the initial or potential kinks and issues have been resolved.

Some products require significant further innovation before they change the market. For example, stents used for heart surgery are continually improving, with each new product introducing incremental changes. However, there is still a need for a breakthrough innovation to resolve the problem that they become clogged within a relatively short amount of time (approximately five years). Such an advance may be possible with the use of biological materials.

- How wide is the gap between you and your competitors in terms of technology and R&D potential?

  o Entrepreneurs may be certain that they have achieved a major technological breakthrough which places them far ahead of their competitors. However, this evaluation needs to be examined objectively. Entrepreneurs also need to realistically estimate how quickly the competition can catch up. The amount of time it will take your competitors to catch up and introduce the same innovative features is called "lead time," or the period between the beginning of a process or project and the emergence of results. During this period, you enjoy a technological advantage over your competitors and are alone in selling the innovative products. In your business plan, make prudent evaluations of the lead time that you will be able to enjoy, and take into account your competitors' potential actions.

o It is easier to estimate the technological gap if you are working with an experienced R&D team. An established team with years of experience can predict time frames more accurately, and usually less optimistically, than a less experienced one. This is important both in measuring the scientific gap and in preparing R&D schedules.

o The science or technology gap concerns all areas of expertise related to your product and field. It will be an important gauge of your advantages or disadvantages as an entrepreneur in your business sector.

o If your product sells well once it is on the market, there will be a race to duplicate it. Unfortunately for the original engineers and company, the process of reverse engineering for replicating products is usually much faster than the original development. If the innovation is protected by patents, or if the company has a very unique knowledge base, there will be more time to sell the product without competition. However, despite the protection mechanisms you may have, competition will probably arrive if the market is a lucrative one.

- Is your technological advantage sufficient and the lead time reasonable enough to enable you to penetrate the market?

The answers to these questions depend on how open the market is to innovation, and how your competitors will react to the introduction of your product. Sometimes a new technology will render older products so irrelevant that they will quickly become obsolete. In this optimistic scenario, you can look forward to a smooth entry into the market. But this eventuality is rare. In some cases, your customers may not be convinced of the advantages of upgrading the product they are currently using. Other times, the innovation is too expensive to compete in the market, or there are other insurmountable obstacles stalling entry into the market.

In many cases, you can attract enough market attention to get your product tried and evaluated, at least by some of the more adventurous customers. If your product generates a favorable response, and you are then successful in pitching your product to the rest of the market, you can look forward to a period of growth. The CD is an example of a product which was initially evaluated concurrently with records and cassettes, and managed to completely replace the competing products over a period of several years. Thirty years later, CDs are in the process of being phased out and music has made a transition from store-sold merchandise to electronic downloads made directly from the Internet to mobile phones, iPods, digital music players and other electronic devices.

3.7   The Financial Environment

The financial environment plays a decisive role in the life of a company. It will determine your likelihood of success in several ways. To become familiar with the financial environment, answer the following key questions:

- What are your financing needs?

  Setting up a new company is not cheap. Financial needs differ from one company to another. Some examples of major financial expenditures include:

  o Research and development
  o Machinery and equipment
  o Land and buildings
  o Marketing
  o Working capital

In financial planning, consider not only the total amount of funds needed, but also the cash flow over time. Which payments are immediate, which will be made at a later stage, at what stage will cash be generated from your customers (not necessarily at the point of sale)?

- What are the available financial resources?
  - o What are your internal resources? Do you have retained earnings from previous activities which can be used for funding your new venture?
  - o What financial resources will be provided by the shareholders, whether as an investment or a loan?
  - o What type of external debt, including bank loans and supplier credit, can you raise?
  - o What kind of capital can you raise? Often companies turn to venture capital funds, institutional investors or "angels" to raise money in exchange for a share of the equity.
- What is the cost of financing raised from each of these channels?

A basic financial principal is that any form of financing, even using your internal resources or shareholder financing, has a price. Calculate the cost of each option so that you make a wise decision when choosing the form of financing for your company.

We will expand on these questions in more detail in Section 4.5 on the financial plan. Because the entrepreneurial team is not always familiar with financial terms, this book will define the basic terms and recommend further reading to enhance your knowledge as needed.

3.8   The General Environment: Economic, Trade, Political, Social and Legal Factors

Earlier in the chapter we described external factors which impact your business directly, including the marketing environment and the technological environment. We now turn to other external or environmental factors which influence not only your specific business but a wider market; perhaps the entire regional or national market and, in some cases, even international markets. It is essential to understand these factors, as they may have a major influence on the business' future, and some of them present significant factors of opportunity or risk.

To gain a good understanding of the general environment it is important to carefully study the different factors described in this chapter on a regional, national and international level.

3.8.1 *Economic and Trade Factors*

- Economic trends are apt to change very quickly. A recession may be followed by a period of growth, and stability can occasionally turn quickly into instability. Some examples of major economic crises which had tremendous repercussions in many areas of business include:

  o The 1970s energy crisis, which arose because of substantial petroleum shortages, only partially real, caused price inflation together with stagnant economic growth. Because of this crisis, interest in alternative sources of energy, such as solar and wind turbines, increased. The search for alternative energies has generated considerable research and a new generation of startups.

  o The dot-com bubble, when prices of Internet related stocks rose precipitously, began towards the middle of the 1990s. The rapid rise in equity value peaked in March 2000 but the bubble deflated shortly thereafter, causing the collapse of numerous Internet-based companies and services.

  o The financial crisis which began in July 2007 was triggered by high default levels of subprime and adjustable rate mortgages (ARM) in the United States, eventually causing a liquidity shortfall with worldwide repercussions. It was accompanied by a severe recession in the American and most European economies. The housing industry in the United States and other countries, including England and Spain, crashed, with new housing projects dropping to less than half of their 2006 levels.

- Inflation
  Inflation levels in the United States and most of Western Europe have been relatively low for many years. However, in many countries, inflation continues to be a significant factor to contend with in international dealings. Negative inflation (deflation) is a warning sign of market stagnation and decline.
- Currency Fluctuations and Policies
  A glance at the euro-U.S. dollar exchange rates for the five year period from early 2010 through early 2015 (shown in Figure 3.10) reveals how strongly currency fluctuations can influence the profitability of an international business. During this period, the exchange rate rose as high as 1.47 dollars per euro and then dipped as low as 1.13 dollars per euro. If your inputs, such as raw materials, labor and rent are in one currency and a good share of your sales are in another currency, such fluctuations can drastically affect your profitability.

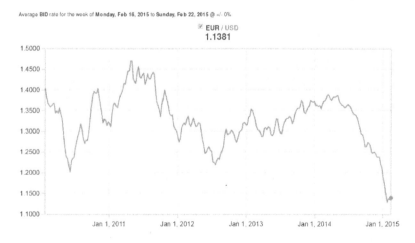

Figure 3.10:   Euro-U.S. Dollar Exchange Rates Jan 2011–Jan 2015

- Changes in the standard of living and consumer confidence levels will influence consumer decision making.
- The national balance of payments (BOP) and the existence of a national surplus or deficit will affect import and export terms and limitations.
- Customs policies and trade barriers are important considerations in determining the final price to the consumer. Some countries enjoy "free trade zones" with others (such as NAFTA between the US, Canada and Mexico, and EFTA within the EU) — which simplifies international trade substantially. Conversely, some countries create high trade barriers, with the intention to protect their domestic suppliers at the expense of importers. Trade barriers can appear in the form of tariffs, quotas, boycotts, demand for licenses and standards, or subsidies to local businesses.
- Much can be learned from the leading regional industries. Some industries are more sensitive than others to fluctuations in world markets. Regions where sensitive industries are a major component of the local market are more economically vulnerable than areas containing mostly less sensitive industries. For example, the economy of the oil producing nations is highly dependent on the price of oil. In order to hedge against this, Saudi Arabia and the Gulf states have invested massively in other business sectors, locally and internationally.
- The capital market will determine how easy it will be to raise capital from internal and external sources, whether private or public. Money can be raised locally or in foreign markets. Questions to ask include:

  o Which capital markets are relevant?
  o How many public offerings take place?
  o What is the volume of trade?
  o What are the interest rates?
  o How welcome are outsiders?
  o What is the current market trend?

- It is easier to raise capital in markets with major venture capital and private equity funds. In addition, the availability of angels and angel clubs can indicate the availability of seed money for startup ventures.
- The labor market is one of the significant features of an economy. Factors to consider include the type of skills available, employment levels, salary and benefit levels, trade unions, labor laws and even the frequency of labor disruptions, such as strikes.

3.8.2 *Political Factors*

- Long-term political stability is a very significant factor in doing business with different countries, particularly developing countries. A business may be affected not only directly through its own business interests in unstable countries but also indirectly through the business interests of major suppliers or customers in countries facing upheaval. Brazil became much more attractive to business during the presidency of Luiz Inácio Lula da Silva (popularly known as Lula) which stabilized the political governance there, at the time. Many African countries have not been able to attract businesses from the United States or Europe due to their constant political instability.
- The characteristics of the political regime will weigh heavily in planning the marketing strategy to a given country. For example, in China, a large proportion of the business world is controlled by government-owned companies and various governmental barriers are imposed (e.g. restrictions on removing funds from the country). In most of Western Europe and North America, many imports enjoy free market conditions, making entry easier.
- Researching the tax rates and tax breaks for various industries will provide valuable information on the ease of conducting a business in a given country or region. Many governments, at a national or regional level, provide different forms of

incentives to attract new business, based on specified criteria. These plans and benefits are created in order to increase economic activity. Ireland is an example of a country which successfully attracted innovative companies by offering substantial tax breaks.

- You may find that prejudices about your nationality and/or the geographic origin of your products may exist in different regions. This can work both ways. Some countries might be very enthusiastic about products with a specific foreign origin, such as French wines, Italian marble, Swiss precision items, German manufacturing etc., and others might have a preference for locally made items. For example, in Australia, there is a strong preference for Australian food and agricultural products. In many places, there is a certain ambivalence regarding products from China. While China is producing many high quality brands on a large scale at lower production costs than in many other countries, there is growing concern about ecological and labor law issues in China, including child labor and labor exploitation.

3.8.3 Social Factors

When you are active in foreign countries, you must be aware of the different effects of social factors

- Employment concerns: As Figure 3.11 shows, the number of hours in a work week varies greatly among countries, and this is a significant factor to take into account. Other employment issues include policies on employee strikes, which occur fairly regularly in some European countries, such as Italy and France, and work ethics, which are very different in each country.
- Ethnic differences.
- Local and national attitudes and characteristics: While these are not always easy to define, they may include openness to foreigners, management styles, and other cultural differences.

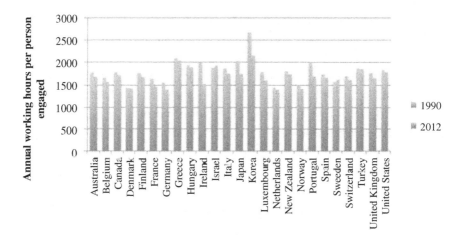

Figure 3.11: Working Hours in 1990 and 2012, OECD Countries

Source: The Economist, available at: http://www.economist.com/blogs/freeexchange/2013/09/working-hours

- The current local or national state of mind: This may be influenced by a particular event or date. For example, the Olympics are always a great attraction, with a flurry of local activity and entrepreneurship leading up to the great event. However, this effect may not always be positive in the long run. Other types of events which influence the state of mind might include a war or an economic recession.
- Trends and fashions are among the social factors to consider in choosing a region for your activities.
- In many countries, there are laws concerning minimal wages and working hours, which affect the cost of labor. In some countries, it is extremely difficult to terminate employment, even when there are major issues of productivity or work disruption.

3.8.4 *Legal Factors*

Legal conditions vary greatly from one area to another; even within one country it is important to understand the local legislative conditions. These include:

- Antitrust and competition laws: These exist in most countries. Some common examples are restrictions on monopolies and cartels, or against pricing discrimination. Many countries, particularly those with emerging economies, require some local ownership of businesses. Many countries have restrictions and limitations on foreign real estate investments.
- Legal requirements: Legal requirements apply in all areas. A few examples are health, environment, safety and labor.
- International trade laws can be complex and affect areas such as transfer pricing, taxation treaties between countries and international trade and customs laws.
- The stability of the legal environment should be considered. How likely is it that radical changes will take place during the lifetime of your business?

3.9   Gathering Information

One of the significant challenges in the business plan process is collecting accurate and relevant information, which entails spending a significant amount of time and resources. If done well, this work is well worth the effort. Information sources are often categorized into three groups:

- Internal Sources: Most entrepreneurial ventures already have a lot of valuable information and personal knowledge within the organization, which can be a terrific resource that should not be overlooked. Be sure to create channels of communication within the startup team and to document and preserve important knowledge.
- External Primary Sources: These are direct contacts that can be established with active market players, including suppliers, marketers, end users, expert advisors and consultants, industry organizations and others. These contacts

are best made directly through face to face meetings or teleconferences. Sometimes questionnaires are useful ways to gather information, particularly from end users. If you are planning to work in different geographic locations, try to establish primary sources in each location, since market conditions vary greatly from place to place, as discussed earlier in this chapter. Be aware that any information that you try to get from afar, via telephone or email for example, may not be as complete as that obtained from good direct contact with a local market expert, who can often overcome the language and cultural barriers and provide you with the most accurate data.

- External Secondary Sources: There is a tremendous wealth of written information out there, if you know how to access it. Secondary sources include scientific and other professional journals, statistical publications and a variety of information and brochures advertised by active companies in the industry. In addition, follow industry experts' websites and blogs, which are invaluable tools for keeping up with the market.

The Internet is a vast resource and it is worth spending time to seek out the relevant websites, blogs, articles and publication for your needs. The challenge is not always finding the information, but learning how to weed out the less relevant parts and keep the important information and updates accessible. Another challenge is verifying the reliability of the informal sources offering information on the Internet, which can be biased and may lack objectivity. Be sure to check whether your sources are reputable and trustworthy.

Numerous government sites have helpful links for different types of business resources, and in many industries you will find useful information through trade associations and statistical bureaus. See Figure 3.12 for example, which shows the opening page of the United States government site for foreign businesses at:

http://www.usa.gov/Business/Foreign_Business.shtml

Foreign Businesses Doing Business in the United States

For foreign business owners desiring to invest in the U.S.; create import and export opportunities; build partnerships; and learn more about the U.S. economy.

On This Page

- Economic Statistics
- Energy, Transportation, and Telecommunication
- Finance and Development
- Frequently Asked Foreign Business Questions
- International Fishing

- International Trade
- Labor Issues
- Non-Government Resources for Foreign Business
- Professional International Exchange Programs

Economic Statistics

- Bureau of Economic Analysis, U.S. Department of Commerce
- Fedstats
- Foreign Labor Statistics, U.S. Department of Labor
- Foreign Trade Statistics, U.S. Census Bureau
- More Business Statistics
- U.S. Economic Indicators

Figure 3.12:   From the United States Government Site for Foreign Businesses

This is just one of many pages of links you can access through this site, and there are many such sites for different countries, trades and industries.

It is generally unwise to rely on one resource only. Try to access many resources and analyze the information from different viewpoints to compose as accurate a picture as possible.

How much information is enough? There is no good answer to that question. On the one hand, by digesting the maximum amount of information available, you will improve your chances of obtaining the most accurate picture. On the other hand, you will encounter a lot of duplications and "noise" to filter through which will make the task very difficult to manage. Some of the information, such as expert reports, is expensive, and analyzing a lot of information is very time consuming. The trick is striking the right balance so that you can gather the information you need without missing out on important sources or wasting valuable resources. The decision on how much time and money to spend on information is a matter of weighing the costs and benefits. In summary, choose the information upon which you will build your plan very carefully. You want to be sure that your sources are relevant, reliable and also affordable.

Initially, you will be learning about the market in order to first prepare your business plan. This will be your most intensive research effort. Following this stage, information gathering should be continued over the life of your enterprise, and periodical updates are necessary, particularly when the environment changes. When the changes are significant, your business planning will probably also require an update.

Cases in which you will be most in need of accurate and relevant information include:

- particularly innovative ventures
- ventures in which a substantial investment is required
- high risk ventures
- ventures in a dynamic market

In all of these cases, do your research well. You are likely to find that quality information can save you valuable time and money. Your strategy will enjoy a stronger foundation, which increases your prospects of success.

Chapter 4

Planning

Once you have completed the stage of gathering information and analyzing the business environment, you are ready to make the most important decisions for your business and to begin preparing your plan. This plan will be invaluable as a management tool. It will be the heart of your written business plan, as we will show in Chapter 5.

When planning, try to focus on two primary questions:

1. What are your new enterprise's goals and aims?

   You may have encountered many young businesses that systematically avoid providing a clear-cut answer to this question in an effort to keep their options open. We strongly recommend that you be prepared with an unambiguous answer. It is impossible to make efficient decisions if you do not know what your goals are. A clear statement of your goals ensures that your resources, including your marketing communications and your R&D, are dedicated directly towards reaching those goals. And if you can't state your goals coherently, you will be much less likely to attract investors and business partners who will seek well-defined answers and plans. You will also lose the valuable benefit of word of mouth:

when you cannot describe your goals clearly, others will not be able to either. Explicit goals will also help you measure how far you've come and how well you are doing over time.

2. How can you optimally achieve these goals and aims?

During the planning stage you will construct a work plan for accomplishing the goals and aims you have established.

Your objective during the planning stage is to set a well-defined business strategy, which will be reflected in the business model. During this stage, you will be concentrating on five primary areas: the marketing plan, the R&D plan, the production plan, the management or organizational plan and the financial plan. These plans will also provide the basis for your sales and cost projections, as discussed in Section 5.6.

The Marketing Plan Components

- Target markets based on market segmentation
- The product mix
- Distribution and marketing channels
- An advertising plan
- Pricing
- Customer credit policy
- Pre- and post-sales support and technical assistance, service and warranties
- Business locations
- Brand and product names

The R&D Plan Components

- The R&D work plan, describing the work to be done in-house, outsourced, or bought from other parties
- R&D goals
- The schedule and time frame for each of the R&D activities
- The R&D staff required and their work plans

The Production Plan Components

- The division of production between in-house production and subcontractors
- The production technologies to be used
- A detailed schedule of the equipment and raw materials required
- The physical location of the production plant
- Logistic and shipping considerations
- Manpower requirements
- Purchasing policies
- Inventory policy
- Quality assurance processes
- Alternative supply routes

The Management or Organizational Plan Components

- The management structure and decision-making framework
- The company's operating plan
- The company's management policies and compensation and benefits policies

The Financial Plan Components

- The capital requirements for equipment, labor, inventory and activities
- The capital structure
- Financial forecasts

These five elements of the business model interact with each other, and decisions made regarding one of the elements will affect the others. Together, these elements make up the action plan based on the business strategy. Chapter Four will examine these five elements in more detail.

4.1   Business Strategy

4.1.1 *What is a Business Strategy?*

The word "strategy" derives from the Greek word "στρατηγία" (strategia), which is the office of the military general. Used in the military sense, strategy refers to the buildup of military forces and assets and their application towards achieving military goals. Military strategy is built based on the general's understanding of his own forces, the enemy forces, the terrain and the potential moves available to each side. Time is a significant factor, and the general needs to be able to predict changes and enemy actions in real time, as developments take place. A strategy is not the same as a plan. A plan is based on known, fixed facts, while a strategy is developed under uncertain and changing conditions.

The analogy to the business world is clear. While soldiers' lives are usually not at stake when it comes to business strategies (outside of the arms industries), a business's life, products and livelihood all depend on correctly analyzing the situation in real time, seizing opportunities and skillfully managing business maneuvers.

> *The Business Strategy involves setting goals and planning how to achieve them efficiently.*
>
> It determines how the business can optimally benefit from opportunities arising in the business environment and how it can successfully contend with risks that appear. A good strategy is built on a sound understanding of the strengths and weaknesses of your business compared with the rest of the market, and on an optimal amassment and use of resources over time.

Since the term business model is often used, this would be a good place to differentiate it from the business strategy. The business model describes what the business is, how it will work and how the company intends to address specific issues, such as the type of company it will be, what products will be sold, the sources of revenue, and many other operational questions. The business model usually specifies the mid-term revenue and expense stream.

The business strategy refers to how the business interacts with the dynamics of the market and how it will deal with competitors and meet longer-term goals, such as achieving a certain market share or an international foothold.

Amazon's original business model in 1994 was based on providing customers with access to a huge selection of books through their Internet website. They advertised that over 2.5 million titles could be ordered through their system. Initially, the company planned to serve as a middleman only, and to avoid the expense and effort of opening its own warehouses. Eventually the business model changed, as the company found that it could improve its service significantly by opening its own warehouses, and the company became an operational wonder. These developments relate to the business model. One of Amazon's top strategic goals from the start was to grow quickly, and the company invested its efforts and money in achieving rapid recognition as the online address for the largest selection of books at the best prices, with the most convenient and cheapest deliveries. Amazon did so by aiming to be "Earth's most customer-centric company," and to dominate the market by consistently providing an excellent customer experience, not only through competitive pricing but also through having excellent distribution, warehousing, logistics, inventory management and customer support. Amazon indeed grew rapidly enough to grab the lion's share of the online books sales market and retain it for close to two decades. They have further extended their business model to include sales of electronic equipment, computer accessories and many other products and services beyond books, including electronic readers and media devices, fulfillment services and more.

Another illustration of the difference between a business model and a business strategy is the success of Walmart, which did not actually develop a new business model, but used a model very similar to that of Kmart, which operates the same type of stores and sells similar products. However,

Walmart's strategy differed from Kmart's, with Walmart focusing on providing a presence in small towns rather than large cities and on guaranteeing everyday low prices.

Facebook did not have a clear business model originally, although its strategy was very clear. It aimed to become the largest social network, and it has accomplished this and maintained its status successfully, to date. Facebook is also an example of a company that did not have a clear revenue model for a number of years. However, it did recognize that having a large customer base would eventually translate into profits. And so it has: with revenues of $12.47 billion, Facebook earned a net income of $2.94 billion in 2014.

4.1.2 *How Far Ahead Should You Plan Your Business Strategy?*

Your business strategy pertains to long-term goals. The precise time frame depends on the nature of your business. Two important factors in determining the time span are:

* The amount of money invested
* The length of the product life cycle

Industries which require large investments in manufacturing plants will have longer-term plans, particularly when few alterations are expected in the end product over time. A nuclear power plant requires a very heavy investment of billions of dollars and can produce energy for an extended period of time. This industry will have long-term plans of 30 years or so. The auto industry also plans its construction facilities for the longer term. Auto models will typically be around for a decade or more, and the assembly lines are designed to accommodate the various changes that are introduced over the life of a particular model. These changes include small mechanical and electronic changes and alterations in appearance. Energy and chemical plants also require long-term planning spans of 10–20 years or more.

The electronics industry has a much shorter life span, as we discussed in the section on product life cycles (see Section 3.6). Computers, cellphones and other electronic devices are continuously changing as new technologies and applications are introduced. We differentiate between the planning span of a particular device, which might be two to three years, and the planning span of the production facility, which is intended to accommodate several generations of a particular device using most of the same equipment and machinery. Over the past several years, many production facilities have had to be updated more frequently than originally forecasted because of dramatic technological advances.

Although some industries require longer-term plans, the business strategy should be reviewed and reevaluated over the life of the business, undergoing adaptations and revisions as the environment changes. Like the business plan itself, it is valuable only if it is up-to-date, relevant and relatively responsive to change.

4.1.3 *How Do You Plan a Business Strategy?*

Plan your business strategy only after conducting a study of the environment, as described in the previous chapter. Once you are fluent in everything relating to your product, market, environment, etc., you can begin to address each variable. Although you should systematically tackle each area independently, you will soon discover that there are strong interdependencies between them. A decision made on one variable will create a new reality which will inevitably affect other variables, whether directly or indirectly. For example, your marketing team's sales plan will affect your production plan, just as your production capacity may make you reevaluate your marketing plan. If you aim to successfully compete with a product already competing in the market, your production and marketing strategies will also be affected. And whatever your ideal strategy may be in any area of your business, it must be consistent with your financing plans and prospects. These interdependencies make strategic planning a complex task demanding a lot of thought and a good amount of healthy intuition.

There are different ways to tackle the job of creating a comprehensive strategy. This chapter presents our own methodology, beginning with the marketing strategy. While there may be other ways to begin, we will explain why we prefer to begin with marketing in Section 4.2. Even once you have completed a section of your business plan, be prepared to keep going back for corrections and adjustments in response to the dynamics of interdependencies between the variables which we described. Reviewing and revising are part of the strategic planning process, which is a continual effort requiring a lot of patience and wisdom.

4.1.4 *Strategic Plan or Action Plan?*

Just as we differentiated between the business model and the business strategy, it is useful to distinguish between your strategic plan and your action plan.

The strategic plan determines your business policy for the long run, similar to the way in which a government might set its policies in the areas of economics, social welfare, foreign policy, education, etc. The action plan, which is more of a tactical plan, relates more specifically to the actual practical steps which need to be taken to realize your strategy, even though at times you may make practical decisions that slightly deviate from your strategy due to short-term constraints. Some of the practical decisions that will be part of your action plan include:

- Work plans
- Work schedules, complete with milestones to measure progress
- Human resources requirements, recruiting schedules and organizational charts

- Schedules of the required equipment and facilities
- Inventory schedules
- Purchasing policies
- Management plans, delegations of authority and responsibilities
- Administrative needs
- Internal policies, e.g., financial policies and quality assurance (QA) policies

The strategic plan sets long-term goals for the firm, emphasizing the strength of the business and the opportunities available. It indicates how to overcome possible weaknesses and work within the given constraints, which can include limited financial resources, limited manpower or limited skills, for example.

4.2   The Marketing Plan

A business stands on several pillars: production, R&D, marketing, management, customer service, etc. The best product may never succeed if its production is faulty or too expensive, if the QA processes aren't good enough or if the marketing strategy is ineffective.

Many Chief Marketing Officers (CMOs) and top executives consider marketing strategy to be the very heart of the overall business strategy, with the most influence on the potential success of the business. Apple is an example of a company which has been consistently outstanding not only in its innovative products, but also in its creative marketing which has generated a fascination with its products and a tremendous, loyal customer base.

Increasingly, over time, and particularly during the last two decades, the consumer market has become customer-centric, and products or services must be adapted to what the customer wants or needs. Bearing in mind that the marketing strategy has to be realistic and well-coordinated with the company's technological and financial capabilities, the best way to begin your strategic planning is by determining which market you are targeting and with what line of products. For these reasons, we recommend beginning with your marketing strategy.

An example of a critical strategic marketing decision is IBM's decision to sell its PC division to the Chinese manufacturer, Lenovo, and concentrate on B2B IT services, software and high-end computers instead. Apple's decision to enter the market for consumer electronics, particularly the music market, helped establish Apple as a leading company now enjoying the highest market value in the world.

The marketing plan is the result of a long series of interdependent decisions. The exact components will differ from one industry to the next, and even between competing companies in the same industry. We will describe the most central components of the decision-making process to be considered when developing your marketing strategy including:

☐   choosing the target markets
☐   developing a product mix
☐   building a distribution system to get your products to your customers
☐   advertising and promotions
☐   pricing
☐   customers' credit policy
☐   post-sales support
☐   location of operations
☐   branding

• **Target markets**

The decision of which markets to target is perhaps the most important a business can make. It is also one of the two decisions you should make first when building your marketing strategy; the second involves your product mix, which we will describe next. These decisions will become the basis of all the other decisions in subsequent stages of your marketing plan.

Choose your target markets only after becoming completely familiar with your different options, and determining which have true potential. Once you have chosen your target markets, you will know:

o   What groups of customers you will serve
o   When to begin marketing to each group of customers
o   What areas of expertise your business will focus on
o   What competitive environment you will be working in

You may have such a unique product or service that you will be alone in the market. Alternatively, you may face an intensely competitive market. Don't limit your vision to the current situation; you have to be able to predict future developments. Even in a market which seems quiet at one point, your competitors may have competing products in their pipelines which can quickly change the dynamics of the market.

Some of the considerations in choosing markets and market segments include:

o   Are your sales plans and goals achievable in these markets?
o   What are your company's strengths and weaknesses within these market segments?
o   Can you maintain a strong presence in these markets over time? What would it take to do so?
o   What is the level of activity in these markets? Are they growing markets, mature markets or declining markets?
o   Will you be able to obtain a significant share of the market, both in terms of quantity and revenue?
o   Are the markets well-located geographically, allowing you to provide products and services efficiently?
o   What is the cost of penetrating these markets? What are the barriers to successful penetration?
o   What type of customers will you be serving?
o   Is the market affluent or financially constrained?

- **Product mix**

  This is the second decision which, together with the target markets, will govern the rest of the decision-making process in your business. We stress again that this is a continual, iterative process, and in later stages of the planning process, you may find that you should revisit and alter your product mix. This could happen for many different reasons. Here are a few examples:

  o Your market research shows that there would be a stronger demand for a different mix of products and or features

  o Your R&D or production departments can't deliver all of the features on the products that you originally planned, or has come up with interesting new solutions which were not originally available

  o Your proforma financial results show that you can't finance the planned product mix and you have to scale down features or product selection.

  So although the product mix and target markets are the best place to start, they are also interdependent on many other variables in the business strategy.

  > *The product mix* is the portfolio of all of the products and/or services that you propose to offer your customers.

  The product mix should be composed very carefully and meticulously to meet the real needs, tastes and desires of your target markets. The product mix is heavily influenced by your decision about target markets. For this reason, you need to take both of these factors into account simultaneously as you seek to identify the right market for a realistic product mix that you can offer.

Some of the main decisions which will determine your product mix include:

o Are you offering a wide or narrow selection of products?
o Which, if any, of your products are customized, and which are standardized, off-the-shelf products?
o What is the short-term product mix you will offer, and what is the longer-term product mix you are planning?
o Is each individual product that you are offering adding value to your product mix?

Once you have answered the preceding questions, you can continue to:

o Identify which customers will be interested in each of the products in your mix
o Assess the profitability of each product
o Check the feasibility of successfully making each of the products in your product mix available to your customers
o Evaluate how your product mix will impact your company's image, for sales purposes and for your current and future business interests
o Evaluate customer interest
o Determine whether this product mix gives you a unique position or an advantage in the market

Determining your target markets and your product mix ahead of time will help save many costly mistakes. Even very large corporations with successful products and excellent market research capabilities have overlooked important factors in introducing new products, or existing products to new markets. A recent example is Amazon with its smartphone, the Amazon Fire, which was launched to compete with the Samsung Galaxy and the iPhone, but failed to catch on. Target's launch of 133 big box stores in Canada in March 2013 ended with a decision to shut all operations in Canada less than two years later.

- **Distribution Chain**

  Physically getting your product to your customer is an important part of the sales process, and is accomplished by setting up a distribution system. Some of the important factors in choosing the distribution chain include:

  o   Direct or Indirect Distribution?

  The distribution chain can consist of one level or many levels, depending on the complexity of the distribution systems and the parameters of the target market: location, size, spread and level of expertise. Often, in a multi-level distribution system, some levels will be managed by in-house sales personnel or a subsidiary located within the target market, and some will be managed by external distributors/resellers (wholesalers and retailers active in the market), sales representatives, agents or local partners.

  A decisive factor in setting up your distribution system is your customers' preferences. Will a direct relationship with your customer be beneficial? This is often the case with tailor-made products, such as advanced technological solutions. However, often it is advantageous to work through an indirect channel and benefit from a professional distributor's existing relationships with the market and your target customers.

The Distribution Chain is the process of getting your product to the consumer through a chain of intermediaries. This should be differentiated from the Supply Chain, which is the process of getting the raw material needed in your production process from your suppliers to your business, also usually through a chain of intermediaries. These functions are often managed by a logistics and supply chain manager. Managing these functions well is essential for cost reduction, efficiency and customer satisfaction.

o   Sales Representatives ("Reps") or Distributors?

When you work with external sales reps, you are essentially granting them the right to represent your company for the purpose of product sales, in a manner very similar to that of your own sales personnel. The reps are expected to bring experience and connections in the market. Their income is often totally or primarily derived from commissions on sales. A sales rep approaches customers directly, and is usually not greatly involved with major marketing efforts, such as advertising campaigns (although they will have very valuable customer feedback). In some cases they maintain contact with the customer even after the sale has been made (for post-sales support, technical support, handling claims, logistics, etc.). In other cases, post-sales support will be handled by specialized personnel in the company.

Distributors work as independent businesses buying products and selling them to end users. They generally buy products "in bulk" at a heavy discount and profit from the sales margin between the customer's price and their costs.

Distributors often run active campaigns, promotions and programs to target new customers, and usually provide post-sales support.

Distributors and sales reps generally work with a portfolio of products. This has its advantages and disadvantages. On the positive side, the customers turn to the distributers or reps knowing that they are authoritative on a range of products, and your product can benefit from the customer base built over time by the distributer. Your product may complement other products handled by the distributor. This is often helpful in introducing new items into industries and markets that are difficult to penetrate. On the negative side, your product may not enjoy the distributor's undivided attention as it is likely to be presented along with other products, sometimes even products that directly compete with yours. The distributer or rep may prefer to promote a competing product from their portfolio, if they expect it to have better growth or a higher profit margin. It is important to research the distributer or rep and their product portfolio in advance, to ensure that your product is well-placed and that earnest sales efforts will be made.

The choice of selling directly or with a distributer or rep is often determined by the market and the product, and may differ from one region or product to another.

o   <u>Exclusivity</u>

In light of the above issues, granting exclusivity for your products could be a way to guarantee the loyalty and dedication of a distributer or sales rep to your product. Exclusivity contracts are often conditional on commitment to a minimum sales level. But granting exclusivity can also create some problems:

- By putting all of your eggs in one basket, you are extremely dependent on one channel of distribution. If it is not successful, you will have lost a lot of valuable time and money without generating enough sales.
- Customers may find that their access to your product is not convenient if they have only one source for orders.

Working with several distributers or reps is a more intensive and diverse way to get your product out to customers and to increase your sales potential. But overlapping customer bases can also cause rivalry, discontent and eventually decreased motivation.

If you do decide to sign exclusivity contracts with distributers or reps, it is essential to include specific parameters, such as: duration, geographic area and/or clearly defined customer bases. The contract should also specify clear milestones to be met as a condition for maintaining exclusivity.

Distribution is often one of the most sensitive components of the marketing strategy. Distribution systems take a long time to establish and depend on establishing and nurturing a loyal customer base and maintaining healthy long-term relationships with multiple parties.

o Franchising

Franchising is a widely used means of multiplying a business model and building profits without the heavy investments required for building more and more businesses. The differences between franchises and chains are not always apparent to the customer. Whereas Starbucks is actually a giant chain of over 19,000 company-owned coffee shops in over 60 countries, McDonald's, 7-Eleven and Subway are popular franchises. Franchises extend beyond mini-markets and fast food places, and include restaurants, gasoline stations, hotels, spas, fashion stores, car rental agencies and even hospitals. The franchise model is a simple one. After building a successful business and a brand name, usually based on some unique or innovative features, the owner (franchisor) offers the same model to other investors (franchisees), who open similar businesses of their own. The new franchises use the identical innovative elements created by the original business, including the business name and reputation, which made the original business a success. Franchising uses the technological, marketing and management attributes of the original business to multiply and create new businesses. Some of the benefits of becoming a large-scale operation lie in purchasing leverage, advertising and promotions and legal and financial management costs. In many countries worldwide, as in the United States, customers often prefer to buy a familiar brand, where they know precisely what they are getting. This is the main advantage of opening a franchise of a familiar brand. For example, in some locations, a hotel owner might find it easier to attract customers as part of the Hilton group of close to 4,000 hotels worldwide, with established brand names including Hilton, Waldorf Astoria, Hampton Inn and others, rather than operating on their own. However, other customers dislike franchises and prefer a local business.

For the franchisor, franchising facilitates rapid growth with a low direct investment. The franchisor enjoys revenues from franchising fees and other revenue streams from the new franchises, with differing terms from one franchise to another. The disadvantage of franchising is that it is much more difficult to guarantee the same quality level of product and service that you can provide within your own business and your own employees.

- **Marketing communications**

An important component of your marketing strategy is delivering the right message to your potential customers. The goal is for customers to understand your offering and choose it over other competing products, and optimally to become loyal to your company and product. This is accomplished by establishing communication platforms. Some of the typical communication platforms are shown in Figure 4.1.

Advertising	Sales Promotion	Public Relations	Personal Selling	Direct Marketing
web sites	fairs, trade shows	press kits	sales	e-marketing, web sales
banners	premiums, gifts	news releases	presentatons	mailings, email
print ads	samples	webinars, seminars	incentive programs	catalogs
broadcast ads	contests, games,	blogs	fairs, trade shows	telemarketing
internet ads	sweepstakes	annual reports		
symbols and logos	coupons	publications		
packaging	rebates	lobbying		
videos	financing, trade ins	special events		
audio-visual materials	customer loyalty	community activities		
brochures, booklets	programs	and charities		
billboards, posters				
display signs				
point-of-purchase displays				
sponsorship				

Figure 4.1:   Marketing Communications Platforms

The marketing information strategy determines:

o   What information will be communicated?

o   Which information channels are most suitable?

o   Which of these information channels are realistic choices when considering cost factors?

o   How will the campaign be divided between the different channels, now and over time?

Some channels are best for creating initial interest, and other are best for providing detailed information, such as technical data, prices, payment terms and warrantees. Different channels are used during different stages of the diffusion process.

o   How will the advertising and promotions budget be allocated? What proportions will be allocated to the company and to the distributers?

• **Pricing**

Pricing is a major component of your product package. Your price should fill three requirements:

o   It should attract customer interest and generate product or service sales.

o It should be consistent with your product image.

o It should yield profitable results which are in line with your sales and profit projections for the product.

Pricing also plays an integral part in your marketing strategy. Like any other aspect of your business strategy, it must be consistent with your financial goals, but it is not part of your financial strategy. In determining price, you need to ensure that it covers your costs, on the one hand, and fills the requirements listed above, on the other. A few key questions are:

o What area of the price scale fits your product? Is it the low end, for price-sensitive markets? Or the high end, where prestige and quality are strong factors? Figure 4.2 shows many more related pricing strategies.

o Would price differentiation be beneficial, with different prices for different market segments, geographical areas or according to other considerations? Some other criteria for price differentiation include:

▪ The type of customer. Prices will differ for distributors, wholesalers, retailers, end users, preferred customers, etc.

Price

		High	Medium	Low
Product Quality	High	Premium strategy	High-value strategy	Super-value strategy
	Medium	Overcharging Strategy	Medium-value strategy	Good-value strategy
	Low	Rip-off strategy	False economy strategy	Economy strategy

Figure 4.2: Creating Perceptions of Value with Pricing Strategies

Source: *Philip Kotler, Marketing Management.*

- The value of your product to the customer.
- The value of your customer to your business. This is especially important when you are penetrating a new market and are trying to establish some reference customers who are pivotal for attracting the more conservative market. Customer value is also extremely meaningful for industries where customer loyalty and maintenance are crucial, such as telephone companies and banks.
- The sales volume to a particular customer.
- Payment terms.
- Geographic location.

The goal in pricing is to achieve the maximal profitability in each of the market segments. However, there are many customers who will do some market research and won't appreciate being charged a higher price than others, unless there are good justifications for your differential pricing. Remember that today it is relatively easy to compare prices for many products over the Internet. It is also important to research the laws and

---

Reference Customers

Reference customers are objective customers who have bought your product and are satisfied with it. A good reference customer will serve as a positive example to hesitant customers who may not want to be the first to try out a new product.

In the medical instrumentation and the pharmaceutical industries, for example, reference customers are essential.

Sometimes reference customers can be enthusiastic proponents of your product. Reference customers that are highly regarded in the marketplace are extremely valuable when building your business.

regulations regarding differential pricing in each geographic area, as there are can be restrictions and limitations regarding price discrimination.

o   Once you have determined your entry price, be sure to consider your strategy over time. Sometimes you will set an entry price knowing that you will adjust it over time. At other times the price can be stable over a long period of time. And sometimes changes in the market lead to the making of a price adjustment which you did not initially anticipate. Keeping current with market changes and your competitors' pricing is critical. Two of the best-known strategies for setting your entry price at a different level than the price you expect at a later stage are skimming and penetration pricing:

Skimming entails setting a price that can generate higher revenues from the least price sensitive customers for as long as possible. It is a good strategy for products which have obvious competitive advantages or are appealing in other ways. Once the fat has been skimmed, the price is gradually adjusted to a competitive level, which attracts the more price sensitive segments of the market. Examples of such products include popular products and gadgets, such as smart phones (see Figures 4.3 and 4.4), tablets and game consoles, such as the Sony Playstation, Microsoft Xbox and Nintendo's Wii U series. Designer clothing is also priced to first draw the fashion leaders willing to pay the highest prices. Skimming helps build a high quality prestigious product image.

Penetration Pricing sets lower prices at the entry stage. The goal is to penetrate the market and achieve a large market share quickly. This strategy is often used to bypass competitors and attain market leadership, and can prove successful in a highly price-sensitive market. At times it is used at later stages in the product's

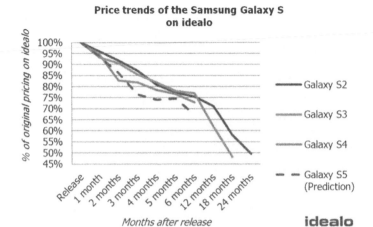

Figure 4.3:   Smartphone Pricing Trends Example

Source: http://bgr.com/2014/02/12/galaxy-s5-price-details-sale/

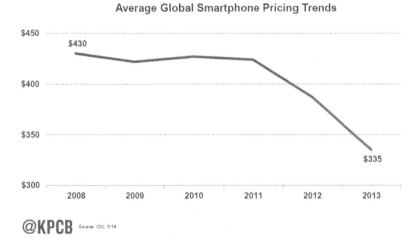

Figure 4.4:   Average Global Smartphone Pricing Trends

life, either to boost business quickly or expend spare production capacity. Penetration pricing is often successful with products which have related complementary or captive products. For example, your printer

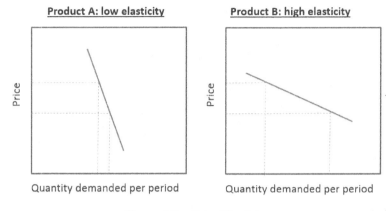

Figure 4.5:   Price Elasticity

In the graph on the left, an decrease in price raises the demand for product A only slightly, compared to much higher demand for product B created by the same same decrease in price.

might be priced at a low level, or even at a loss, but the ink cartridges might have a high markup. Low-end cellphones are sometimes priced at rock bottom levels, but bundled with service packages with high

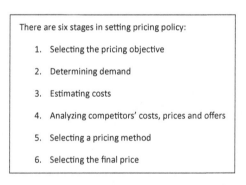

Source: Philip Kotler, Marketing Management

Figure 4.6:   Setting Pricing Policy

margins. Penetration pricing is only possible if you can ramp up production very quickly. If so, you may enjoy the benefit of economies of scale which give you a higher margin per unit. But if you don't succeed in achieving the market share that you had hoped for, or if your competitors follow suit, your penetration strategy may fail. In such a case, you can find yourself with lower revenues than anticipated and excess production capacity and/or product.

Before deciding on your pricing strategy, analyze your competitors' strategies, or the successful strategies in close, comparable markets. Also, try to estimate the price elasticity for your product or service, i.e., how changes in pricing will affect customer demand. See Figure 4.5.

A popular strategy for penetrating markets quickly, particularly with Internet products, is called "freemium." Freemium services, sometimes augmented by advertising, offer a basic version of a product or service which is enjoyable or useful enough to attract sufficient free users to build a large client base. Clients are able to use the basic version indefinitely, or per the specific terms set, but are also offered an upgrade which enhances their product experience (e.g., by removing ads, adding services or providing other features and benefits), at a cost. For example, most users use LinkedIn for free, but job hunters or recruiters may choose the paid premium version. Evernote offers its note-taking and information organizing software for free, but many subscribers pay for the premium version offering additional features, such as a larger upload capacity and better sharing options. And many cloud storage providers including Google Drive, Box, SugarSync and Dropbox provide free storage ranging from 2–15 GB, and charge only for larger storage capacity and other premium services. Freemium products range from a tremendous variety of apps for personal use to full business software packages and management systems. Freemium models are used when companies expect to create more revenue from monetizing existing freemium

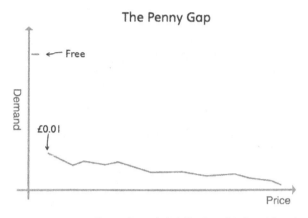

From a diagram by Josh Kopelman, First Round Capital

Figure 4.7:   The Penny Gap in Freemium Models

customers who upgrade to the paid premium version, than could have been achieved by attracting paying customers through advertising alone. However, companies should be aware that a large user base that enjoys and utilizes products as free users will not easily convert to a paid service. Even a small charge may deter the majority of users, as illustrated in Figure 4.7.

- **Customer Credit**

  An important component of the package you offer your customers lies in the credit terms. Credit is given for large and small transactions. Household items are often bought on credit through credit card companies, and in larger transactions, the payment terms might be set directly between the seller and the buyer. On average, larger transactions have longer payment plans. For example, cars or machinery might have payment plans which extend over three to five years. Other products might be paid in 3–12 monthly installments. Common supplier credit terms are net 30, net 45 or net 60, in which the payment is due at the end of the indicated number of days from the date of the invoice. An earlier payment often entitles the customer to a discount.

There may be different government incentive packages for either financing and/or insuring the credit, usually in specific industries which the government is seeking to promote. There are also insurance tools (e.g., for export), as well as banking tools which offer coverage to the supplier against credit risks. Customer credit is another element of the marketing package which has significant financial implications. Extending credit lines to your customers will alter your working capital and influence your financial needs. This will be explained further in Section 4.5.1.

- **Post-sales support**

For many products, particularly technology-based products, post-sales support is a vital feature. Post-sales support is the package of services rendered to the customer throughout the life of the product. The support might include training packages, a help desk, warrantees, upgrades and repair services. If you sell your product to distant locations, it may be complicated to provide this support. In these cases many companies provide post-sales support through third-party local companies, or by relying on remote support provided by phone, web or email. If you are introducing an innovative product, customers will often need and expect exceptional post-sales support. Post-sales support is also provided for non-technological products, as can be seen, for example, in department stores and various business chains, which maintain customer support desks to handle all types of inquiries, complaints and returns. Many companies set up call centers for providing customer support. These may be established inside the company but are often outsourced to call center providers.

In many companies, local post-sales support has been replaced with support from remote locations, where labor is less expensive. This applies especially to software and peripheral computer devices, where software and patches can be downloaded and support personnel can be allowed access to computers from any location to virtually any destination in the world to help resolve issues.

- **Location of operations**

The location of a business's production facilities, warehouses and operations may not seem to be part of the marketing plan, but because it has such a major impact on the realistic target markets, location needs to be in the picture when making marketing decisions. The cost of labor, rent, transport and other operational expenses can be significant and will ultimately impact your product costs. When transport becomes a big component in the overall cost of the product, it may be more economical to make the product in proximity to its market. Location also determines how quickly you can make your product, services and post-sales support available. The tax and legal environments are also a function of location. For these reasons, the marketing department needs to be involved in decisions regarding the location of operations.

- **Branding**

Branding is an important ongoing marketing activity, which begins with choosing a brand name and continues with establishing your brand within the market through a wide range of branding activities. The American Marketing Association (AMA) defines a brand as, "a name, term, design, symbol, or any other feature that identifies one seller's good or service as distinct from those of other sellers. The legal term for brand is trademark." A good brand should represent your product well and convey a message that motivates customers to buy your product and remain loyal to your brand. Brand names include the main brand representing the brand's full product line, such as Nike, McDonalds or Daimler-Benz, as well as the individual product names themselves, such as the Nike Air Jordan series, the Big Mac or the Mercedes-Benz C-Series. Apple's product portfolios, where the iPhone and iPad are brands in themselves, provide another example. A lot of work goes into choosing brand names, and they have a strong impact on customer perception. Consider that until 1971, the Nike brand was called Blue Ribbon Sports.

Of course, the easiest products to brand are the truly great ones. Once a great product takes off, it can go viral. Part of branding your product is making sure that your customers are aware of what it does and how to use it, and how it compares with other competing products. One of the results of a successful marketing campaign is to establish your brand as the immediate choice that leaps to the mind of your customer.

Large corporations do not always identify all of their brands with the corporate name, in order to create separate independent brand identities. For example, Cadillac and Chevrolet are both General Motors brands, but General Motors is not featured in their ads, and the luxury Cadillacs have very different marketing campaigns than the more down-to-earth Chevys.

The final stage of preparing the marketing plan is building the sales projections, which will be discussed in more depth in Section 5.6.3.

4.3   The Research and Development Plan

Companies that develop their own technological expertise do so through research and development activities. Only a small proportion of businesses rely solely on their own R&D departments. Most productive companies acquire the technological capabilities that they need by purchasing machinery, equipment, designs and sometimes even finished products. Others outsource their R&D activities to companies with expertise in the relevant areas. R&D is often the key objective in joint venture agreements, or other forms of cooperation.

Some companies will not attempt to lead at all in the R&D arena, and will prefer to be market followers. They keep an eye on the R&D leaders who are busy inventing new technologies and then race to imitate them. Sometimes they will invest more in design or in promotion to differentiate their products. Even the most dominant companies are constantly following market developments and incorporating new features to keep up with their competitors. One example is the market reaction to Apple's launch of the iPhone with a touch screen in 2007. This was quickly imitated by several other companies, including Samsung with the Galaxy series and others competitors who introduced new products, some of which boasted enhanced features including larger screens, improved resolution, a better camera or other components. In fact, Apple did not invent touchscreen technology. The first touchscreen phone was the IBM Simon, released in 1992. However, Apple recognized the appeal of touchscreen and invested in acquiring and developing this technology for the mass market.

The choice between outsourcing your R&D and developing it in-house is a very substantial one. Technological expertise which is for sale may be far from cutting-edge technology and chances are that developers are continually working on even newer and more modern technologies. Still, one of the advantages of acquiring technologies is that conducting your own R&D can take a great deal of time, and there is no guarantee of success. On the other hand, running your own R&D department may result in competitive advantages, including an additional source of income, if you can capitalize on the expertise itself. In-house R&D can also increase the value of your company, raising your equity price. Some companies choose to initially outsource the R&D, and then work in-house to add value, improve the technology and position themselves as R&D leaders.

In many areas, and especially in the high tech markets, companies with proprietary R&D are more attractive to investors. The Israeli high tech market is an interesting case. Although Israel has few natural resources, the country has managed to produce a tremendous amount of valuable R&D as a result of a very strong technological infrastructure, partly because of the country's military industry. Israel has also promoted this industry with economic and financial incentives which have induced numerous international corporations to build R&D facilities there over the past 30 years. This has resulted in a further strengthening of R&D expertise and the creation of a wide range of spin-offs and new technologies, which have, in turn, drawn investors, including the major global Venture Capital funds and strategic investors. Israel's outstanding record in R&D and entrepreneurship has been documented the book *The Start-Up Nation* by Dan Senor and Saul Singer, published in 2009.

Planning R&D is a significant part of the company strategy. It is also one of the most challenging areas to plan, because of the difficulty of accurately predicting timelines and milestones. The output of the R&D department, where expertise, human resources and equipment are invested to attain a higher level of knowledge, is also very hard to quantify. Complicated as it is to measure the efficiency of an R&D team, it is critical to define milestones and achievements. Some of the considerations in setting up an R&D division are:

- **In-house development vs. outsourcing**

  The primary decision in R&D is what elements are best developed by your own team as opposed to what you can outsource, as described in the preceding paragraphs. To make this decision, you will need to do some market research, ascertaining what technological elements are available, from whom and at what price, and weigh this against what your own team can do. The military industry and the nuclear industry are good examples of industries where there is a lot of knowledge available on the market, but using outsourced R&D is expensive and only possible under strict limitations. However, in various civilian industries, from microelectronics production through software development, there is a wide range of products available, sometimes off the shelf, which can save expensive R&D resources and reduce the uncertainty of the process. Still, outsourcing can be expensive, and can create excessive dependence between companies.

In-house development involves hiring researchers, developers and other staff, buying equipment and setting up laboratories. This can be worthwhile in companies in which ongoing development is anticipated for the long term and when the company has the skill and expertise to surpass competitors. Another advantage of in-house development is that there is no question about the ownership of the intellectual property and the fruit of your R&D work. If you don't need to have the R&D in-house, it may be wiser, and it is often faster, to rely on other R&D companies in which the infrastructure is already up and running, and which are willing to outsource their services. If you are outsourcing, it is essential to enter into sound contracts establishing who owns the R&D results and guaranteeing confidentiality. While we recommend performing background checks and assuring the reliability of all of your suppliers and business partners, this process is even more critical when choosing an R&D contractor, since your business and success will rely heavily on the contractor you choose.

It is also quite common to cooperate with universities and research centers in order to develop new products, particularly in the areas of medicine, medical instruments, chemistry and nanotechnologies, among other fields. Many universities have centers which facilitate the cooperation between the institution's R&D teams and corporations seeking to strengthen their R&D activity. This association is often a win-win situation, where the corporation benefits from the academic research, and the university benefits from the commercialization of its findings. However, when the technology is jointly owned, the university will often share in the rewards, taking a share of the profits.

- **Development goals**

  Research and development involve a lot of creativity and the R&D team sometimes overflows with ideas and directions. This is a positive situation and can lead to unexpected breakthroughs. The challenge is to channel that creativity and make sure that your team knows what your development goals are, and is working towards them. Your time and financial resources are limited, and they must be allocated towards achieving productive results. Steve Jobs was known for his leadership in setting specific goals for Apple's long-term plan. Many companies, including IBM, have special labs which allow the scientists complete freedom to innovate and explore new ideas. Smaller companies have considerably stricter limitations in resources and need to work with a clearly defined plan. Companies that cannot afford to invest in R&D beyond a certain point will work with what they have and focus their efforts on improving production capabilities, or on developing new applications for existing technologies and products.

  The pharmaceutical industry is a good case in point. Market leaders in this industry concentrate on developing completely new products and improving existing products. Other companies in this sector focus mainly or solely on generic products which require production expertise, but far less R&D. The same holds true for the electronics industry, the food industry and the cosmetics industry, among others.

- **Allocation of R&D resources**

  Even a small R&D team requires a clear plan for allocating its resources, as there are often several projects in process concurrently. In fact, the question of how to allocate resources among projects presents a serious dilemma. On the one hand, it is advantageous to spread your R&D resources and not work only in one direction. By running several projects simultaneously, you improve the odds of success; even if most of your projects don't yield good results, there is a chance of some of them succeeding. On the other hand, you do not want to disperse your resources too thinly. By investing more in one particular project, you are increasing the chances of its success. There is no one solution to this dilemma. Companies involved in R&D should consider these issues when deciding upon their R&D strategy, and make their decisions based on what they believe can be achieved by the company, with an eye towards the market's needs at all times.

  When working on multiple projects, you should still make sure that they share a common goal. Projects with related directions can give rise to a shared experience effect that leads to better results all around. All projects should be consistent with the company's strategy. This approach will achieve better and more significant development results. In addition, having focused and consistent goals makes a company more appealing to investors and business partners.

- **Keeping the applications in mind**

  In a business oriented lab, the research and development goals are not merely academic, but must result in practical applications which can be sold. There are countless startups headed by scientists from universities and industries with patents and other intellectual property which are the result of years of research. Some have made unique discoveries, spending valuable time and effort on further R&D, only to discover that the market is either not interested in the proposed technology, or is not willing to pay for it. Or even worse, that a competitor has already beaten them to the market. Sometimes there are significant gaps to close before the market can widely adopt a technology. Consider robotics, which is a highly developed science with incredible capabilities. Unfortunately, the costs are still so prohibitive that the adoption of robots to date has been far below forecasts, and they currently perform only about 10% of manufacturing tasks, according to The Boston Consulting Group (BCG). However, BCG forecasts that this will change dramatically in the coming years due to declining costs and improved performance in robotic systems.

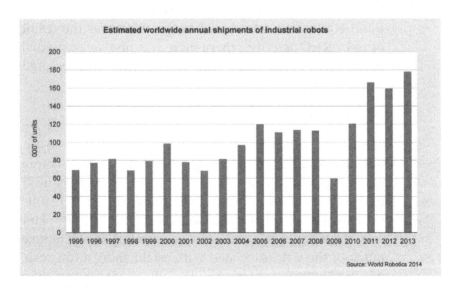

Figure 4.8: Adoption of Robots 1995–2013

Many products in the medical diagnostics field failed because they didn't find a good fit with any market segment. For example, they were too expensive for small clinics and at the same time they could not compete with the sophisticated equipment that large medical centers and hospitals could afford. Here again, we encounter the significance of good market research and understanding exactly who your potential customers are, what they need, at what price and with which specific features. Your market research may indicate that you need to change the course and objectives of your R&D. There are exceptions to this rule. Henry Ford is popularly quoted as saying, "If I had asked people what they wanted, they would have said faster horses." Whether or not the quote is genuine, it certainly raises the issue of the extent to which customer attitudes can influence innovation. Cars, PCs and microwave ovens are among the breakthrough technologies which completely redefined the market and created demands that customers themselves would not have anticipated. Other examples can be found everywhere. GE's garbage disposal equipment introduced in the 1950s was the result of risky R&D activity, where there was no way to predict the market's reaction, and the market was created through educational campaigns.

- **Pilot plants**

Setting up full-scale production is not only very costly, but also involves some retrials and adjustments before obtaining good results. Often the same parameters used under laboratory conditions will produce different results in full-scale production. Although setting up a pilot plant is in itself expensive and time-consuming, it can reduce much of the risk associated with establishing a full-scale production facility. Moreover, the pilot plant can serve the company on an ongoing basis, for small-scale production, especially on trial series of new materials and process.

- **Employment terms**

High quality R&D recruits are vital for a company that relies on development. R&D personnel often come with a great deal of expertise, and deepen and increase their knowledge throughout the course of their employment. This creates both a strong reliance on them, and a concern about the knowledge base that the team could potentially take with them upon leaving the company, and relay to your competitors, or use in a new firm of their own. For these reasons, employment terms for R&D staff are structured to reward the employee well on the basis of success, and ensure long-term loyalty to the company. Often, enduring loyalty is encouraged through options packages and other benefits that vest over a long-term period. It is also particularly important to have these employees sign non-disclosure and non-competition agreements. However, even these agreements have their limitations and are enforceable only according to the constraints of the local laws.

- **Managing R&D**

Scientists with the necessary technical knowledge do not necessarily have business and management skills. Yet these skills are indispensable for managing the employees, projects and milestones effectively, and for aligning the R&D activity with the company's business goals. In addition, in order to run the department well and obtain good results, the R&D manager must be an expert on the technical and scientific aspects of the work. An R&D manager with both skill sets is ideal, but hard to find. It is important to set clear parameters for success and work according to approved plans with precise timeframes and budgets.

- **Economic evaluations of R&D projects**
  It is not easy to quantify the benefits of R&D projects, even when the costs seem straightforward. There is a great deal of uncertainty regarding time frames and results, and an economic evaluation of the R&D projects will involve many estimates and assumptions. Still, an estimate is usually better than no evaluation at all, and we recommend evaluating each project's performance to the best of your ability.

- **From development to production**

  One of the critical moments in a product's life is when the decision is made to move it from development to production. The timing of this decision can have a major impact on the success of the product and even of the company. On the one hand, the product is never complete, and R&D can continue working on improvements and enhancements endlessly. And on the other hand, at some point, you will need to stop investing in R&D and get the product out to the markets, especially if you have competitors rushing into the market with their own products.

  There is no formula to determine when the time is right. It is important to have clear objectives from the marketing department and understand which features must be ready before the product moves to production and which features can wait to be introduced with the next generation of products. A long, drawn out R&D process has its price, both in company resources and in delaying the arrival of the product to the market.

  Many companies, particularly software companies, release beta products, or test products. These are released to gain market interest, as well as benefit from significant testing and feedback before delivering a finalized product. New Internet-based products and services are launched and constantly revised in real time, often with active help from users. We can often find premature, incomplete products on the web which later blossom into great successes.

4.4 The Production Plan

4.4.1 *Companies with Products in Development*

Production planning and setup begins at some point during the development stages, depending on the amount of time it will take to set up production. During the early stages, the production facility will be planned only in very general terms. Some of the decisions that will be made include:

- The selection of a production technology: Research the market to find out what production technologies are available, and choose the one that best suits your needs. Some of the considerations may include the level of automation, the volume of the output in the near future and the potential for scaling up and expansion.
- Machinery and other equipment: Even at an early stage, it is important to determine what items you will need, who the suppliers are, the cost and the delivery timetables. Consider whether to have your production facility set up by one vendor as a turnkey project, or whether you will purchase each individual item and set up the facility yourself.
- Location: We discussed the marketing considerations for location in Section 4.2. Now consider location from the logistical view point. Is the location convenient for finding employees and shipping raw materials and finished goods? Does it offer convenient enough access to manage it well? Consider the necessary infrastructure, such as power lines and waste removal. A location which is close to an airport or a shipping dock will reduce logistic costs and time. Some localities offer various financial incentives to certain types of industries they are interested in attracting. Consider what location suits your company's image and needs, whether the best fit would be a prestigious facility in a modern industrial park surrounded by leading companies, or perhaps less appealing surroundings in a low end industrial area at a much lower cost.

- Production Layout: A thoughtful and thorough layout plan for your facility will enhance efficiency and cut costs. Consider:

  o   The number of facilities and their sizes
  o   Storage areas for raw materials and finished products
  o   Production areas
  o   Quality assurance
  o   Packaging
  o   Transport of goods from one area to another
  o   Administrative and support functions

  You may decide to set up the facility gradually, beginning with a smaller production volume, and expanding as the business grows.

- Production Manpower: Decide on the different types of skills that your production staff will need and how many production workers you will need for each skill set. You can then prepare work plans and consider where you can recruit and train the employees. Depending on the size of the facility and the type of tasks, you can decide on the organizational plan for the production staff. You may need a few teams and managerial levels, with specific tasks for each of them.

- Safety and Ergonomics: Creating a safe, comfortable and sensible work environment will increase employee satisfaction and efficiency and decrease risks to employees and work interruptions. The safely mechanisms that you employ must comply with local rules and regulations.

- Environmental considerations, particularly pollution, power consumption efficiency, renewable raw materials etc., have great import, not only from a conservationist's point of view, but also in terms of regulatory compliance and costs.

Your decisions on the production facility will be based on multiple factors. Consider, for example, a medical instrumentation company, built around a new and innovative development. The ideal location for the head offices and R&D center may be close to a major medical center, where experiments can be carried out. The location of the plant, on the other hand, might be determined by the proximity to transportation hubs or special tax and other financial incentives. The initial decisions, especially whether to manufacture the entire device in one plant or to outsource the production, should be based on the estimated sales over time. It may make sense to use one strategy in the near future, and move over to a different strategy as sales increase.

These decisions will heavily influence your logistic plan, which deals with the management of the flow of goods, information and other resources between the point of origin and the point of consumption, and includes the storage and transportation of raw materials, inventory and finished goods. A logistics plan is necessary for all companies, whether producers or service providers. Some of the main components of the logistics plan are shown in Figure 4.9.

Together with the decisions on production and logistics, consider the locations of your head office and additional marketing offices. If you are providing web services, consider

The logistics plan includes:

- Demand Forecasting
- Procurement
- Material Handling
- Warehousing and Storage
- Order processing
- Packaging
- Inventory Control
- Transportation
- Handling Returned goods

Figure 4.9: The Logistics Plan

whether you will be setting up your own servers (and where) or outsourcing. The outline of the logistic plan is important at the early stages of the planning process, and is often an important factor influencing many parts of the production plan.

4.4.2 Established Companies

If you are introducing a new product in an existing company which already has production facilities set up, strive to ensure that your new production plans are compatible with the rest of the company's activities. You will need to plan production volumes based on the marketing plans, as well as on the available production capacity, considering the rest of the products in the production line. There are numerous details to be examined, and, without careful planning, you can miss your production schedules for any number of reasons. For example, if your marketing plan forecasts sales of ten million units annually, but your production capacity is eight million units at most, the shortage of production capacity must be addressed quickly. If your production plan requires a certain volume of raw materials, you will need both sufficient storage space and transportation capabilities to meet your schedules, and you will need to place orders with the suppliers early enough to ensure their timely delivery.

An established company should reassess its production facilities and adapt them as needed. Sometimes the existing production facility can accommodate the new products, and other times, changes must be made, whether through in-house development, purchases of additional equipment or the hiring of employees with more specific skills. Many factories become more automated over time, and that too should be evaluated periodically with an eye towards new developments in the market.

Some of the important decisions to be made include:

- Inventory management

  The production facility requires an inventory of raw materials and will create an inventory of finished products. A good inventory management system will ensure adequate raw materials for production, track inventory levels and optimize storage, both at the production facility and at the distribution centers. There are different approaches to inventory. The "Just-In-Time" strategy is to keep minimal inventory, and add to it as needed. The advantage is that it is cost efficient. The disadvantage is that there is a high risk of business disruption if inventory is lacking. It is not suitable for industries in which there are fluctuations in the supply time and availability of raw materials, or for products which have fluctuations in their order levels. These companies must plan to maintain larger inventories, which are more costly, but decrease the risk of disruption due to unavailable materials or insufficient finished products.

- Production engineering

  A well-planned production facility will be structured with various needs in mind including:

  o   Minimization of downtime
  o   Ongoing maintenance
  o   Repairs
  o   Future upgrades for improving output efficiency and product quality
  o   Future capacity growth

- Quality assurance

  Innovation often captures market attention, and is certainly a very appealing element of your product. But quality assurance is equally important, and, in some cases, even more so, for attaining and maintaining a sizable and loyal market. Whatever your product is, customers have very low tolerance for faulty products, and some market segments require extremely high quality standards. Markets such as the medical, security, defense, automotive and luxury markets, for example, all require the most stringent quality standards for most of the products they buy. A number of recognized international quality standards help provide this type of assurance. The leading standards organization is the International Organization for Standardization (ISO), which has been developing standards in a wide variety of areas since 1987. Most ISO standards are highly specific to a particular product, material, or process, with over 18,000 ISO standards now in use. ISO 9001, relating to quality and ISO 14001, relating to environmental performance, can be applied to any organization, whether it provides goods or services.

In some countries, there are active local standard institutes, such as UL (Underwriters Laboratories) in the United States and TüV in Germany. MIL (United States Military Standard) is used in security and defense in the United States and is also adopted by other countries. In other industries, large manufacturers have their own sets of standards, with which their suppliers must comply.

There are many products which require formal approvals from government authorities before they can be sold. These might be departments of health or environmental protection agencies, for example, as well as national standards institutions. Approval from the United States Food and Drug Administration (FDA) is required for marketing a wide variety of products in the United States (see text box). FDA approval also provides marketing advantages, including targeting more specific markets, pricing and quality positioning. For example, skin care products, such as products for acne, eczema and dandruff, can be found both in cosmetics departments and as over the counter or prescription pharmaceutical products. Many products which fall between both categories in terms of usage are sometimes referred to as "cosme ceuticals". Even if no medical claims are made, these products must be tested for safety and cannot be sold at all, even as cosmetics, without FDA approval. The same products will require a much stricter FDA process involving more stringent clinical testing and quality assurance to be sold as pharmaceutical products with specific medical claims. This course is more complicated, but can result in marketing and pricing advantages.

Quality assurance is important for the following reasons:

- Faulty design can lead to dangers, damages or even injuries for which your company will be liable.
- Quality processes increase productivity, output, consistency and reliability.
- Defective products or services will lead to lost business.
- Quality assurance costs money, but a good QA process is likely to make financial sense in the long run.

What does the FDA do?
(Source: *FDA website*)
The FDA is responsible for:

- Protecting the public health by assuring that foods are safe, wholesome, sanitary and properly labeled; ensuring that human and veterinary drugs, and vaccines and other biological products and medical devices intended for human use are safe and effective
- Protecting the public from electronic product radiation
- Assuring cosmetics and dietary supplements are safe and properly labeled
- Regulating tobacco products
- Advancing the public health by helping to speed product innovations
- Helping the public get the accurate science-based information they need to use medicines, devices, and foods to improve their health

- In-house production vs. outsourcing

  Setting up a production facility is costly and takes time. Sometimes, using subcontractors for all or part of the production process makes sense. In many cases, there are existing production facilities that already have the necessary production expertise and equipment and are capable of producing parts of your product or even the end product itself almost immediately. This can save time in getting your product out to the market, and can save the substantial costs of assembling the production facilities, hiring the production employees and training them. However, the cost of producing through subcontractors will affect your bottom line. In the past, the rule was that the higher the volume of production, the more likely it was that companies would eventually set up their own production facility, or purchase one that suited their needs. This is still often the case. In electronics, certain components have become commodities which are mass produced by third parties, especially in East Asia. Even the largest producers buy components ready-made according to their specifications. A common example of this is the computer keyboard.

  In comparing in-house production to sourcing from another company, some of the advantages of in-house production are that you have greater control of:

  o Quality
  o Technology
  o Confidentiality
  o Delivery schedules

- Manual labor vs. automation

  Most modern production plants use automation to some degree. However, automation in general and robotics in particular can be prohibitively expensive. The more automation there is, the higher the set-up and maintenance costs will be. As part of your planning process, calculate the costs and benefits of different configurations of manual labor and automation to determine your best option.

* Second sourcing vs. sole sourcing

Consider a computer manufacturer with an ongoing contract with a graphic card producer. The graphic card producer must provide the computer manufacturer a steady supply of graphic cards, regardless of any local issues which may affect its own plant. If, for example, the graphic card plant is located in an area prone to strikes, transportation disruptions or military conflicts, the steady production both of the graphic cards and ultimately the computers could be adversely affected. The computer manufacturer would be wise to find a second source of the graphic cards, or demand that the graphic card producer do so, and this is often stipulated in critical supply contracts. Another solution in cases of sole sourcing is to create a safety stock in a different location, in case of problems with the ongoing production.

Second sourcing and safety stock are serious factors to consider during production planning, as they affect major decisions, such as location, capacity and the total capital investment required. Having more than one supplier may also be helpful when negotiating preferred terms and conditions. However, too many suppliers are also problematic. The more suppliers you work with, the more effort you'll need to invest in managing them and monitoring their standards. In addition, using multiple suppliers means that your orders from each one will be smaller, and you can lose the cost advantage of buying in bulk.

The importance of second sourcing or creating a safety stock is illustrated in the example of the 1995 earthquake in Kobe, Japan, when the global electronics industry suffered significant disruptions because of the heavy reliance of the industry on semiconductor plants in Kobe.

4.5   The Financial Plan

The main objectives of the financial plan are to summarize the information in the business plan in financial terms and to provide support for decisions which will affect the firm's profitability.

The financial plan is the place where all of the information regarding the company is translated into financial terms and summarized, with a measurable bottom line. This enables you to review all the business decisions you need to make concerning production, R&D, marketing, manpower, etc., in light of their financial consequences for the business, and evaluate whether your business will be profitable and achieve its financial objectives. By processing the information in financial terms, you will be able to calculate the costs and benefits of different activities. You can then go back and eliminate aspects of the business that might be a financial drain with lower benefits, or invest more in the areas which can have a positive impact on your bottom line. This holds true for non-profit organizations as well. Although these organizations aren't seeking a profit, they do want to achieve the best outcome for the money invested, and this can be best accomplished through creating a financial plan.

There are three main elements of the financial plan:

- The Capital Requirements: the financing which will be needed for the business
- The Capital Structure: the sources of the financing
- The Financial Performance of the company: the financial performance measurement evaluates the results of the company's planned activities.

The methodology for preparing the financial plan will be described here. The written plan will be further described in Section 5.10.

There is no need to include all of the detailed financial schedules in your business plan. The business plan usually includes just a summary of your pro forma profit and loss and cash flows. However, preparing the detailed schedules is extremely important for several reasons:

- Planning purposes
- Internal management
- Further clarification and justification of business claims, as needed
- Negotiation purposes

4.5.1 *Capital Requirements*

One of the first things to do when preparing your financial plan is to define all of the capital requirements. These include:

- Machinery and equipment
- Plants and buildings
- A marketing and distribution infrastructure, including branches in other locations
- IT systems
- Logistics
- Research and development
- Offices (administration, computers, furniture)
- Working capital (elaboration follows)

Once you have defined your capital needs, you will know how much money you need to raise.

The actual capital requirements differ from one company to another. A company which is in the earlier development stages will have a more detailed R&D plan which might specify capital needs for R&D, such as:

- A structure for the laboratory
- Laboratory equipment
- Raw materials
- R&D labor
- Management costs
- Patent search and applications
- License and royalty fees

A company which already has an innovative product and is working on adapting a production line and creating a market for the product will need a large share of the capital for production, logistics and marketing, including:

- Production costs
- Raw materials
- Labor
- Utilities
- Logistics: storage and transportation costs
- Sales and marketing

    o Sales offices and manpower
    o Advertising
    o Promotional campaigns

The data needed for preparing the financial plan varies at different stages in the company's life. For an initial feasibility plan, rough numbers which are typical for similar companies might be used. However, at some point, your business plan will require more detailed information, and then it is important to use verified data, relevant to your particular needs. Get quotes from several suppliers for equipment and raw materials when calculating your financial needs. Determine how much the office space will cost in the various locations needed. Use real numbers for your payroll estimate. Evaluate different options from a financial perspective. For example, calculate whether buying or leasing machines is more economical. Compare your estimates with similar companies, both to see whether your results make sense, and ascertain whether there are better options for you to consider.

Time is a significant factor. To calculate how much money you will need as you proceed, establish the timing and payment terms of each capital investment. Payment terms can be very significant in evaluating the project, especially when raising capital is difficult. For example, if you are paying for most of your equipment over a three-year period, and expect to have incoming cash flow from revenues from the 15th

month onwards, the incoming cashflow may be sufficient to cover some or all of your equipment costs from that point in time onwards. In such a case, you won't need to raise the full cost of the equipment in advance, assuming the business grows as forecasted. We recommend making realistic assumptions here! Take into account that at times, the in-flow of cash can be lower than expected, or delayed. Prepare contingency financial plans for those scenarios.

The financial plan should cover a period over which the company gradually becomes self-sufficient and can finance its own future activities. For many companies, the financial plan includes a five-year forecast. In industries which require a major long-term investment, such as energy, chemicals and aerospace, the planning horizon will be even longer. In the services industry, however, the planning horizon might be shorter. And in the computer and Internet areas, it is wise to keep to a detailed planning span of two to three years, because of the rapid changes in market needs, competition and prices.

Working Capital

The calculation of your working capital, or your operating liquidity, is too often neglected, and this can be disastrous for the business. Even a profitable company with valuable assets can suffer from lack of liquidity, which can evolve into an operational nightmare. Working capital measures the difference between cash outflows and inflows during a given period, usually between a quarter and a year. Net cash flows are often very different from accounting net earnings, and this difference can cause even a profitable firm to become illiquid at times, which can potentially stall activities or even halt them altogether.

Net working capital is most often calculated in financial projections as the current assets minus the current liabilities. If your current assets are lower than your current liabilities, you have a working capital deficit. Your current assets are those assets that can be converted to cash or used for your ongoing operations within 12 months. These include:

- Cash and short-term investments, including all types of cash equivalents
- Inventories of raw materials as well as of semi-finished and finished products
- Accounts receivable (amounts due for payment by your customers within the given timeframe)
- Prepaid liabilities

Current assets are also referred to as short-term assets or STA.

You current liabilities are basically everything you need to settle in cash within the short term, usually within 12 months. These include:

- Accounts payable: Amounts due for payment over this time period. This includes amounts due to your suppliers and service providers for goods and services as well as payments due for taxes, license fees or other payables which need to be settled during this time period.
- Payments due over the short term for financing

Current liabilities are also referred to as short-term liabilities or STL.

The amount of working capital that you require depends on many factors, including the payment terms to your suppliers and from your customers, and how difficult it is to raise short-term debt in a crunch.

Working capital funds are usually needed for the ongoing use of the company within a year. Storing sufficient inventory is a necessity for the operation of your business. You will require raw materials at the start of the production cycle, and there will be an inventory of finished products at the end of that cycle. These will all eventually generate revenues, and the value of the raw materials, work in progress and finished products will be converted to cash when the products are sold to customers. This cash will then be available for the ongoing needs of running the business, such as buying more raw materials.

If the company extends credit to its customers, it will have a balance sheet asset of accounts receivable which will be converted into cash within a short time, depending on the payment terms: for example, 30, 60 or 90 days. This amount is also part of the working capital.

On the other hand, when the company receives credit from its suppliers, it registers a balance under accounts payable which will have to be paid over the short term, but in the meantime, the company has cash available for its ongoing activities. This balance is in effect vendor financing which is available to the company. It creates a liability, and this is a negative working capital balance.

The bottom line is that the company needs to finance the excess of short-term assets over short-term liabilities in the short term. As the company grows, both the short-term assets and the short-term liabilities may grow, and this will usually increase the working capital required.

The ratio of current assets to current liabilities is known as the current ratio, and is often referred to as STA/STL (short-term assets/short-term liabilities). The golden rule

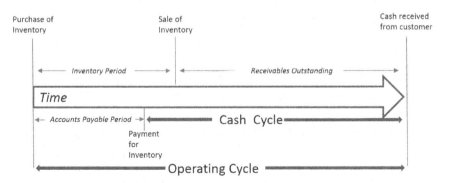

Figure 4.10:   Cash and Operating Cycle Example

holds that current assets should amount to double the current liabilities. Banks often use the current ratio to evaluate firms trying to borrow money, and firms with a current ratio of less than one, i.e., with negative working capital, will be considered high risk borrowers.

Although the working capital balance can be calculated from the financial statements, the accounting value does not reflect the cost of the working capital. If vendors extend a 90 day line of credit to the company, the company does not have to raise these funds by liquidating other assets, which will hopefully be earning interest or value. Nor, in the more common scenario, will the company need to increase costly debt during that period. These are important considerations in the business model, and particularly in calculating a healthy level of working capital for the company. The obvious rule is that less cash tied up in working capital is better for the company from a financing point of view, provided that the company has adequate inventory to manufacture products on time. Working capital models which typically have high current ratios are the various prepaid services, such as memberships and subscriptions. In these cases, the company generates cash before it provides the service or pays its vendors, and can use these funds to expand the business more rapidly. The working capital balance is an interest-free form of valuable cash available for the company's use over the short term. However, many prepaid subscriptions are sold at a discount over pay-as-used services, so the question of the profitability and financial value of prepaid vs. pay-as-used can be more complicated, and should be considered carefully.

You should calculate the working capital that you will require by building a cash flow model for all of the company activities. The cash flow model incorporates all of the cash collected and paid for current company activities. It does not include capital investments or long- and medium-term financing, apart from the current payments which are due over the period of one year, in the case of loans.

The difference between the incoming cash and the outgoing cash will indicate how much working capital you will require. A large amount of working capital is usually invested at the start of operations, after which there are additional incremental increases, depending on the needs of the company at the various stages of its life. Growth firms will need to invest more funds in working capital during their expansion period.

4.5.2 *Sources of Capital and Capital Structure*

This section describes the sources of financing for investments required in the company and for its ongoing operation. In the early stages, before the company has any revenues, it is utterly dependent on owner equity and external financing, which will usually be sought from the founders' family and friends and from angels. These funds are referred to as seed money. Companies with an innovative product or technology are often eligible for grants which can provide partial funding. At later stages, many companies seek financing from venture capital funds. Once the company has sales that generate cash, these activities will provide self-financing. As the company grows further, it can raise additional funding either through a private placement or a public offering of its shares. All of these terms will be explained in this chapter.

The decision of where to raise capital is an important one, and must be considered very carefully. Most entrepreneurs would benefit from professional advice, as there are numerous issues at stake here, including:

- Ownership and control of the company
- Taxes
- Financial and business risks

For example, when financing with debt, the owners benefit both by keeping a greater share of the equity and from the fact that the interest on debt is usually a tax deductible expense, regardless of who made the loan, including the owners themselves. However, the interest rates on external debt are likely to be high, and debt increases financial risk. In addition, if the company is not profitable during its first years, or if the company is entitled to tax breaks, for example, through government incentive packages, there may be very little benefit from the interest expense deductibility. Another consideration is that once a company has raised a large amount of debt, the level of existing financial leverage may make it harder to obtain additional credit in the future. Large equity investments are regarded by bankers and suppliers as a sign of financial strength and owner confidence in the success of the company, whereas high debt levels raise concern.

One of the additional advantages of equity investments is that eligibility for grants is often contingent on a minimal level of equity investment. A company with low debt levels is also much more appealing to venture capital funds, who are understandably not interested in providing financing for preexisting debt. In fact, it is very common for VCFs to demand that debts to the owners be converted to equity as a condition for funding, to ensure that the new money invested will be used exclusively to expand the business.

Sources of capital are described further in the following two sections:

4.5.2.1   Non-Equity Sources of External Financing
4.5.2.2   External Financing from Equity Investments

4.5.2.1 *Non-Equity Sources of Financing*

- Self-financing

  Some businesses are able to self-finance, or rely completely on owner loans or equity. For example, a project on any scale, even a very large one, which has enough upfront or early payments to finance the company through to the completion of the project, will be self-sufficient and will not need to raise money. An owner who can finance the company until it has sufficient cash flow generated from its business activities will not need to turn to external financing sources.

Such self-financing businesses are the exception to the rule. Most companies will require some external financing.

- Debt and bank credit

Financing that does not involve ownership of the business creates a liability, such as debt or credit. This type of financing is typically provided by banks and other lending institutions, suppliers or bondholders. Company shareholders also provide loans to their companies at times. These types of liabilities usually have predetermined repayment terms over a given period and bear interest. Loans from the owners are the most flexible, and repayment can often be planned according to the company's abilities and needs. The risk level of the debt depends on the level of risk in the company. If a company has a healthy cash flow or appreciable future orders, it can demonstrate its ability to repay the loan on time and is more likely to receive loans for financing. Lending money to a company just starting up is a high risk proposition and repayment is not guaranteed. The interest rate is calculated accordingly, with a high risk loan carrying a higher risk premium. Because debt holders do not benefit from the upside of a company's potential growth, they are more interested in seeing some form of assurance that the loan will be repaid than in estimates of remarkable growth potential.

In planning your company's capital structure, you will need to carefully consider what will be optimal for your company and how much financial leverage is advisable. Financial leverage is the ratio of total debt to total assets. The higher the level of external financing by debt, the more financial leverage the company has.

Financial leverage: the ratio of total debt to total assets.

Financial leverage allows you to increase sales and earnings without further reducing your equity, but increases the risk of default and bankruptcy. Even when your cash flow is insufficient, you will still need to make the interest payments on your loans. Leverage poses special risks for the equity investors, because the debt holders have a prior claim on any company funds for repayment of their loans with interest.

If you can raise money from your bank, you can attain financial leverage without reducing your equity. This is excellent for a company poised to achieve early financial independence. For other companies, however, bank financing may make it harder to find equity investments at a later stage, thus increasing the risk of default and bankruptcy.

Banks generally require collateral against funding, particularly with young startups which usually have no assets other than ideas and know-how. With more mature companies enjoying both more experience and solid sales records, banks may offer credit, especially against sales contracts or account receivables. As banks tend to be conservative and usually subject the firm to a due diligence process, bank approval for a loan can be considered a positive signal.

Since the late 1990s, some banks have been giving loans to high tech companies at the usual business interest rate, but with the addition of receiving options on the company's shares. These options are called warrants. The banks take a higher risk on these loans in exchange for a potential capital gain if they exercise the warrants. This type of activity dropped drastically after the dot-com crash of 2000–2002.

- Supplier credit

  Supplier credit, which appears in the financial statements as "accounts payable," is an important source of financing common for many types of businesses of all sizes. It allows the buyer to receive the products or services and pay for them at a later stage, generally one to three months after receipt. The payment period might be considerably longer for heavy machinery, even extending to several years in some cases. As described above, supplier credit is very important in calculating the working capital needed. If products are turned around and sold quickly, supplier credit can eliminate the need for external financing to cover payments for the products ordered. To use a simple example, a retailer who orders goods, receiving 60 days of credit before payment is due, and can usually sell the goods within 30–40 days for cash, does not need to invest funds in the goods stocked. Once the cash is collected from the customers, the retailer has the funds available on time to meet the scheduled payments to the supplier. Of course, the retailer must still take into account other funding needs and potential fluctuations in the sales levels.

- Leasing

  Leasing is an important tool which should be considered carefully in the financial plan. In leasing agreements, the lessee or the receiver of the leased assets, such as machinery, trucks, or other items, may use those assets in return for a predefined series of payments. The types of assets which may be leased include:

  o   Land
  o   Buildings
  o   Machinery and manufacturing equipment
  o   Cars
  o   Computers and IT equipment

The principal advantage of leasing is that instead of these items being paid for in full in advance, they are immediately available for the company's use in exchange for low monthly payments, which are usually tax deductible. The disadvantage is that for long-term use, the cost of leasing generally is higher than that of outright purchase. In any case, it is important to consider the tax and other financial considerations, including depreciation, tax breaks, VAT and financial incentives which may be available with capital investment.

The two common types of leases are financial leases and operating leases.

Financial Leases: Financial leases are in fact financing plans in which the lessee makes monthly installments with the option of purchasing the asset at the end of the lease period. These leases are usually long-term, for the full economic life of the asset.

Operating Leases: These are straightforward rental contracts, which run for shorter terms and not for the full economic life of the asset. Here the lessee uses the asset, sometimes together with other services. This is a very common type of lease for companies that expect to renew or replace equipment frequently. Among the most common forms of operating leases are those for cars, trucks and even aircraft.

- Incentives for capital investment

Many countries have capital investment incentive programs for helping companies with their initial setup costs or expansion costs by partially offsetting the cost of the capital investment. These programs can contribute a certain percentage of the costs of technologically advanced machinery, clean technology, equipment, software and hardware, up to a certain predefined limit. For example, a program might contribute 25% of eligible capital investments, with a minimum investment of $50,000 and a ceiling of $2,000,000. These programs are often designed with export in mind, with preferential terms for exporters in qualified industries.

Capital investment incentive programs are available for different industries in the United States, Canada and many European and Asian countries. We recommend that you do the research and find out what is available to you in countries where you intend to do business.

- Incentives for R&D

Another common type of incentive program is funding for R&D projects. These programs usually require very detailed plans describing the R&D project, its applications and its market potential, as well as ongoing reporting of timeframes and resources allocated to the project. These efforts are often worthwhile, as you may be eligible for a research grant to help offset the high costs of research, or other R&D incentives.

- Business Incubators

A fledgling company just starting out will often need management guidance, offices, administrative staff, labs and financing. Business incubators are designed to provide young businesses with many or all of these, together with professional advisors, networking activities and other resources. Business incubators have been around since 1959 and have expanded significantly since the 1980s. They have been shown to increase the likelihood that a startup company will stay in business for the long term after leaving the incubation environment. A business incubator's main goal is to produce successful firms that will become financially viable and independent. Incubation activity is taking place worldwide, in both developed and developing countries.

According to The National Business Incubation Association (NBIA) in the US, the earliest incubation programs focused on a variety of technology companies or on a combination of light industrial, technology and service firms, today referred to as mixed-use incubators. However, in more recent years, new incubators have emerged targeting specific industries, such as food processing, medical technologies, space and ceramics technologies, arts and crafts, and software development. Incubator sponsors have also targeted programs to support microenterprise creation, the needs of women and minorities, environmental endeavors and telecommunications.

More information can be found on the site: *www.nbia.org*

- Export incentive programs

Many nations throughout the world have government sponsored programs to help companies start exporting and which provide support for developing and increasing exports. These programs often offer training programs, assist in drawing up business plans for exporting and provide valuable knowledge, such as market research and information on foreign buyers. Equally important, they often offer financing programs or opportunities to enhance your exports by participation in trade fairs or through sharing some marketing and other costs.

In the United States, visit the government website at *http://export.gov*. In other countries, be sure to inquire what services are available to you. There are likely to be some programs that can help you develop your business.

- Grants

There are many publicly funded programs which are designed to encourage new and growing businesses. The rationale for many of them is to encourage companies that can potentially bring jobs and prosperity to their neighborhoods and cities. The grants are usually distributed through various government ministries, departments and agencies, both nationally and locally. Many companies that are developing new products or technologies are able to fund part of their activities through research grants. These grants are often provided by government institutions as part of government incentive packages for technological advancement. Such grants usually demand regular progress reports, and in some cases, a share in the intellectual property and royalties from the end product, in return for which the firm is given conditional loans to be returned only if the project is successful and profitable.

During the early stages of a new enterprise, particularly before deciding on the location of the business, it is often advisable to do some research on the grants and conditional loans that may be available to you in different locations.

- Crowdfunding

  A new form of funding for new enterprises has developed over the last few years, known as crowdfunding. Harnessing the pervasiveness of social media, crowdfunding platforms enable businesses to present their business plan or product to a large number of individuals in order to raise money. While each individual contribution may be very small, when thousands of participants are involved, the total funds raised through crowdfunding can be very significant. There are currently countless crowdfunding platforms worldwide, funding everything from businesses to social causes and artists. The ability to access individuals who are willing to support ventures and causes has had a significant impact on many companies and causes, with over $16 billion invested worldwide in 2014 through these platforms. The concept of crowdfunding is not new, and was used as far back as the 17th century to finance book printing by hopeful purchasers. The Internet has created an opportunity to combine this concept with the direct access to unlimited potential investors for new ventures.

There are several crowdfunding models, including:

1. Rewards Crowdfunding: Contributors place advance orders for the product or service that the business is planning to develop. While this may sound ideal, as it enables businesses to raise money without incurring debt or sharing equity, it also has its problems. Many companies that raised funds using this model have incurred many difficulties along the way, including sales tax issues, difficulties delivering huge back orders on pre-sold products, etc.

2. Equity Crowdfunding: In this model, participants receive shares for their funds. This is a straightforward equity investment, as described in Section 4.5.2.2, with a wider distribution of shares than a private placement and a smaller one than an IPO. While the business benefits from the funds raised, it also sacrifices equity and incurs obligations to a very large number of equity holders. Legal requirements for companies seeking to raise capital through equity crowdfunding differ from country to country. In the United States, the Jumpstart Our Business Startups (JOBS) Act was signed in April 2012 to provide an online mechanism through which companies can sell securities or equity in their businesses to non-accredited investors. However, the U.S. Securities and Exchange Commission (SEC) has not yet determined the final rules for this legislation. Get advice on what legal obligations you may incur before choosing to use this channel to raise capital.

3. Debt Crowdfunding: In this model, potential borrowers and lenders are matched on crowdfunding platforms.

There are also many non-business crowdfunding platforms, including royalty-based and charity crowdfunding platforms which match donors with charitable causes.

Category	Description	Examples of Crowdfunding Platforms	Best For
Rewards	Contribution in exchange for a good or service	Kickstarter, Indiegogo, RocketHub	Projects with pre-sale items
Equity	Investment in exchange for equity	AngelList, CircleUp, Seedinvest	Growing companies with an exit strategy
Royalty	Investment in exchange for royalties on future revenue	Upstart, Bolstr	Companies seeking to pay only from profits
Debt	Loan, receive interest on principal	LendingClub	Companies with cash flows and collateral
Donation	Straightforward donation	YouCaring, DonorsChoose, WeDidIt	Non-profits, medical emergencies

Figure 4.11:   A Summary of the Main Crowdfunding Models

4.5.2.2 *Equity Investments*

A company's equity for accounting purposes is comprised of equity investments and retained earnings. Equity investments are made when partial ownership of the company is sold in return for funds provided to the company. The individual or firms purchasing a part of the company's equity in the form of company shares become partial owners of the company, together with the other shareholders. In the early stages, equity investors are often friends and family of the founders as well as angel investors, who will be described later. The percentage each investor owns is determined by the terms of the equity agreement. There will often be a few rounds of funding. At each round, the company is valued and the stock price is negotiated. As the company grows and becomes profitable, the retained earnings, which can be used for expansion or for dividend payments, increase the equity of the company. Equity in accounting should not be confused with the company's value; in fact, there are often significant differences, particularly in technologically based start-up companies. The book value or accounting value of the equity can be very different from the economic value the same equity has for investors or shareholders. Many start-up companies that invest heavily in R&D may have a negative book value, yet their economic value may be very high.

If the company is successful, the company's owners will ultimately benefit from their investment, both from dividend payments and from an increase in the value of their capital investment.

Growing companies don't usually pay dividends for the first few years, instead keeping their funds available to invest in expansion. Microsoft, for example, paid its first dividend in 2003, a full 28 years after its founding.

There are many famous success stories, particularly in the Internet world, where founders and early investors successfully sold part or all of their shares at incredible profits. Pierre Omidyar founded AuctionWeb in 1995, with a minimal investment. In 1997, Benchmark Capital invested $5 million in AuctionWeb, for 21.5 percent of the company. This was the only round of funding for the company, now known as eBay (Echo Bay Technology Group). The company continued to grow and when eBay went public, it was valued at $2 billion.

Facebook.com, founded by Mark Zuckerberg while he was a student at Harvard University, is another outstanding case. Enjoying the support of venture funds along the way, the firm reached a market value of $100 billion at its IPO in 2012, with a price/earnings ratio of over 200.

Success stories like those of eBay and Facebook have become legendary, but should not mislead you when making your own financial projections. The majority of successful companies can expect more moderate growth and should build a realistic business plan. Investors will appreciate reasonable assumptions based on an excellent product or service and well-researched data far more than unrealistically optimistic scenarios. Bear in mind that because neither dividends nor an increase in value can be guaranteed, investing in equity in a new company involves a high level of risk.

In privately held companies, the major equity investors, apart from the owner, are often angel investors and venture capital funds (VCFs). At a later stage, the company may choose to offer equity to the public in an initial public offering (IPO). Secondary public offerings may be made following a successful IPO.

The Stages of Raising External Funding Through Equity Investments

As a company develops, there are different stages of funding which may be provided by different sources of funding, including venture capital:

o   Pre-seed funding: Your first funding is often raised from friends and family, enabling you to work on your idea and create a workable plan.

o   Seed Money: This early funding is provided to help entrepreneurs prove the viability of their new ideas. Initial seed money is often provided by angel investors (see section on angels below).

o   Startup: Companies with a proven concept need funding for developing their product and other functions of a new company, such as marketing and initial production.

o   First Round (Series A round): This round is targeted towards production expansion, following development of a working sales model.

o   Second Round: This funding is typically targeted towards expanding marketing, increasing the existing revenue level and becoming profitable.

o   Third Round: This round is also called mezzanine financing, aimed at preparing the company for an IPO.

o   Fourth Round: This round of funding is often a public offering, and sometimes provides veteran shareholders an opportunity to liquidate part of their holdings.

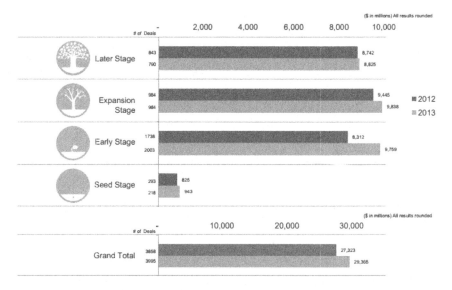

Figure 4.12:   Venture Capital Investments in the USA in 2012 and 2013 by Stage
Source: PricewaterhouseCoopers/National Venture Capital Association Money Tree™ Report, Data: Thomson Reuters).

- **Raising money through angel investors**

Private individuals seeking to invest money in young startups are called angel investors, or just angels. Many angels are active or retired entrepreneurs or senior executives with interests in particular business areas. Apart from funds, they also can provide mentoring and important business experience and contacts.

Angels fill the gap between whatever funds the entrepreneur has managed to raise on his or her own, or from friends and families, and what the company needs before it is ready to turn to VC funding. Angel investments typically range from $25,000 to $500,000, but they can be lower or higher. The higher the investment, the more control and influence the angel is likely to seek. An angel may seek approval rights or a seat on the company's board of directors.

> **Preferred Shares**
>
> Some early external investors in startups negotiate for preferred shares, while the founders and other early investors hold ordinary shares. The preferred shares give their owners equal partial ownership of the company similar to that of the other shares, but also provide some additional advantages. For example, in the event that the company is liquidated, the preferred shares have priority over the ordinary shares. In any distribution of funds, the holders of preferred shares are entitled to repayment of their initial investment before additional funds are distributed equally to all other shareholders.
>
> Some preferred shares include a ratchet. The ratchet provides additional protection to the shareholders whereby, in the event that additional funds are raised at a lower evaluation, the preferred shareholders' investment will be protected from dilution. For instance, if they invested in three shares at $20 per share and in the new round, shares are valued at $15 each, they might receive an additional share to readjust the size of their stake.
>
> Ratchets can prove very constraining and problematic in future rounds, and should be offered with great caution.

Some angels form groups and work together. This enables them to each invest in several companies, thereby diversifying their investment portfolio and reducing their risk. When pooling together, a typical investment in a startup can be as high as $5 million. When raising money from a large group of individuals, consider the legal requirements. Some countries may require a prospectus when an investment is offered to more than 35 individuals, as it may be considered a public offering.

Total angel financing is substantial, with $20.1 billion invested in the United States in 2010, in a total of 61,900 companies. This is nearly as much money as the VC funding during this period, but the angel funds were invested in over 60 times as many companies (Source: Jeffrey Sohl, Center for Venture Research).

- **Raising money through venture capital funds**

  Professionally managed venture capital funds as we know them today have been around for over 50 years, operating mainly in the United States. A huge venture capital boom took place in the late 1990s, peaking in 2000 with $105 billion invested in over 8,000 deals. However, following the dot-com crash that began in March 2000, many venture capital investors sought to reduce the size of the commitments they had made to venture capital funds. Today, there is a sizable venture capital industry, with approximately $30 billion invested in the United States alone in 2013, representing over 4,000 deals. Of this amount, only 6% was invested as seed money. The funds were mostly invested in early stage and expansion

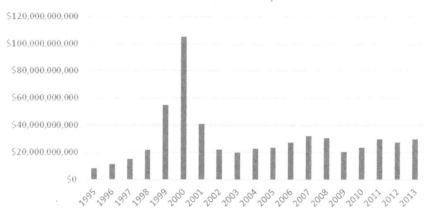

Figure 4.13:   Venture Capital Investments in the USA Since 1995

Source: PricewaterhouseCoopers/National Venture Capital Association Money Tree™ Report, Data: Thomson Reuters).

funding (Data source: PricewaterhouseCoopers/National Venture Capital Association MoneyTree™ Report, Data: Thomson Reuters).

Venture capital funds invest in a share of the company's equity. Originally, venture capital funds worked individually, but over the past several years, funding by groups of VCFs is commonplace. VCFs differ from one another and develop different areas of expertise. Some focus solely on certain industries or geographic locations, while others have more varied portfolios and operate worldwide. Some are interested in fledgling companies, and others focus on more mature companies.

VCFs' expectations and involvement with the companies they invest in also vary. Some become actively involved in the company's management and have veto rights over critical decisions, including changes in the company strategy, executive hires, investments, mergers and acquisitions and other major decisions.

VC funds are interested in profits and target their investments towards companies with strong potential. Some of the elements they look for include:

o   a well-founded business plan
o   an excellent management team; team members with proven track records are a great asset
o   an outstanding product or service which either solves a pressing problem or provides a clear benefit or "customer delight"
o   dedication and passion in the company
o   a high return on their investment; VCFs generally seek successful exit potential

VC funds are set up for a limited period of time, often 10–12 years. During the first few years, the fund invests the capital in a portfolio of ventures. After investing, the VC fund is usually active in helping their companies maximize their

Firm	City	# of Deals
Kleiner Perkins Caufield & Byers LLC	Menlo Park, California	103
First Round Capital	Philadelphia, Pennsylvania	94
New Enterprise Associates, Inc.	Menlo Park, California	83
Andreessen Horowitz LLC	Menlo Park, California	73
Draper Fisher Jurvetson International. Inc.	Menlo Park, California	68
True Ventures	Palo Alto, California	62
Innovation Works, Inc.	Pittsburgh, Pennsylvania	61
Google Ventures	Mountain View, California	61
500 Startups, LP	Mountain View, California	55
Battery Ventures LP	Waltham, Massachusetts	54
U.S. Venture Partners	Menlo Park, California	51
Intel Capital Corp.	Santa Clara, California	50
Bessemer Venture Partners LP	Larchmont, New York	49
Polaris Partners	Waltham, Massachusetts	47
Greylock Partners	Menlo Park, California	47
Sequoia Capital	Menlo Park, California	47
Atlas Venture Advisors Inc	Cambridge, Massachusetts	44
Ben Franklin Technology Partners Southeastern PA	Philadelphia, Pennsylvania	44
General Catalyst Partners LLC	Cambridge, Massachusetts	43
Canaan Partners	Menlo Park, California	43
Domain Associates LLC	Princeton, New Jersey	43
Khosla Ventures LLC	Menlo Park, California	41
SV Angel II Q LP	San Francisco, California	41
Norwest Venture Partners	Palo Alto, California	40
Lightspeed Venture Partners	Menlo Park, California	39

Figure 4.14: Most Active Venture Capital Investors in the US, 2013

Source: PricewaterhouseCoopers/National Venture Capital Association Money Tree™ Report, Data: Thomson Reuters).

potential. Successful VCs open new funds regularly. Some of the leading VC funds worldwide are listed in Figure 4.14.

- **Private placements and public offerings**

  Once the business model has proven successful, funds can be raised for the company by selling shares either through a private placement or a public offering. In a private placement, the shares are offered to a select group which may include private individuals, institutional investors, VC funds or other funds. In a public offering, the shares are sold to the general public. The first public offering is known as the initial public offering (IPO) and subsequent offerings are called secondary offerings. Some issues to consider with this type of funding:

o The size of the company and its readiness for a public offering

Public companies are listed on a public stock exchange and any individual can buy a share at the listed price. Private companies are held by only a select group of investors. There is a minimum size requirement for companies that want to go public, and the company must have a few years of operating history. Public offerings are relevant only when a company seeks to raise a significant amount of money and the investment bankers and underwriters predict a successful outcome.

o Costs

A public offering is expensive. The direct costs to a large, established company can be in the range of five percent of the funds raised, and for a small and risky company, they can reach twenty percent. These costs include payments to the accountants and attorneys working on the disclosure documents, payments to the various underwriters and investment bankers or consultants, distribution costs of the shares, etc. There are also numerous indirect expenses for public relations and company executives' time during the long and challenging process.

While a private placement is comparatively inexpensive, there are fewer potential buyers and the stock may be sold at a lower valuation than in a public offering.

o Tax considerations

Capital gains often have different tax levels depending on the type of ownership of the shares and on the law governing the company. It is advisable to get some expert advice when deciding on where to set up the company.

○   Disclosure

When making a public offering, the company is required to make a full public disclosure of any financial information which may be of public interest. The company publishes a prospectus describing the company's business, including financial statements, biographies of officers and directors, and detailed information about senior executive's compensation, any litigation that is taking place and any other material topics. The company must be prepared for audits by the regulators, such as the Securities Exchange Commission and the Stock Exchange, to ensure that full disclosure has been made. Once the company has gone public, it will have to continue to report on all of its activities, including any major new agreements or changes in senior management. Private companies do not have the burden of this type of ongoing reporting.

○   Corporate governance

In 2002, the United States government set new regulations for all American public company boards, management and public accounting firms. This legislation is known as the Sarbanes–Oxley Act (or SOX). Under this legislation, top management is personally obligated to certify the accuracy of financial information, among other matters. This imposes additional costs on managing a publically traded company. Other countries have imposed similar rules.

○   Future funding rounds

A public offering allows a large number of investors to acquire a share of the company. This broadens the capital base and often increases the share value. A higher share value is beneficial to all of the shareholders, including the founders and initial investors, and future funding rounds are likely to yield a higher value if the company performs successfully. Often future funding rounds will facilitate mergers and acquisitions which have been planned as part of the company's growth strategy.

o   Management time

There is a great deal of time invested in a public offering, both before and after the event. Senior management will typically spend about six to twelve months of intense work with the underwriters, attorneys, accountants and public agencies on the offering. A considerable amount of work goes into the negotiations, contracts, prospectus, and pricing. Many offerings are preceded by a "road show" during which the company visits prospective investors and investment bankers. Preparations for the road show are intensive and can take months out of valuable company time.

Once the public offering has taken place, there is continual scrutiny of the company's disclosure

Global IPOs by number of deals and capital raised

* 2013 IPO activity is based on priced IPOs as of 2 December and expected IPOs by end of December. *Source: Dealogic.*

Figure 4.15:   IPOs — 2001–2013

Source: Global IPO Trends, Ernst & Young

which entails ongoing reporting and auditing, which is also time consuming and expensive. The company's management must maintain relationships with the investment bankers, analysts and major investors.

To summarize, a public offering is a very weighty undertaking, which can yield excellent results but may not be suitable for all companies.

• **Raising capital offshore**

In the past, most financing for technological startups and many other new ventures came from the United States. Cross-border listings began in earnest in the 1990s and have been growing significantly over the past 10 years. We also see many cases of joint listings. Multinational companies choose to raise capital through foreign exchanges for many reasons, including:

o Higher valuations
o Access to new investors
o Expansion into new markets
o Maintaining an international presence

With United States stock exchanges subject to more severe regulatory restrictions, and Europe and the United States facing financial instability, many companies have turned to Asian markets over the past years to raise funds.

In January 2010, the world's largest aluminum company, Rusal, became the first Russia-based company to list on the Hong Kong stock exchange, raising $2.2 billion. The same year, Avangard, Ukraine's largest egg producer, raised $187.5 million through an IPO on the London Stock Exchange. Notwithstanding China's attractive markets, 2010 also saw 41 Chinese companies newly

Quarterly IPO deals by region

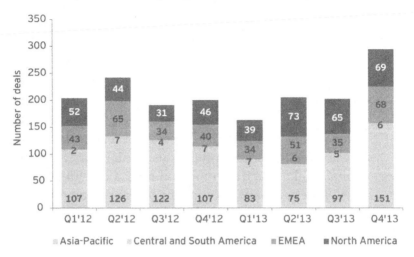

* Q4'13 refers to projected IPO activity, which consists of priced IPOs as of 2 December and expected IPOs by end of December. *Source: Dealogic.*

Figure 4.16:   Quarterly IPO Deals by Region 2012–2013

Source: Global IPO Trends, Ernst & Young

listed on the American exchanges, the majority of which enjoyed an excellent reception.

The increase in cross-border IPOs is enabled by technological advances that give investors access to real time trading data on stock markets anywhere in the world.

When deciding where to list, companies should carefully consider many factors, including regulatory requirements, speed of listing, the investor base, valuations and cost.

Summary: Capital Structure

Every company aspires to become financially independent and profitable. Once the company enjoys healthy sales and is able to pay off its debts, the remaining funds can be used for the ongoing financing of its operations. This enables the company to operate independently without increasing debt or equity investments. As the company accumulates reserves, it can finance expansion and investments for continued growth without additional funding.

Many companies can and should take advantage of various programs which offer them debt at lower interest rates or grants, although these programs do have strings attached in the form of reporting requirements and other compliance terms. These can help with part of the financing. For the remainder of your funding needs, you will probably have to consider whether you prefer raising debt or raising equity capital. Make this determination after a careful study of the possibilities available to you. The business plan must address the capital structure in general terms, and include details of the short-term plans.

A Few Words on ESOP

A discussion of capital structure would not be complete without mentioning Employee Stock Option Programs, also known as ESO or ESOP. Such programs issue stock options to employees in order to enhance their loyalty to the company and give them an incentive to remain with the company for the long term. These are plans in which employees are issued options which vest over a period of time. For example, a plan might grant 3,000 options which vest evenly over three years, with 1,000 vesting each year. Once the options have vested, the employee can buy the agreed amount of company shares at a predetermined price during a limited time period. This is known as exercising the options. The unvested and unexercised options usually become void once the employee leaves the company. These programs are particularly important for the retention of senior staff, but many companies offer them to almost all employees. Facebook's IPO created hundreds of new millionaires due to its ESO program, which has been extended to most of the company's 3,000 or more employees worldwide. While there are many people who have acquired wealth through employee option programs, there are also many people who have been disappointed when their options became or remained worthless, especially after the dot-com crash.

ESO programs are considered so valuable that many venture capital funds require them as part of their standard investment terms. In such cases, the company's owners hand over ten to twenty percent of the ownership of their company to current and future employees by allocating equity to the ESOP. The most senior and valuable employees will usually be offered longer-term programs.

Before structuring an ESO program, get legal and tax advice on the implications of different possible ESO structures. These can have very significant ramifications on the value of the options.

4.5.3 *Financial Performance Forecast*

At any stage of the company's life, and particularly when seeking external funds or business partners, the financial performance forecast is an invaluable tool in assessing the company. This is true not only for business enterprises which are built with profitability in mind, but also for non-profit organizations and philanthropic projects, in which there may be no material profits. Any organization needs to demonstrate a clear justification for the allocation of funds to show that resources are being used optimally.

The financial performance forecast is the place where all of the plans and actions detailed in the other sections of the business plan are quantified and translated into financial terms. The result is a plan, complete with financial targets which the business will aim to achieve.

Most investors and partners will evaluate the business based on its financial potential, and will invest only in a potentially profitable business. The original entrepreneur may be less objective and more willing to follow a dream even without a solid financial justification. But potential investors usually evaluate many other alternative investments, ranging from dozens to hundreds or even thousands of other companies. And as the VC community has experienced over the past 20 years, investors will divert their funds from venture capital to less risky investments, such as fixed income deposits or government bonds, if they believe they will not receive a high average return on capital from VC activity. Keep in mind that investors can compose an investment portfolio of their choice from publicly traded companies and/or indices through the stock market. Consequently, the benchmarks to beat are these alternatives, which also usually have the advantage of being much more diverse, liquid and transparent.

Measuring the value of a company is a complicated task, and there are many methodologies for doing so. We will review some of the main methodologies in this chapter, and in Appendix I, but for a more complete familiarity with valuation and measurement theories, please refer to the literature on this topic.[1]

We often recommend leaving the valuations outside of the actual business plan, or including them in an appendix, and allowing the pro forma financial reports, such as the projected financial results, to speak for themselves. The reasoning behind this is that investors have various interests and needs and will analyze the data in different ways. What is important is performing the evaluations and making the financial justifications available as needed. This will aid you in your own decision-making process and reinforce your confidence that you are not wasting your time, money and energy. It will be invaluable to you when managing future processes, whether you work with external investors and partners or not.

---

[1] An excellent resource is R. Brealey, S. Myers, and F. Allen, Fundamentals of Corporate Finance (2013, 11th edition), McGraw-Hill.

Two of the main approaches to financial performance measurement are:

1. Evaluation based on accounting methodologies
2. Evaluation based on corporate financial theory, usually based on discounting expected net cash flows

Using Accounting Methodologies to Measure the Company's Performance

When using accounting methodologies to evaluate your company, create straightforward projections according to the accepted accounting standards, such as the International Financial Accounting Rules (IFRS), which are accepted in many countries throughout the world, or the General Accepted Accounting Principles (GAAP), used in the United States. These evaluation reports are called pro forma reports, and include profit and loss statements based on the planned activities, and often contain balance sheets and cash flow statements as well. We will describe these reports in detail in Section 5.8.

The proforma reports will show the company's projections for income and expenditures, including:

- Revenue

  The company's revenue, or income, is based on the sales projections and pricing which were provided in the business plan.

- Cost of Goods Sold (COGS)

  COGS is defined as the direct costs of producing the units being sold, including:
  - Raw materials and supplies
  - Production labor costs, including associated costs such as payroll taxes and benefits
  - The costs of running the production facility, such as utilities expenses, machinery depreciation, etc.

  o The accounting depreciation of the plant and equipment involved in the production, reflecting the allocated costs out of the investment in the production line. This is a non-cash item but may have large impact on the results from an accounting perspective. Depreciation is briefly explained in Section 5.7.

  o Overhead of the business which can be allocated to production.

  COGS is calculated at the time of the sale. At this point, the units are removed from the inventory, with the finished goods reflecting their production costs. A sample table of COGS is provided in Section 5.8.

- Gross profit

  Gross profit is calculated by subtracting the COGS from the revenue. Gross profits represent the profits after paying the direct costs of producing the units sold, and before deducting the remainder of the company expenses, which are called operating expenses.

- Operating expenses

  The main categories of operating expenses are:

   o Sales and marketing expenses

    The costs of implementing the sales and marketing plans are calculated and appear in the operating expense section of the pro forma profit and loss statement. This can help you determine whether the planned expenses are proportionate and reasonable, considering the expected revenues from sales. During the initial stages in the life of a company, these expenses will be very high relative to the revenue, but they should later drop to resemble industry norms. A sample table of sales and marketing expenses is provided in Section 5.6.

   o Research and development costs (R&D)

All research and development costs will appear in the operating expenses section of the pro forma profit and loss statement. A sample table of R&D expenses is provided in Section 5.7.

o   General and administrative expenses (G&A)

All general management, office and administration expenses will appear in the operating expenses section of the pro forma profit and loss statement.

• Financial expenses

All costs associated with external financing will appear in the financial expenses section of the pro forma profit and loss statement. Report the costs of long-term loans separately from the short-term financing costs. Another important component of the financial expenses is the cost of working capital. Be sure to specify and detail both the nominal and real costs.

• EBIT or EBITDA pro forma reports

Some pro forma reports describe the forecasted results without including tax and interest in the calculations. These reports provide Earnings Before Interest and Taxes (EBIT) forecasts, which has a forecast of revenues, COGS and expenses, without interest and taxes. EBITDA reports go a step further by also excluding depreciation and amortization, which are non-cash items, as seen in Figure 4.17.

The pro forma profit and loss statement (P&L) is usually detailed on an annual basis and covers three to five years. Prepare the P&L on a quarterly basis for the first two years, as a benchmark for planning the cash flow statements and understanding your financing needs in greater detail.

Potential investors may look for different things in the pro forma P&L. Those who are very sales oriented will scrutinize the financials to see whether there is good sales potential, whether sales are ramping up well over time and

Forecasted P&L Results (in USD, $K)								
	2014		2015		2016		2017	
Income	3,125		7,171		17,451		36,037	
COGS	1,418	45%	3,212	45%	7,652	44%	15,816	44%
Gross Profit	$ 1,707		$ 3,959		$ 9,799		$ 20,221	
	55%		55%		56%		56%	
Expenses								
R & D	384	12%	852	12%	1,784	10%	2,577	7%
Sales and Marketing	1,133	36%	2,167	30%	3,296	19%	5,352	15%
G&A	631	20%	902	13%	1,351	8%	2,091	6%
Other	319	10%	681	9%	1,399	8%	2,659	7%
Total Expenses	2,468		4,601		7,830		12,679	
EBITDA*	-761		-642		1,968		7,542	
	-24.3%		-9.0%		11.3%		20.9%	

EBIT	-24.3%	-9.0%	11.3%	20.9%
R&D	12.3%	11.9%	10.2%	7.1%
Sales and Marketing	36.3%	30.2%	18.9%	14.9%
G&A	20.2%	12.6%	7.7%	5.8%
Other	10.2%	9.5%	8.0%	7.4%

* Earnings before interest, taxes, depreciation and amortization

Figure 4.17:   Sample Profit and Loss Report

whether there are repeat sales, when relevant. Others are seeking a good technology, or a great management team, or all of the above. Although there have been many products that became extremely popular without a revenue model, with Google, Twitter and Wikipedia being outstanding examples of products or services which became household names even without revenue models, they are the exception rather than the rule. Most companies will be required to show that there is money-making potential before they can raise funds, and that is what the pro forma financials aim to do. This also holds true for companies that are working purely on R&D. Although such companies show only expenses for long periods of time, the pro forma financial statements help to quantify and manage these costs, and also demonstrate when the knowledge can become valuable. This is important when trying to raise financing.

Again, it bears emphasizing that the "one size fits all" model does not work well in the business world, and there are many exceptions that must be dealt with. If your company is

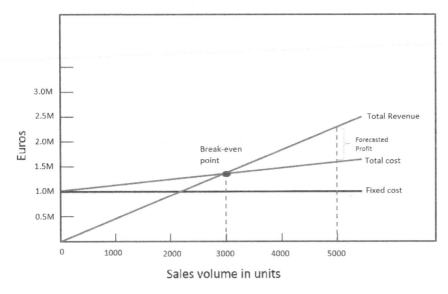

Figure 4.18:   Break-Even Analysis

In Figure 4.18 above, the company forecasts 1M Euros in fixed costs, and additional incremental costs per unit sold. The break-even point in this example is when the company sells 3,000 units. The company expects to sell 5,000 units in the given period, and the forecasted profit is shown above, as the total revenue minus the total cost.

developing a new cure for skin cancer, the critical factor is medical success and the business plan will focus on the R&D activity and milestones, and much less on pro forma analysis.

When preparing pro forma financials, keep in mind that these are projections and are therefore likely to change under different circumstances. Because of their sensitivity to change, it is important to update them continuously, consider different possible outcomes, and perform a sensitivity analysis accordingly, as shown in Appendix II.

Another important form of analysis is finding the break-even point in the project. Break-even analysis identifies the minimal level of production and sales at which the company covers its operational costs. Fewer units sold will lead to losses, and more units sold beyond the break-even point will lead to profitability. See Figure 4.18 for an example.

Using Financial Methodologies to Measure the Company's Performance

When using financial methodologies to evaluate your company, you will measure the net cash flow generated by the project. The net cash flow equals cash receipts minus cash payments over a given period of time. It can also be calculated by taking the net profit before financial costs and adding back the amounts charged for any non-cash expense, such as depreciation and amortization.

The timing of cash flow receipts and payments is critical when planning your business activity, and will dictate how much financing you require. When using financial methodologies to measure the performance of a project or company the financing costs must also be considered. Any cash tied up in the company could theoretically be used to earn money in different ways over time. For example, money could be closed in a time deposit and earn interest. It could also be invested in different projects. One of the important principles to understand is the time value of money, which is related to the time dimension of financial assets. Using financial methodologies, we analyze whether the project has a financial justification in light of the cost of the capital and the potential value of alternative investments. In addition to time, we also take risk level into account. For example, investors can always invest in traded securities, including corporate bonds or stocks. So there is a base for comparing the investment in your venture to an investment with a similar risk level in more liquid securities.

Three of the basic financial metrics used to analyze projected cash flows are: NPV, IRR and Payback Period. We will explain these briefly below and in Appendix I.

- **Net Present Value (NPV)**

  The NPV of your project is the value of the stream of future net cash flows presented in today's dollars. Net cash flows are calculated by subtracting the cash outflows from the cash inflows for each period. By measuring the investment required in the project against the total value of the future net revenues, NPV will help you evaluate if it is worth proceeding with your project. A simple example can illustrate NPV:

Consider a project requiring a $200,000 investment at the start of the first year of operation. This investment is expected to yield a six year net cash flow of $50,000 per year. On the face of it, $200,000 paid today will yield a cumulative future cash flow of $300,000. However, we must apply a discount rate to this revenue stream so that it can be measured against an alternative investment, such as a six year bond with an annual coupon. The discount rate is specific to the area of business and reflects the value of the money as well as the risk of the project. It also reflects the fact that a revenue stream of $300,000 gained over six years in installments of $50,000 per year is worth less than $300,000 in the bank today, and may be worth significantly less when the venture is a risky one and the company has a high cost of capital. The more uncertain we are about receiving the $50,000 in any future period, the higher the discount rate must be. The cost of capital is a weighted average of the financing costs through the various financing channels, such as debt, equity, credit etc.

To calculate the future cash flow stream, add the value of all the revenue streams and deduct all the operational and management costs, before any financial expenses.

The formula for NPV is:

$$NPV = -I_0 + \frac{NCF_1}{(1+r)^1} + \frac{NCF_2}{(1+r)^2} + \frac{NCF_3}{(1+r)^3} + \cdots\cdots + \frac{NCF_n}{(1+r)^n}.$$

I_0 is the value of the net cash flows at the start of the project, usually the initial investment. Because it is an outflow, it is negative. NCF_1 is the net cash flow at the end of Year 1, and so forth, until Year n, which is the final year calculated in evaluating the project. The variable r is the discount rate used. NPV therefore reflects the economic value of the project, or its added value.

Choosing the appropriate discount rate is a complicated task. We recommend using the discount rate of similar companies in the industry, and performing a sensitivity analysis. We will expand on this in the appendices.

A positive NPV indicates that the project is worthwhile and should be pursued. A negative NPV is a sign that there are better alternatives for the money invested, and that the project should be rejected. The NPV is the value of the entire project in today's currency, or the price which would be worthwhile to pay today for the future cash flows.

- **Internal Rate of Return (IRR)**

The IRR gives you the discount rate that sets the net present value of the cash flows to zero, i.e. the discount rate at which the investment breaks even. It is the rate of growth a project is expected to generate. To give a simple example, if you invest $200,000 today, and expect a net cash flow of $300,000 in one year, the IRR is fifty percent. In other words, if we replaced r in the formula above with fifty percent, the NPV would be zero. In this case:

$$NPV = -2000,000 + \frac{300,000}{1+0.5} = 0$$

IRR:

$$0 = -I_0 + \frac{NCF_1}{(1+IRR)^1} + \frac{NCF_2}{(1+IRR)^2} + \frac{NCF_3}{(1+IRR)^3} + \ldots\ldots + \frac{NCF_n}{(1+IRR)^n}.$$

Generally speaking, the higher a project's internal rate of return, the more worthwhile it is to undertake the project. As such, IRR can be used to make investment decisions.

- **Payback period**

  Payback Period is a financial metric that addresses the question of the length of time required to recover the cost of an investment. In essence, the payback period is the length of time required for the cumulative incoming cash flows to equal the cumulative outgoing costs, including the initial investment. It is usually measured in years. The advantage to a short payback period is that the investment costs are recovered sooner and are available again for reinvesting in a new project. It is usually assumed that a project with a longer payback period is riskier than one with a shorter payback period.

  For example, if a project costs $200,000 and is expected to return $50,000 annually, the payback period will be four years.

  The payback period is easy to calculate, but it has significant drawbacks. It is not a measure of profitability, since it ignores all cash flows after the payback period. It also ignores the time value of money, which we have seen is a significant factor.

Evaluating your project's performance using financial metrics is complex. In addition to making projections on your incoming revenues and costs, you need to take into account numerous other factors which affect your net cash flow, such as tax deductions resulting from applying the corporate tax rate on annual net profits, which include depreciation costs and interest payments.

In many cases, the business plan provides details of the expected cash flows, and leaves the financial analysis to the readers, who must rely on their own understanding of the industry and similar companies, as well as their tax considerations and cost of capital. This is particularly true in innovative technologies, where there is a great deal of uncertainty. If you do decide to perform an analysis using one or all of these metrics, we advise further reading in financial literature for a more comprehensive analysis.[2] It is also prudent to discuss your analysis with professional advisors.

Using Marketing Indicators to Measure the Company's Performance

Beyond the classic metrics described above, it is worth noting that there are many other tools used to estimate a company's value. Over the past 20 years, there has been considerable discussion about alternative valuation models which apply to the new business models in the Internet age. One of the most relevant metrics for application developers and Internet companies is the number of users, and the growth rate of the user base.

Some models, such as the CLV model presented below, value the company through customer worth in dollar terms. Another approach is to target the acquisition and retention of a large user base as a strategic goal.

- **CLV models**

    Marketing managers often use Customer Lifetime Value models (CLV or CLTV models). In these models, CLV is usually defined as the present value of all future profits obtained from a customer for the duration of his or her relationship with the company. This resembles the discounted cash flow approach described above, but when used at a more detailed level, the CLV provides information at the level of individual customers or customer segments, and allows for differentiation between types of customers and various levels of profitability. The CLV

---

[2]An excellent resource is R. Brealey, S. Myers, and F. Allen, Fundamentals of Corporate Finance (2013, 11th edition), McGraw-Hill.

models also incorporate the prospect of gaining new customers or losing customers to competitors in the future.

For example, a cellphone service provider will have a good estimate of the net value generated by a customer, the cost of retaining a customer and the cost of acquiring a new one. This information, together with the relevant probabilities of retention and acquisition, enables you to calculate the expected present value.

- **Targeting the acquisition and retention of a large user base as a strategic goal**

This strategy assumes that if the company can attract and sustain a significant user base, it will eventually be able to offer paid services and generate revenues. Or alternatively, that the massive interest generated from a large number of users will attract advertisers, creating revenues from banner placements, click-throughs and other advertising models.

This type of valuation was widely prevalent with new Internet-based technologies, particularly towards the end of the 1990s, but has been used with much more caution since the high tech bubble burst in March 2000. While the number of users remains a compelling and relevant parameter, most investors will still want to see the business model behind the venture.

The market values of the IPOs of Google and Facebook were based not on their revenues and business models at the time, but rather on the number of users they had. The expectation that these companies would develop a number of different ways of generating future cash flows was based on their strong user base. These companies have indeed been able to generate high profits from their user base, but many other companies have not been able to translate a strong user base into a profitable business model.

4.6   The Organizational Structure

We have repeatedly stressed throughout the book that a good product is not enough. But even a great product and a great team are not enough. A company must be structured well and managed well. And while good management requires a lot of personal skills, as well as experience, knowledge and even intuition, it also involves structuring the company so that the appropriate authority and responsibilities are delegated and information is made available to the decision makers. Not all entrepreneurs are good managers, and vice versa. And competent managers of small organizations may not be right for large corporations.

Efficiency and cooperation in an organization are fundamental for both internal and external purposes. Internally, processes run more smoothly and decisions are more coherent. Externally, the company presents itself as a well-oiled machine that is equal to the tasks it aims to perform, and this is important to future partners, investors, employees and customers.

Many technology-oriented companies don't pay enough attention to organizational structure. They are busy working on product development, and don't spend the time and resources needed for good management. Often these companies are run by engineers and scientists who lack managerial knowledge and skills. We see many companies with great ideas and even great products that never manage to take off at all, or that seem to take off, but then crash because of poor management. Even more tragically, many of these companies could have succeeded, but failed to heed good advice that they received from different advisors and investors, convinced that they were working on a new frontier where the rules of the game had changed. This was indeed the case with some Internet companies in the past, but conditions have changed. Finding the right balance between exploring new ground, yet using solid business sense will facilitate the success of your company.

4.6.1 *Planning the Initial Organization and Management*

Consider the following factors when setting up your company:

* **Decision-making**

  A young firm faces many challenges, in particular those related to its small scale at the early stages. There are few managerial resources, and even fewer professional managers. While product development and creating a marketing strategy are often central, don't let those pressures obscure the importance of management.

  Even a tiny company has to determine who is ultimately responsible for the different tasks that need to be performed and how information will be made available. It is not uncommon for one person to have more than one role in a young company. For example, the head of development might also manage or assist with production. But having everyone doing everything is not healthy, and can lead to confusion and lack of accountability. Roles should be defined, together with detailed responsibilities.

  Establishing decision-making processes is also vital. During the early stages, there is often a lot of informal decision making. While informal discussions, brainstorming and involving as many employees as possible should be encouraged, the ideas from these informal sessions should always be evaluated and tested. As the company grows, the decision-making process should be structured so that decisions can be made at different levels and the senior managers can focus on the main issues, rather than be involved in every minute detail.

  An office manager or executive secretary who makes the decisions on vendors for various items and services, such as copy machines, printing services, communications and much more, and handles the day to day office management, takes a significant load off the other managers.

In fact, many senior advisors stress the importance of having a good office manager even at the early stages, when the role of office manager is often overlooked because the focus is on other key hires, such as developers and marketing managers. Yet these very tasks which can easily be delegated can overwhelm the CEO, just when he or she should be thinking about the more important issues which give the company its competitive advantage. The same holds true for all areas of responsibility that can be delegated to other staff members. When delegating tasks, set aside adequate time for receiving updates and making joint decisions on important issues.

Employees at all levels will want to feel that they are valued. One of the key ways to retain satisfied employees is involving them in decision making and allowing them to influence company decisions. This helps them identify with the company and feel that they share in the company's success. Consider how to do this wisely, giving each employee an area of influence and an opportunity to be heard, without creating overwhelming and time-consuming decision-making forums. Structured meetings at all levels give everyone a chance to raise important issues and be heard. When all decisions, large and small, are made from above, employee satisfaction is low.

Another key way to motivate employees is to give them opportunities to grow within the company. Enabling them to learn new skills, and offering employees who excel new opportunities within the company, help to maintain a high level of satisfaction.

Of course, the compensation package itself should be planned carefully. Because new companies are often on a tight budget, they frequently enhance the compensation package with employee stock option plans, known as ESO, or ESOP, which are described in Section 4.5.2. By granting employees the opportunity to benefit directly from the company's success as it grows, you increase both their compensation and their loyalty.

All these factors will help keep your employees involved and excited about the company and its activities. Important information should be made available to employees as needed at important milestones in the company's development.

- **Organizational structure**

The company's organizational structure will evolve as it grows. During the early stages, it tends to be quite simple, and its primary purpose is describing company functions and areas of responsibility. But as the company grows, and you need to expand the management team, and eventually hire middle management, it will become essential to define different functions and divisions based on the critical areas of responsibility.

Check Point Software Technologies Ltd., which is a global provider of IT security solutions, best known for its firewall and virtual private network (VPN) products, was established with a tiny budget in 1993 by three founders. Today, the company has over 3,000 employees all working within a well-managed organizational structure, run by the company's current chairman and CEO, Gil Shwed. These employees are dispersed throughout the world, from the headquarters in Israel and the United States, to approximately 40 other countries worldwide. Multinational companies like Check Point, Intel and many others typically have several management levels, as well as management on both a regional and corporate level.

Such multi-level organizational structures should be created only when the time is right. Consider how to keep your organizational structure effective and cost efficient. As levels increase in an organizational structure, the information channels become longer and more complicated and the costs increase.

- **Board of directors**

  A board of directors is appointed to oversee the company's activities. Typical duties include:

  o   Establishing high-level organizational policies and objectives
  o   Selecting and reviewing the performance of the company's chief executive officer (CEO)
  o   Supporting the executive decision-making process
  o   Reviewing the risk exposure of the firm and how it is managed
  o   Reviewing and approving annual budgets
  o   Planning and supporting the execution of the financial strategy
  o   Reporting to the stakeholders about the organization's performance
  o   Setting the standards for the senior management's compensation packages

  The structure of the board of directors is an important strategic decision. Some entrepreneurs and investors seek to recruit very senior and influential board members. These may be successful people from various backgrounds, including business people, politicians or experts in the relevant industry, such as military experts, leading doctors or scientists. These board members can contribute a lot of valuable expertise and experience, as well as connections to relevant external entities. In addition, they may lend credibility to the company. The general assumption is that if such leading figures are associating with the company, they have carefully inspected and approved the company's products, strategy and management. This presents the company in a very favorable light to the general public, and is especially valuable if the company hopes to make a public offering.

  The board has an important role in maintaining a more objective perspective of the company than the internal management can. It oversees and audits the company's activities, and can offer considerable constructive strategic advice, as well as valuable professional contacts.

Alongside the many benefits a senior board provides, there are also significant expenses involved. Board members have diverse compensation packages, which may include fixed compensation together with options and/or stock packages. Electing senior board members often won't be realistic for very young companies, but should be considered as the company grows. In addition to the expense of a senior board, you may find that senior people are less available to devote time to the company's affairs.

When electing board members, carefully consider their voting privileges. The board of directors is not run democratically. In some companies, the voting privileges are closely related to the capital structure, where each investor is granted voting rights according to the amount of capital held. Sometimes the founders will have special privileges, such as veto rights in certain areas.

Any manager, whether of a new venture or an existing one, should be aware of all of the changing legal requirements that are emerging with respect to corporate governance issues. These include enhanced responsibilities of board members and greater independence in their decision making.

4.6.2 Planning and Managing the Organization Past the Early Stages

Once you are past the start-up stages, reconsider the different ways that you manage the company:

- **Decision-making**

  As your organization grows, you will need to structure the information flow and the decision-making process very clearly. Each manager should know who reports to him or her, and to whom they themselves report. In addition, managers should understand which decisions they can make alone, which decisions should be joint ones, and which decisions are beyond their domain or authority. A structured reporting process is important to ensure that scheduled updates are made. These updates help managers keep tabs on the most up-to-date information.

- **The Organizational Structure**

An explicit organizational structure is fundamental for an established company with many employees. The internal organizational structure should be clearly illustrated

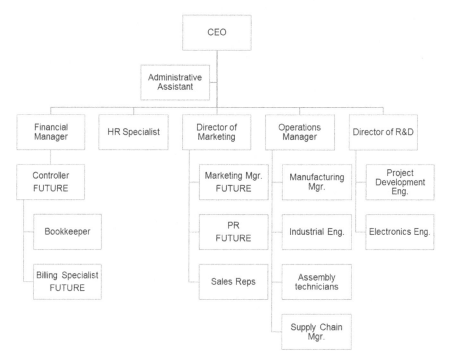

Figure 4.19:   Organizational Chart

In Figure 4.19 above, we see an example of an organizational chart. The structure of the organizational chart is based on the functions within the organization, which differ from one company to another.

using organization charts, and should be communicated both internally as well as externally. The organization chart should reflect the responsibilities and authorities of the managers as well as the lines of reporting and information flow. The structure describes the various divisions and department, the managers' positions within those divisions and departments, the hierarchy and subordinate relations. A high rank within the organizational structure signifies a higher level of responsibility and deeper involvement in the company's decision-making process. It is often helpful to inform vendors, subcontractors, customers and investors of the company's structure, to make sure that they understand who is responsible for interfacing with them.

When the organizational structure is not sufficiently clear, or does not reflect the de facto decision-making process, employees at all levels will encounter difficulties in coordinating and communicating across the different parts of the company. This will lead to unnecessary complications in the company, wasting valuable time and resources.

On the other hand, a well-structured and logical organizational plan will help keep motivation high and make all of the work processes more efficient. Because of the importance of the formal structure, hierarchy and internal delegation of authority, we recommend devoting the necessary attention to these decisions and periodically reviewing them.

- **Job titles**

  New companies that are short on cash have been known to award job titles prematurely to employees with insufficient skills and experience, in order to maintain their job enthusiasm and as an alternative form of compensation. Later on, it can be costly and disruptive to remove these loyal employees from their positions and responsibilities to make way for managers more suited for these jobs.

As realities change, organizational structures may need to change too. A major organizational restructuring is called for when a firm is merged into another company, purchases another activity, or undergoes other significant transformations. To have a successful merger of activities and functions, a new structure should be agreed upon and implemented by all parties.

In more mature and larger companies, individual divisions grow and are often headed by more senior "C-suite" executives, including the CFO (Chief financial officer), CMO (Chief marketing officer), COO (Chief operations officer), CIO (Chief information officer) and CHRO (Chief human resources officer), with the company being headed by the CEO (Chief executive officer).

- **Choosing the right structure**

There is no single structure that is right for every company, and you may face many dilemmas regarding the optimal structure. For example, the marketing department might be set up as one unit under a marketing manager and be responsible for all of the products in the company. Alternatively, some companies may prefer to manage each product group separately under the appropriate division within the company, assigning an independent marketing unit to each division. These are two entirely different strategies, and the selected strategy should help the company attain its goals. Regardless of which structure is chosen, coordination across departments and divisions will be needed.

A similar quandary may arise in planning the R&D structure. The R&D for the entire product portfolio might be managed in a single R&D department, or R&D may be managed within each individual product line separately. The same dilemma applies to business development, and even financial and administrative support.

Choosing the right organizational structure for your company depends strongly on the company strategy. A company with very diverse activities and product lines, or great geographic distances between units, might do well do manage each one separately, while structuring an organizational matrix in which reporting and information sharing take place not only within a particular division, but across all of the divisions which may benefit from it. On the other hand, there may be strong similarities between the various product lines, in which case it makes sense to have one department handling all of them. Brand management will also determine organizational structure. Many corporations with multiple brands choose to manage each brand as a separate entity, with its own production, marketing and other departments. Proctor & Gamble, Unilever and General Motors are examples of such companies.

4.6.3 *Delegation of Authority*

Even in a small company, it is essential to delegate sufficient authority to ensure smooth and efficient processes. When too many decisions have to be made by a single manager, bottlenecks are created, and less work gets done. Many first time entrepreneurs find it difficult to delegate authority and prefer to retain full control. But eventually, they must realize the importance of delegating authority and the benefit of team work. At this point, they must find methods for assuring the flow of information in the firm, or they will not be able to perform well.

So, in addition to determining who manages whom within the organization, and who is in charge of what project, decisions must be made regarding the scope of the authority for individual employees and managers. Some examples include:

- If a project needs certain services or products, such as a market research report, is the project manager or department manager authorized to make the purchase order decision independently, or does the marketing manager have the responsibility? Or perhaps a more senior manager will make the decision.

- If some software development is required for several different projects at once, and not enough programmers are available, who is responsible for prioritizing the projects?
- Will internal resources always be used, or will individual project managers have the authority to bring in their own subcontractors?

Many of these questions are answered by setting up a clear organizational structure with well-defined decision-making processes. One way to grant more independence to individual managers at all levels is by having pre-authorized work plans and budgets which are prepared and reviewed periodically. The budget describes the planned activity within the individual unit, department, division and ultimately the company, together with the schedule and cost for each activity. If these are pre-approved on an annual basis, with quarterly or monthly reviews, individual managers can work independently within the scope of their budgets, without the need for more senior approval for each decision. Of course, things tend to be very dynamic in many companies, so there will always have to be some flexibility built in.

Part 3: The Written Business Plan

Chapter 5

Writing the Business Plan

The written business plan serves many functions, both internally and externally, as we discussed in Chapter 2. It includes much of the material and knowledge acquired during the information gathering stages, integrating it all into a working plan. The presentation level of the material is extremely important. The business plan must be concise enough to be easily read, yet thorough enough to tackle all the essential questions. The presentation must be clear and visually appealing.

A well-presented business plan will help open doors. A badly presented one may result in a missed opportunity, even if the project is a good one.

For these reasons, it is vital to make a great business plan a top priority. This chapter will describe the process of writing the business plan, and its structure.

5.1 Who Does the Writing

The business plan is a comprehensive document. The writer must be completely familiar with the project goals, the knowledge accumulated during the pre-planning stages and the full details of the chosen business strategy. It might seem that the ideal candidate is the entrepreneur or project manager, with the help of the rest of the team. Unfortunately, the entrepreneurs or project managers are usually unable to dedicate full attention to this task. And although they may be gifted as entrepreneurs, they may not have adequate writing skills. The solution is often to delegate different parts of the business plan to other team members, according to their areas of expertise. This is possible when the entrepreneur or other senior executive stays at the helm and takes on the role of the chief editor, compiling and unifying the various parts. Of course, when the business plan is written by more than one individual, it is important to maintain a consistent style and structure.

In larger and more established firms, the CEO is unlikely to have the time needed to personally write and edit the document. In such cases, the task is delegated to other senior employees, such as an analyst reporting to the CFO.

Another solution is to hire a professional business plan writer from outside the company for this job. This is especially recommended for entrepreneurs who find it difficult to translate their plans into a written document. A professional writer will free up the start-up team and enable them to dedicate more of their time to the ongoing work of creating or expanding the company. Professional writers usually have the advantage of previous experience in writing and editing business plans. They can also have a more objective view of the company, which may be more similar to that of the targeted readers of the business plan. The business plan is written with the close cooperation of the founding team and different managers, who should supply all the required information, as if they themselves were writing the document. A good professional writer will take all of this knowledge and use it to prepare a single, coherent, well-written plan. This process often helps refine and specify the business strategy, which delivers benefits above and beyond the written business plan itself.

The project managers should be closely involved in the writing process to be certain that the written document accurately represents their plans. Even when a professional is hired, it may be a good idea to have the first rough draft prepared by the entrepreneur. This will help the entrepreneurs consolidate all their plans and consider all of the issues, thus ensuring that the business plan reflects their vision for the enterprise.

Once there is a written draft, we recommend that the company's legal counsel, and patent attorney if applicable, review it to ensure that the claims made are substantiated and will not cause legal complications. Other professional advisors' input is also valuable, such as that of accountants and business advisors. It is also important to get feedback from business partners and investors. Because their viewpoints may be somewhat diverse, their input will be valuable in creating the final draft.

5.2 The Principles of Writing a Business Plan

Earlier chapters discussed the information gathering stage. This stage often yields a tremendous amount of material, not all of which can or should be used when presenting the business in the written business plan. While the building blocks of the plan must be as detailed and accurate as possible, the written plan itself must be concise, readable and clear. It should inspire trust. The best written plan will serve as a springboard for serious discussions and negotiations. Deciding what information goes into the plan and what information will serve as backup to it requires a deep familiarity with the business together with sound judgment. There are four main principles guiding this decision:

1. Conciseness
2. Focus
3. Clarity
4. Organization

We will now describe these four principles in more detail.

- **Be Concise**
  When you send your business plan off to an investor, it will often be added to a stack with dozens, if not hundreds of other plans. For the investors, going through one business plan after another, finding the few that may interest them is a tedious task. Don't waste their time with irrelevant information and long explanations. Make sure that your message is delivered in a direct, clear and succinct manner. At the same time, being too minimalistic can also be problematic. The document should provide enough information to convey an unambiguous and complete plan. A document of 20–40 pages is generally acceptable, and the plan can sometimes run as long as 50 pages, particularly when there are numerous significant issues to cover. If you would like to provide more documentation, you can state that it is available upon request. Another option for entrepreneurs who feel strongly that their business plan is incomplete without more documentation, is to include the information in the appendices, which can even be submitted in a separate file or binder to avoid overloading the business plan. Submitting a separate appendices binder makes sense when additional supportive technical information needs to be available for various advisors, but should not be included in the main document to be read by the investors.

- **Focus**
  If you have reached the point at which you are ready to write the business plan, you have probably accumulated a great deal of information and knowledge. Yet, the business plan should include only the most relevant material. How can you determine what should be included and what must be left out?

  First, keep the primary features and goals of your venture in mind. A few examples:

  o If your venture is based on a technological breakthrough which will save time and money compared to the existing technology, stress the technological features and the comparison with currently available alternatives. Demonstrate why your technology is not available to your competitors, and estimate a reasonable lead time.

o If you are introducing a completely new innovation, focus on proof of your concept, market potential and your marketing strategy. For example, Internet software developers often have a beta version already being used before they turn to investors. The beta version indicates that there is a potential user base and provides valuable feedback.

o If you are seeking a marketing partner, stress the advantageous features of the products or services themselves. Highlight the potential benefits from the partnership.

o If you are pitching a strategic change in an existing company, stress relevant advantages to the company, whether in terms of brand development, IP, market share, sales or profits. Compare these proposals to the current situation.

Second, remember who your potential readers may be. Business plan readers can have very diverse interests, depending on the proposal. They may be investors or potential partners in the areas of marketing, development, production or more. Their focus will vary accordingly. Your business plan has to provide the specific information they require to make their decisions. A few examples:

o Investors seeking return on capital will require a highly detailed plan, beginning with a description of the company and the project and ending with precise and well-grounded financial projections. They will want to see how profitable their investment is likely to be, with a clear analysis of the risks involved. This type of business plan is the most comprehensive kind.

o Plans for potential marketing partners can usually be less financially oriented. Marketing partners will benefit from a highly detailed description of the products, the markets and the competitive environment. This information will help them decide whether to take on the challenge of marketing the products and determine what kind of outcome can be expected.

o Plans for potential R&D or production partners must be more technically oriented. The focus in such cases will be on the compatibility between your products and the partners' plans, know-how and facilities. Elements to stress in this type of plan include your technological skills and experience, profiles of your leading team members and technological achievements to date. Because this type of partner will not necessarily be taking on the marketing, your company may need to address the marketing plan in detail within the business plan.

Business plans vary widely due to the different goals they are pursuing and the readers they may address. We will discuss the structures of different business plans in this chapter. In fact, there may be several versions of the same business plan, each serving a distinct purpose: one for investors, another for marketing partners, etc. If you are working with several versions of your business plan, be sure to keep them consistent, or your integrity may be called into question.

- **Clarity**
  Keep your business plan reader-friendly. It should be easy to understand and interesting to read. Some pointers:

  o Use clear and consistent wording and avoid unnecessary complications. Bullet points with the essential information are more effective than wordy texts.
  o Clearly titled chapters, subchapters and itemized paragraphs help break down the text clearly, and help direct the reader to the most relevant sections.

o Charts and diagrams are very effective for conveying numerical data.

o Use graphics whenever possible to keep the readers interested. Submit a slide show or a video presentation with your business plan for more visual explanations.

- **Organization**
  Form is as important as substance in creating positive first impressions. An organized business plan conveys that this is a company with good organizational skills in all areas. A sloppy business plan makes a negative impression. There are many subtle nuances here. For example, investing in an overly fancy binding for a printed business plan can, in some cases, imply wastefulness and poor judgment, or be perceived as an attempt to distract from insufficient or poor content.
  Here are some general guidelines:

  - Use visually pleasing and readable formats and fonts.
  - In a printed business plan, the binding should be nicely designed and durable enough to look good even after several readings.
  - Have the document reviewed for grammar and spelling mistakes.
  - Pages, chapters, tables and diagrams should be numbered and indexed.

Business plans are often written in English, reflecting the needs of the widest range of potential readers in the business world. Even if you are starting your business in a non-English speaking country, you may eventually want to seek partners or investors from other countries. Writing the business plan in English will save you the time and effort of having it translated. However, if your foreseeable activity is within a non-English speaking country, it may be faster and easier to write in the language used most there, particularly if the business community is not fully fluent in English.

5.3   Organizing the Contents of the Business Plan

The easiest way to work on the structure of your business plan is to look through several Tables of Contents, which present examples of different possible structures. Some accepted rules govern the structure of the business plan, so a few of the main chapters are standard. The rest of the subjects which are addressed in the business plan can vary widely, and there is a lot of flexibility regarding the Table of Contents, so long as there is a logical sequence.

As we described in the previous section, the main considerations in determining the content of the business plan are its main goals and the potential readers. The business plan should be structured with these factors in mind.

When there are issues which are elaborated upon more than others within the business plan, consider breaking them down into chapters and subchapters. This will allow for the clearest presentation of the contents, without having overly long chapters or sections.

The first part of the business plan will always be the Executive Summary, which is not numbered as a chapter. Choosing the next section is less obvious, and should be done carefully. To a large extent, it sets the tone and direction of the business plan. Consider these examples:

- In a completely new venture, Chapter 1 will usually focus on the problem the new product or service expects to solve. For example, if the new innovative product is a medical device, the chapter will describe the relevant medical problem and the current devices addressing it. The chapter will demonstrate how the proposed medical device significantly improves the treatment of the problem compared to all existing alternatives.
- When the business plan is for an established company, you should highlight the company itself and Chapter 1 will be

dedicated to a detailed description of the company, including its activities, main assets and policies.

In the next sections of this book, we will review the most important chapters which should be included in most business plans. The order of the chapters can be rearranged to present the company in the desired manner.

Figure 5.1 describes the basic structure of the business plan. The order and contents will change based on the company. Examples of tables of contents from different business plans can be found in Appendix III.

5.4   The Executive Summary

Begin your business plan with the Executive Summary. It should appear immediately after the Table of Contents. In some business plans, it appears even before the Table of Contents, right after the title page, so that the reader plunges straight in. However, we prefer to have the Table of Contents appear at the beginning of the document, as the most convenient place for referencing.

The goal of the Executive Summary is to capture your readers' interest, while treating the following three topics concisely:

1. The Main Topics of the Business Plan

   - The proposed product or service
   - The major markets
   - The advantages of the product or service
   - The company's main goals
   - The business model

2. The Company

   - A description of the new venture
   - The team members

Chapter	Description
Title Page/s	<ul><li>The name of the company or product</li><li>The date</li><li>Confidentiality, disclaimers</li><li>Optional: instructions to return the document</li><li>Optional: the author</li></ul>
TOC	<ul><li>Table of contents</li></ul>
Executive Summary	<ul><li>1-3 pages long</li><li>A summary of the document's highlights</li><li>A summary of the business strategy</li><li>Goals of the document</li><li>A summary pitch</li></ul>
The Opportunity: The proposed product/service	<ul><li>Description of the problem</li><li>The unique solution through the proposed product / service</li></ul>
The Technology	<ul><li>Description of the technological environment</li><li>Description of technology, unique advantages</li><li>Lead time, brief patents description</li></ul>
The Market Environment and Strategy	<ul><li>The market environment</li><li>Description of target markets</li><li>Marketing and competitive strategy</li><li>Sales projections</li><li>Marketing budget</li></ul>
R&D	<ul><li>Goals</li><li>Milestones and schedules</li><li>R&D budget</li></ul>

Figure 5.1:   Sample Business Plan Structure

Production and Operations	• The production plan • The logistics plan • Production and operations budget
The Company	• The organizational structure • Personnel forecast • Budget for Personnel

The Financial Chapter	• Investment plan
	
	• Financing plan
	
	• Summary budget and pro forma financial reports:
	
	   o Profit and Loss Statements
	
	   o Cash flow
	
	   o Sensitivity analysis
	
	• Risk analysis

Appendices	• CVs of key personnel
	
	• Clinical data
	
	• Technical data
	
	• Research
	
	• Case studies
	
	• More detailed financial pro forma reports, including a balance sheet
	
	• References
	
	• Others:
	
	   o Description of agreements
	
	   o Patents summary
	
	   o Certificates and licenses
	
	• Previous financial statements

Figure 5.1:   (*Continued*)

3. The Proposal

- The type of involvement or partnership that the company is seeking from the reader of the business plan
- The opportunity being offered or the value to the potential partner

When the goal is raising capital for the company, the Executive Summary will cover a fourth area:

4. The Financial Returns

- The expected profits and cash flows
- Other possible financial measures, such as NPV, IRR and the payback period (described in Section 4.5.3 of this book)

Do not underestimate the significance of the Executive Summary!

The few minutes that it will take your reader to review it may very well be the most critical moments in the life of your project. If the Executive Summary intrigues the readers, they will read on, which may lead to the beginning of a business relationship. However, if the reader loses interest right from the start, expect your business plan to land on the tall pile of business plans that never enjoy any serious attention.

Most investors and managers are overwhelmed with proposals. In many cases, they will not have time to go through the entirety of the business plans that are sent to them, and they expect to receive the main points in the Executive Summary. Make sure that your Executive Summary is targeted specifically to your readers' interests. In fact, consider preparing a few different versions of the Executive Summary, tailoring them to the primary interests of specific readers.

Get early feedback on the Executive Summary from some outside, objective readers before sending them to your primary recipients. Ideally, these initial readers will not be familiar with your venture and will first become acquainted with it through your Executive Summary. This puts them in a position similar to that of many of your primary recipients. These initial readers can provide you with important feedback on the clarity of the document, its strengths and weaknesses, and their reactions to it. Use this valuable information to improve your Executive Summary.

The Executive Summary is useful on its own, and, by providing a description of the company or project, it can serve as a project information sheet for a wide range of purposes. It can be widely distributed, and can be effective as a networking tool and for raising interest in the company or project. It is easier to skim through an Executive Summary than study the full business plan, and if something in it intrigues specific readers, they can turn to the company for more information. It is widely used as an introduction to the company, and can be sent to potential business partners, VCs and other investors.

5.5   The First Chapter

As mentioned earlier, the topic of the first chapter should be chosen according to the main objectives of the document. We will describe a few possibilities.

5.5.1   *New Innovations*

If you are introducing a completely new and innovative product or service, the first thing that you want to highlight is the product or service itself. This is true whether you are starting a new company, or are working on a new area in an established company. The reasoning is that the reader will first learn about your innovation through the business plan.

Start by introducing the vision behind the new innovation, and continue by describing the proposed product and service in detail, together with an implementation plan and some technical information when relevant. Be sure to address the following areas:

1. The Need for your Product or Service

    Customers want to buy products or services primarily for one of two reasons: either the products or services solve a pressing problem, or they provide some type of major benefit or delight. With technologically innovative products, you will usually briefly describe the limitations of the currently existing products and the difficulties stemming from these limitations. Compare your technology to what is currently considered state of the art and to what is being developed, so that the leap forward you are proposing is clear. For example, Waze, which was purchased by Google in July 2013 for approximately $900 million, offered a smartphone application for navigation. While other navigation systems based on GPS were supplied by many other companies, Waze combined GPS technology with a social network in which the users provide continuous information on the status of traffic, road hazards and other alerts. This unique feature made the real-time information extremely accurate wherever there was a large base of users on the roads and made the application very popular. According to Yahoo!, there were nearly 50 million Waze users at the time Google purchased Waze.

2. Functionality and Benefit

    Describe how your product or service will be used and why it will appeal to customers. For example, Waze uses real-time updates from other drivers on the road to plan an optimal route for its users, taking into account traffic, road conditions and other factors. Waze's large client base shows that this is a significant service which appeals strongly to users worldwide.

3. Characteristics of your Product or Service

    Demonstrate the advantages of the various features of your product or service. Describe how the new innovation you are introducing enhances the product and the user experience. For example:

- It saves time
- It improves quality
- It is more reliable
- Other enhancements that make your product stand out

4. Physical Description

It is a good idea to help your reader visualize your product or service with photos, diagrams, video links or any other graphic depiction you can provide without compromising your intellectual property. In this chapter, the graphic depiction should be user-friendly; this is not the place for complex engineering plans, which can be provided upon request, or included in the appendices if necessary.

5. Approvals and Patents

If you have applied for any patents related to the technology, explain the essential components here. Again, avoid heavily technical jargon. Also note the status of any authorizations and approvals that you have applied for, such as FDA, CE, ISO or others.

The level of technological information you should provide depends on the weight you want to assign to the technological features of your product. The business plan usually focuses on the big picture, including the main features and benefits of the product, and leaves the technological testing and proof for later stages. But you should provide enough of a technical description to convey the level of innovation you are proposing and to prove your fluency in the areas in which you are competing. Discuss the technological level of the industry you are competing in and your expected lead time, or the amount of time you estimate it will take until the competition catches up and introduces a similar product. In cases in which the technical components must be reviewed in depth, you should have a separate chapter dedicated to this purpose, with subchapters as needed.

This chapter should reflect your unique and innovative ideas and plans, as well as demonstrate your team's technological prowess. Lay out your technological plans, but don't get carried away. Closely reference the business context, and keep the technological language at a level that is appropriate for your readers. Don't expect all of your readers to have the same level of technological understanding that you do, and keep their interest by avoiding overly detailed descriptions. It is best to start with more general descriptions and provide the deeper technological picture in supplementary documentation and follow-up meetings.

5.5.2 *Established Companies*

Established companies prepare business plans for a variety of reasons, including raising additional capital for expansion or for acquiring another company, establishing professional relationships with new business partners, developing new distribution channels and many other reasons. For these companies, Chapter 1 following the Executive Summary should describe the company. Although the company may be familiar to some of the readers, you need to present the full company profile to create a comprehensive picture. Describe the following:

- The products or services the company provides
- Recent sales results
- Research and development in the company
- Production
- Marketing channels
- The personnel in the organization, with some details about the key employees
- The company's main assets
- The company's location
- Some company history, with the main events on the company timeline

Chapter 1 serves to introduce the company to the reader. More details can be provided in later chapters of the business plan. For example, Chapter 1 might provide general information about manufacturing, while more detailed descriptions might be provided in a chapter dedicated solely to manufacturing.

All companies, whether startups or established companies, will have a chapter devoted to a description of the company. With new innovations, where the company is just starting out, first explain about the product or service, and describe the company only later in the document. But when the company is already established, the company itself is highlighted throughout the document and should be described first.

If an established company is considering a complete change of strategy and is refocusing on new areas and activities, Chapter 1 will contain information about the company's history and its assets and strengths, along with a description of what has changed and what will ensure its success in its new activities.

5.6 The Markets and Marketing Chapter

5.6.1 *The Market Environment*

Whatever your product or service, your marketing and sales plan represents the very heart of the business plan. Without a potential active customer base that wants your product and is willing to buy it, there is no business case for it. You might assume philanthropic organizations and Non-Governmental Organizations (NGOs) are exceptions to this rule, since their potential users may be receiving a service without paying for it. However, even a charitable organization has no justification without a user base. The money raised by the charity is utilized more effectively by serving a cause with a considerable base of real active users.

A critical step towards proving the feasibility of the business plan is attaining a thorough understanding of the markets, as described in Chapter 3 of this book, which enables you to prepare a better forecast of demand for your product or service.

In the chapter on the Market Environment, as in the other chapters of your business plan, you need to carefully select the relevant information out of the body of knowledge you have accumulated in your research, and present it effectively. Keep your goal in mind. The reader should gain a good level of understanding of the relevant market environment and come to share your conviction that the product or service you are offering has a strong potential in the market if the business plan is followed.

The Market Environment chapter focuses on the following topics:

- A general description of the industry and market environment in which you will be active

  o The predominant problems and needs in this industry which your product or service addresses
  o A risk analysis relating to entry into the market with your product or service

- The target markets

  o The markets in which you intend to be active
  o An informative segmentation of the markets. The segmentation should provide analytical data which is relevant to your sales plan. Expand upon each relevant segment, providing the pertinent characteristics of each segment, such as geographical distribution, ages, gender, average income, etc. See more examples in Figure 5.2.

Identify the most relevant market segments for your product or service, and analyze their size and significance in relation to the entire market. Indicate the price sensitivity in each segment if possible.

Category	Demographic	Geographic	Psychographic	Behavioral
Examples of criteria	Age Gender Occupation Family life cycle Religion Income	Geographic location Urban or rural Neighborhood characteristics Climate	Lifestyles Personality Preferences Opinions Memberships	Purchase occasion Rate of usage Features and benefits sought Loyalty status Price sensitivity
Specific Example	*30-40 year old men with a $50K or more annual income*	*Urban customers within a 10 km radius*	*Engage in sports*	*More than 3 times weekly*

Figure 5.2:   Examples of Segmentation Criteria

- The current level of demand
  Describe the current level of demand together with a fore-cast of the market potential. A graphic presentation is helpful, such as a bar chart showing the level of demand for each period, as shown in Figure 5.3.
- Similar products and substitutes
  If similar products or close substitutes are currently being sold in the market, provide data on the actual sales of these products if you can. For example, if your product is a pain relief medication for migraines, provide data on the existing medications with similar components, together with data on medications using other components that also provide pain relief and that are used for migraines. Consider all of the products that the customers will be evaluating when making their choice, and provide a clear explanation of why

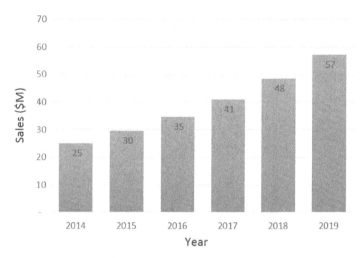

Figure 5.3: Example: Forecast of Total Market Potential (Units Sold/Retail Prices)

customers will choose your product over others. Indicate whether your advantage is due to quality, price or other features in comparison to your competitors.

- The total market potential
  The total market potential reflects the total level of demand for similar products or services, over a given period of time. The market potential should be provided in both units and sales revenue. The time period depends on the industry. A five-year analysis is a good time frame for many products and services, but may not be relevant for others in a rapidly changing market. Figure 5.4 is an example of a market potential analysis in both units sold and sales revenue for a domestic travel market. We recommend using sales revenue figures, as opposed to production costs. This data is more informative for the reader, and will tie in to the financial forecasts which will follow in the Financial Chapter. Even if the product or service is itself a raw material and its target markets are production facilities, we recommend using the projected sales revenue from these customers in your market potential analysis. For example, if you are a producer of digital animation

No. of Total Trips

Market Segment	% of market	2014 (actual)	2015 (forecasted)	2016 (forecasted)	2017 (forecasted)	2018 (forecasted)
Business travel	15%	6,750	7,088	7,442	7,814	8,205
Students/Academics	5%	2,250	2,363	2,481	2,605	2,735
Family visits	28%	12,600	13,230	13,892	14,586	15,315
Vacationers	52%	23,400	24,570	25,799	27,088	28,443
Total no. of trips in all segments		**45,000**	**47,250**	**49,613**	**52,093**	**54,698**

Total Revenue

Market Segment	Average Revenue	2014 *(in $K)* (actual)	2015 *(in $K)* (forecasted)	2016 *(in $K)* (forecasted)	2017 *(in $K)* (forecasted)	2018 *(in $K)* (forecasted)
Business travel	$ 1,000	$ 6,750	$ 7,088	$ 7,442	$ 7,814	$ 8,205
Students/Academics	$ 450	$ 1,013	$ 1,063	$ 1,116	$ 1,172	$ 1,231
Family visits	$ 600	$ 7,560	$ 7,938	$ 8,335	$ 8,752	$ 9,189
Vacationers	$ 555	$ 12,987	$ 13,636	$ 14,318	$ 15,034	$ 15,786
Total revenue for all segments		**$ 28,310**	**$ 29,725**	**$ 31,211**	**$ 32,772**	**$ 34,410**

Figure 5.4: Example: Forecast of Total Market Potential (Units Sold and Revenue) for a Domestic Travel Market

components which are marketed to advertisers for use in televised and online advertising campaigns for their clients, estimate the revenue from the advertisers for the components that you are selling.

The total market potential is extremely important, particularly for venture capital firms. Many VCFs are seeking to invest in companies that are active in sizeable markets and will not enter markets in which the market potential is below a certain threshold.

- The competition

  o The number of active competitors and their main activities

  o The market share of the main competitors. This is easiest to present in a pie chart form, such as the pie chart in Figure 5.5.

  o An analysis of your main competitors' market strategies, particularly those with the most significant impact on your business. Analyze their strengths and weaknesses and recent business trends and try to forecast their next steps.

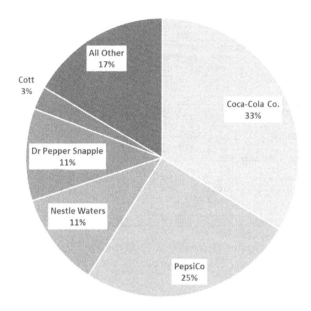

Figure 5.5: U.S. Beverage Business Results for 2014 — Liquid Refreshment Beverage Market Share

Source: http://www.beverage-digest.com

   o The market atmosphere: whether it is an aggressive one where every segment is being targeted by other competitors, or a developing one in which there is relatively little competition, etc.

Make sure that your claims are credible, and back them up with data, listing your sources clearly in the footnotes. Excellent sources of data are industry articles, statistical publications and expert opinions. If you have a lot of such material, choose the most significant for the body of the text, and refer the reader to the appendices or to other sources, including websites, for further reading.

Be sure to give a complete analysis of the competitive environment in the business plan. Present a clear strategy of how you intend to deal with existing threats, and do not whitewash or downplay them.

If similar products and/or good substitutions have been in the market for a while, provide a table with the market distribution going back several years. You can add the details of market size and segmentation to this table, as shown in Figure 5.4. State clearly that these are sales figures from previous years and not projections. By adding in real sales figures from previous years, you can show how your projections tie in with existing trends and make a sensible case for your numbers.

5.6.2   *The Marketing Strategy*

Once you have described the markets, it is time to present your strategy for selling your product or service. This should include strategies for penetrating the market, gaining a stable customer base and expanding that base over time. The forecasted sales should be quantified.

As discussed previously, the focus of your business plan depends on your goals. If you are seeking a marketing partner, you may not need to present a marketing strategy, as that may be the function of the new partner. However, if you are pitching to financiers or VCFs with mainly a financial interest in their investment, the marketing strategy is one of the most critical components of your business plan. Remember that a good idea is not enough, and even a good product or service is not enough. Your investors will want to know that you have a clear plan in place to achieve the projected sales.

The Marketing Strategy should include the following three sections:

- Your product or service and the market's needs

    o Describe the ways in which your product or service fills a pressing need or provides a unique benefit which will appeal to your customers.

Forecasted market share MyTrip (%)

Market Segment	2014 (actual)	2015 (forecasted)	2016 (forecasted)	2017 (forecasted)	2018 (forecasted)
Business travel	0%	0%	5%	8%	11%
Students/Academics	0%	2%	2%	3%	3%
Family visits	0%	7%	8%	10%	12%
Vacationers	15%	18%	22%	26%	31%

No. of Trips Forecasted MyTrip

Market Segment	2014 (actual)	2015 (forecasted)	2016 (forecasted)	2017 (forecasted)	2018 (forecasted)
Business travel	-	-	372	586	923
Students/Academics	-	47	60	75	95
Family visits	-	926	1,167	1,470	1,853
Vacationers	3,510	4,423	5,572	7,021	8,847
Total no. of trips in all segments	**3,510**	**5,396**	**7,171**	**9,153**	**11,717**

Revenue Forecasted MyTrip

Market Segment	Average Revenue	2014 (actual) *(in $K)*	2015 (forecasted) *(in $K)*	2016 (forecasted) *(in $K)*	2017 (forecasted) *(in $K)*	2018 (forecasted) *(in $K)*
Business travel	$ 1,000	$ -	$ -	$ 372	$ 586	$ 923
Students/Academics	$ 450	$ -	$ 21	$ 27	$ 34	$ 43
Family visits	$ 600	$ -	$ 556	$ 700	$ 882	$ 1,112
Vacationers	$ 555	$ 1,948	$ 2,455	$ 3,093	$ 3,897	$ 4,910
Total revenue for all segments		**$ 1,948**	**$ 3,031**	**$ 4,192**	**$ 5,399**	**$ 6,987**
% of Total market revenue		7%	10%	13%	16%	20%
Cumulative Revenue		$ 1,948	$ 4,980	$ 9,171	$ 14,570	$ 21,557

Figure 5.6:   Example: Revenue Forecast for "MyTrip" (Based on Market Data from Figure 5.4)

- A marketing timeline

  o Set targets in each of the market segments in which you intend to be active, both in market share percentage and in sales units and revenues, as shown in Figure 5.6.

  o Use a timeline to describe the penetration sequence into each segment: which segment you will target first, next, etc.

- Plan details
  Your plan should include:

  o Continual market monitoring
  o Advertising and promotional activity
  o Distribution networks

o Pre and post-sales support
o A detailed budget for ongoing marketing operations

5.6.3 *The Sales Forecast*

Your sales forecast is built on the foundation laid out in your market analysis and marketing strategy. The implementation of your marketing plan should yield sales which are reflected in the sales forecast. The sales forecast, such as the one shown in Figure 5.6, typically depends on many estimates and assumptions. These should be consistent with the well-founded data that you have presented in the previous sections. Your sales forecast will be based on:

- The total demand in the target markets in units and sales revenue
- The change in demand over time, or annual sales growth
- The market share that you expect to attain in each segment in percentages
- The forecasted changes in your market share over time, including annual growth of market share
- The change in your forecasted sales price for your product or service over time, whether increasing, decreasing or constant

Because this analysis includes so many estimates and assumptions, it is a good idea to present a range of possible results in the form of a sensitivity analysis. Using this analysis can help you estimate the range of potential errors by seeing how changes in the different parameters affect the end result. For example, you can analyze the sales level using different growth rates. Begin with a reasonable projection, and see how your results change with a slower growth rate, such as five or ten percent less, and with a higher growth rate, such as five or ten percent more. We provide some examples of sensitivity analyses in Appendix II.

We also recommend that you evaluate a few possible scenarios, particularly when the outcome of your project depends on a number of different events, or when you are considering different action plans. Begin with a presentation of the forecast you believe represents the most likely outcome. Follow with another more pessimistic scenario, and also with a more optimistic one. See Figure 5.7 for an example.

Each one of the scenarios in Figure 5.7 leads to completely different results for the company. They affect the sales volume drastically, and as a result, the entire scale of the company's operations changes accordingly. Present each of these scenarios with a different set of sales forecasts for each. Be sure that the different scenarios you choose to present are actual possibilities.

Another approach is to present only the most likely scenario in the Marketing Chapter, and consider all of the risks and uncertainties within the Financial Chapter only, or in an appendix. It is important to show that you have considered the alternatives without making the main presentation too cumbersome or confusing.

A good basis for presenting your sales forecast is the market segmentation you have presented. Chances are that you will have different strategies and designated dates for

Scenario	Description
Most likely	Success in signing up a medium size European distributor to distribute your products in four or five countries in Western Europe within two years.
Pessimistic	The company has to market its products using its own resources only.
Optimistic	Success in signing up a leading international distributor to distribute your products worldwide within two years.

Figure 5.7:　Example: Distribution Scenarios

penetrating the different market segments. Your forecast can be built based on geographical location, type of customers or any other segmentation characteristics which are most relevant.

Present your sales forecast for each segment, and summarize the results into the total sales forecast. See Figure 5.6 for an example. Note that this sales forecast is based on the data presented in Figure 5.4, the total market potential. However, the forecast of the company's market share is usually based on the retail price, and the sales forecast is based on the company's revenue. In many companies, there is a significant difference between the two figures, resulting from all the costs involved in getting the product from the company to the customer. These may include shipping and handling as well as payments to intermediaries along the way. Cost factors vary among different industries. The retail price can be as much as four times the company's revenue per unit or the factory gate price, or more.

An Example

S. Industries is a company that develops equipment to measure and produce gasses. It has estimated that the market potential for gas detectors in the greenhouse industry is $400 million annually, based on the retail price. S. Industries expects to attain a 0.2 percent share of the market in its first year of activity, and 0.8 percent in its second year. This translates to retail sales of $800,000 in the first year and $3,200,000 in the second. If the company income is half of the retail price, this means revenues of $400,000 in the first year and $1,600,000 in the following year from this market segment.

It may be difficult to estimate your market potential and your sales forecast, as in the case of a new innovation. In such a case, you will need to use estimates and assumptions, trying to apply them to realistic possibilities. Make your assumptions explicit and clear.

When the company already has some experience selling the product, be sure to present data for the previous years, as this is helpful in showing any existing positive trends. Even when the trend has not been positive, it is still prudent to present the company history openly and be prepared to discuss why you can expect a different outcome from this point forward.

The sales forecast should include:

- A clear presentation of the main assumptions on which the sales figures are based. This enables the readers to evaluate for themselves whether these assumptions are reasonable or not from their point of view, and whether all of the risk factors have been considered.
- The underlying sales price for each forecast, whether the retail price or the gate price.
- A breakdown of the sales by the main market segments.
- Spreadsheet summaries in which the sales plan is translated into company revenue. The calculations themselves should be based on precise parameters, including price, market share, etc. However, when presenting the data, round up the numbers to the nearest thousand or million. An estimate of $1,125,142.8 in sales may be what your spreadsheet produced, but rounding it up makes the data easier to read and reminds everyone that these are estimates only.
- Choose the most relevant currency for your sales forecast. Particularly when you are active in more than one currency, the data should be consolidated into one total in one currency. This is often the American dollar, or the euro, but could also be your local currency.
- If you expect inflation to affect your sales revenue, you should raise this within the sensitivity analysis, either here or in the Financial Chapter.

When preparing the forecast, find the right balance between providing enough information to explain and validate your projections, and overburdening the document with excessive information which does not contribute to the picture and may compromise your confidentiality.

	(in $K)	(in $K)	(in $K)	(in $K)	(in $K)
	Year 1	Year 2	Year 3	Year 4	Year 5
Product Samples	30	33	35	40	45
Marketing Material - Sales Aids and Brochure	23	24	25	28	30
Webinar & Digital	10	10	10	10	10
Marketing Programs	25	25	25	25	25
Journal advertising	25	25	25	25	25
Ad Agency	45	45	45	45	45
E-Commerce site	15	5	5	5	5
PR Initiatives	25	25	25	25	25
Regional Trade Shows	35	35	40	40	40
Travel	10	12	15	18	20
Salaries and Benefits					
Regional Sales Reps	100	150	200	200	200
Sales Director	85	85	85	85	85
Performance Bonuses	20	30	40	40	40
Total Costs	$ 447	$ 504	$ 575	$ 586	$ 595

Figure 5.8:   Example: Sales and Marketing Expense Budget

5.6.4   *The Sales and Marketing Budget*

End your Marketing Chapter with a table of all of the expected sales and marketing expenses. An example is shown in Figure 5.8. Keep in mind that the types of expenses vary greatly, depending on the company's activities.

When preparing these costs, consider both your expected costs for reaching the forecasted sales levels as well as the marketing costs of similar companies. A new innovation requires a more aggressive marketing campaign over the first years.

5.7   The Research and Development Plan

Many new startups revolve around a promising idea for a technological innovation. Exciting breakthroughs in technology have led to innovative new products in a vast number of areas, such as:

- Medical devices and instrumentation
- Pharmaceuticals
- Cosmetics

- Food products
- Communications
- Computer hardware and software
- Military and security products
- Entertainment

If your new company or project entails innovation, the chapter laying out your R&D plan is of major importance and will receive a lot of focus. Some of the areas to be covered in this chapter:

- **R&D Goals**
  Describe the level of innovation in the planned R&D activities of your company. You may, for example, be working on completely new frontiers and expanding the existing theoretical base. Or you may be relying on existing applications and already have the knowledge needed for your product and/or service.

- **R&D Implementation**
  Describe what elements of your research will be applied to your products and/or services. Provide details on your unique intellectual property (IP). If you have unique IP which is patent protected, share this information.

- **Timetable**
  Supply a timetable based on the important milestones along the way. These may, for example, include the stages shown in Figure 5.9. These milestones will serve as a roadmap and will also enable performance tracking along the way.

A useful tool for mapping out the scheduled activities of a project at different levels is a Gantt chart. Gantt charts provide a horizontal bar chart illustration of the elements of a project, together with the start and finish dates and the relationships among the elements. Many examples of Gantt charts can be found online.

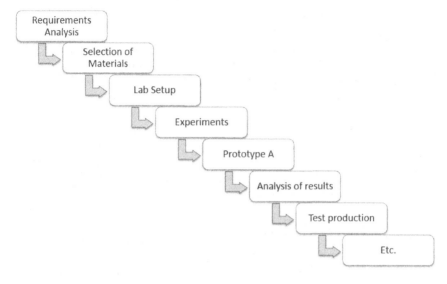

Figure 5.9: Example: R&D Milestones

- **R&D Team**
  In the R&D area, the expertise of your team is a very valuable asset. Describe your team's skills, including their previous experience and the track records of your research and development experts. If you have team members who have already been on the R&D teams of successful products, your credibility in this area will be high, and it will make it easier to raise capital. Serial entrepreneurs have a tremendous advantage with VCFs and angels, especially when they have proven that they can get a great product out to the market successfully. Provide information on any scientific advisors who are helping with the R&D work, particularly if they are leading scientists affiliated with successful companies, research institutes or universities. A brief profile is sufficient for the text appearing in the chapter. Provide more complete CVs in the appendices on your key R&D personnel, particularly if they have impressive track records.

Research Equipment and Materials

Provide a list of the main materials and research equipment that you will be using.

- **R&D Budget**

  The R&D budget will quantify how much money you plan to spend on R&D. Your costs include:

  o Human resources
  o Materials and expensed equipment
  o Depreciation on long-term equipment
  o Subcontractors

  - External labs
  - Research institutions
  - Others

  o Other costs, which may include IP protection, travel, documentation, patent registration and others.

> ### What is Depreciation?
>
> **Depreciation** is a method of allocating the cost of a tangible asset over its useful life for tax and accounting purposes.
>
> To understand the significance of depreciation when new assets are purchased, we need to differentiate between the cash flow and the accounting aspects. From a cash flow perspective, we need to fund one hundred percent of the cost of the assets. But from an accounting perspective, we spread the expense over the life of the asset. For example, if a computer server costs $15,000 and we expect to replace it after five years, we will allocate $3,000 in depreciation expenses each year. However we will need to pay $15,000 when the purchase is made.

Accounting for equipment costs can be tricky. Generally, there are typical depreciation periods for different types of equipment; for example, computers might be depreciated over three to five years (see Figure 5.10). However, if your company is purchasing equipment for a very specific task, and will not be able to use or resell the equipment once the task is complete, long-term depreciation is problematic. In such a case, the entire cost should be depreciated or expensed over the period during which the equipment will be used, if that period is shorter than the depreciation period

Depreciation Periods	New assets' useful life (years)
Buildings	20-50
Computers and Office Equipment	3-5
Furniture and Fixtures	7-10
Machinery	7-12
Vehicles	5-8

Figure 5.10:   Depreciation Periods[1]

according to standard accounting principles. Otherwise, with time, your company will continue carrying costs on equipment which is no longer in use.

Figure 5.10 shows examples of the depreciation periods of different assets over their useful life. The periods differ from country to country. The useful life of your fixed assets will be determined by your accountant.

An example of an R&D budget is shown below (Figure 5.11).

- **R&D Grants**

  As discussed in Section 4.5.2, there are many publicly-funded programs designed to encourage new and growing businesses. They are usually administered through different government ministries, departments and agencies on a national and local basis. You may be able to fund some of your activities with these research grants. Depending on the grant terms and the relevant accounting principles, the grant may appear as a source of income in your budget, or as an offset to the costs, as a negative cost item, as shown in Figure 5.11. In any case, be sure to specify details of the grant together with your full costs.

---

[1] Depreciation periods may differ according to the local tax laws.

	(in $K) Year 1	(in $K) Year 2	(in $K) Year 3	(in $K) Year 4	(in $K) Year 5
Materials and consumable parts	10	11	13	14	17
Subcontractors	10	12	14	16	18
Intellectual Property	12	12	12	12	12
Salaries and Benefits					
R&D Director	70	70	70	70	70
Researchers	45	45	90	90	90
Assistants	30	45	45	45	45
Expenses subtotal	$ 177	$ 195	$ 244	$ 247	$ 252
Depreciaton - Laboratories and Equipment	50	50	50	50	50
Grants	(40)	(40)	(40)	(40)	(40)
Expenses including Grants and Depreciation	$ 187	$ 205	$ 254	$ 257	$ 262

Figure 5.11:   Example: Research and Development Budget

- ## External Resources
  Your R&D activity may be innovative, but it will probably also rely heavily on previous work carried out in the past by other researchers and developers. Some of this knowledge is likely to be in the public domain, having been published in research papers and presented in conferences. However, some of the knowledge may be proprietary knowledge which you can use only after obtaining the necessary authorization. We recommend detailing which part of your R&D comes from in-house knowledge, what is in the public domain and how you plan to obtain authorization to use other researchers' proprietary knowledge. For example, if your work requires software, hardware and communications, and your expertise is in software development, describe how you will obtain the needed expertise in hardware and communications.

- ## Writing the R&D Chapter
  This chapter will hopefully be intriguing enough to interest investors and business partners. If so, it may be scrutinized by experts in your technological area. It must

therefore be credible and professionally written. Some words of advice:

o Involve the scientists and engineers responsible for the different areas and tasks described in this chapter in the writing and editing process.
o Check for consistency with the other references to technology in other sections of the business plan.
o Use accurate scientific terms, but make sure to keep the language uncomplicated enough for any reader, including those who are not technology experts.
o Have readers from different backgrounds, including non-techies, read the chapter and rework it until it is both professionally sound and clear to all readers.

5.8   The Production Plan Chapter

Section 4.4 raised various production strategies. Whichever strategy you choose, if you are selling a product, you need to describe the production process. If you are planning on setting up a manufacturing facility of your own, this chapter will describe the facility and its components and quantify the costs in the production budget. If you plan to completely outsource the manufacturing, describe the manufacturing requirements and costs, which facilities are available and the logistics plan in this chapter. Not all businesses will require a production plan. For example, if your company is a service provider, instead of a Production Plan Chapter, you will have a Service Plan Chapter describing the logistics of providing the services, including the Client Relationship Management (CRM) function.

5.8.1   *An Established Company*

Your production plan will describe your production capacity and your short and long-term goals for the production facility, if your company is already up and running.

Some of the features you should describe include:

- The technologies you are using
- The most important equipment, whether it is significant because of the large investment required for its purchase, or due to the unique contribution it makes to the production process
- The basic floor plan, including total area and functions of the different sections
- The ongoing maintenance plan
- Future plans to replace equipment and/or technologies, such as computerization and automation
- Future expansion plans
- A description of the manufacturing personnel according to the different types of jobs, departments or areas of expertise
- Payroll expenses. It may be a good idea to provide data on similar industries for comparison
- Main subcontractors. Specify how heavily you depend on them
- Quality assurance
- Certifications and standards, such as ISO
- Optimization through shift plans, multifunctioning, etc.
- Critical statistics

  o Quality control
  o Deadlines met or missed
  o Faulty products
  o Returned products
  o Product costs at different production volumes

- Environmental concerns and green technologies
- References and recommendations from customers and partners, if available
- Main policies and procedures, particularly preventive and corrective actions

As with the rest of your business plan, keep this chapter concise and interesting. The above list contains quite a lot of information. Incorporate the leading points in your main text, and provide any detailed schedules you feel are necessary, such as policies, for example, in separate appendices. All of the information provided is the basis for the cost of goods sold, as explained in Section 4.5.3, which will be incorporated into your financial plan. A sample cost of goods sold budget appears in Figure 5.12. The items in the budget are

No.		(in $K) Year 1	(in $K) Year 2	(in $K) Year 3	(in $K) Year 4	(in $K) Year 5
	Factory and Production					
1	Utilities	10	11	11	12	12
2	Quality control	25	25	25	25	25
3	ISO audit fees	12	12	12	12	12
4	Manufacturing subcontractors	70	77	85	93	102
5	Facility rental costs	40	40	40	40	40
6	Storage					
7	Insurance	14	14	14	14	14
8	Subtotal Factory and Production (sum 1-7)	171	179	187	196	206
	Materials					
9	New materials purchased	60	78	101	132	171
10	Materials used from inventory (see below)	13	18	25	36	50
11	Subtotal Materials (sum 9-10)	73	96	127	167	221
	Salaries and Benefits					
12	Production Manager	60	60	60	60	60
13	production workers	45	45	90	90	90
14	Subtotal Salaries and Benefits (sum 12-13)	105	105	150	150	150
15	Cost of goods sold subtotal (8+11+14)	$ 349	$ 380	$ 464	$ 513	$ 577
16	Equipment - Depreciaton	68	68	75	75	90
17	COGS including Depreciation (15+16)	$ 417	$ 448	$ 539	$ 588	$ 667
	Change in Inventory					
	Inventory opening balance:					
	Materials	30	42	59	82	115
	Units in Process	10	14	20	27	38
	Finished units	40	56	78	110	154
	Minus closing inventory					
	Materials	(25)	(35)	(49)	(69)	(96)
	Units in Process	(7)	(10)	(14)	(19)	(27)
	Finished units	(35)	(49)	(69)	(96)	(134)
	Change in Inventory	13	18	25	36	50

Figure 5.12: Example: Cost of Goods Sold

numbered. This is helpful in budgets which include many subtotals.

5.8.2 A New Project within an Established Company

If your business plan pertains to a specific project within an established company which has other production lines dedicated to other areas, try to separate the resources to be allocated to the project from other company resources. Will this new project be integrated into the rest of the company's activities, or will it be managed as a completely separate spin off? In the former case, you may not be purchasing new equipment, but the cost of using the equipment should be quantified, as it is most likely being diverted from other activities.

5.8.3 A New Company

Planning a new production facility is much more complicated than describing the costs of using an existing one. Often, entrepreneurs lack sufficient information about the full requirements for establishing such a facility. Nonetheless, if you are planning to set up a production facility, it is important to start planning it in general terms in the early days, and relate to the principle questions. Then, add details as you go along, and the planning becomes more comprehensive. Production usually has a major impact on costs and the investment required. Some of the topics to cover in this chapter include:

- The production technologies
- The main capital requirements for equipment and facilities
- The expected size of the facilities in square meters
- The preferred location for the production plants. Consider proximity to:

o Raw materials
o Labor
o Shipping facilities
o Subcontractors

Also consider government incentive programs which differ from one region to another.

Provide some information on what aspects of the production can be subcontracted out at different stages in the coming years, and what will be done by company employees.

Even if you don't have all of the information available, this chapter should demonstrate your ability to plan the production facility and eventually implement the production plan. Be realistic in terms of time frames and costs. Production is complicated, and many companies overlook critical factors in the planning stages. Try to gather advice and input from experienced managers in similar industries.

5.9 The Organization, Management and Human Resources Chapter

This is a relatively short chapter in the business plan, which should outline the organizational structure, including:

- The key managers and decision makers. Provide some background on their experience and qualifications.
- The main divisions and departments and their fields of responsibility.
- Company directors and advisors.

Consider other questions. For example, is the management centralized or decentralized? How will the management structure change as the company evolves? Describe the company's contractual and legal obligations, and whether they were entered into electively, for example, providing benefits to senior employees, or whether they are required by law. The latter may include pensions, social benefits, bonuses, employee stock options plans (ESOP) and other forms of compensation.

The level of depth in your organizational plan depends on whether your venture is a new startup or an established company. A young startup can't present a highly detailed plan with any degree of credibility, because it is obvious that the structure is dynamic and many duties are shared, at least at the early stages. Instead, plans for startups should present the basic management layout and divisions in the company, as well as a description of the structure planned for the company after growing and recruiting more employees.

An established company should present the various managers, departments and divisions in the company, together with their respective areas of responsibility. Describe the cross-departmental working relations and connections, focusing on the key players in your project.

When your company relies heavily on subcontractors or business partners, provide details about them and explanations of how they fit into your company's reporting and communications loop. For example, if you are outsourcing some R&D, briefly describe the contractor and the nature of the ongoing working relationship you expect to have.

Employment costs, salary structures, taxes and social benefits vary widely from country to country. Compensation packages can include different components, such as bonuses, company cars and options. Describe the main components of top executives' salaries and compensation costs. Prepare a table of your human resources, like the example in Figure 5.13, detailing the work force in terms of headcount, work hours and costs. Do not include the costs of the subcontractors mentioned in this chapter, which should appear in other budgets. For example, subcontractors for R&D will appear in the R&D budget.

This human resources budget provides a snapshot picture of your workforce, including the costs, and summarizes

Example:

Human Resources Expenses

	Year 1	Year 2	Year 3	Year 4	Year 5
Employees					
Production	3	4	5	5	6
Research and Development	2	5	5	6	6
Sales and Marketing	3	5	5	7	7
General and Administration	2	2	3	3	3
Total Headcount	**10**	**16**	**18**	**21**	**22**
Salaries and Benefits (in $K)					
Production	120	160	184	212	243
Research and Development	120	300	300	360	360
Sales and Marketing	195	325	325	455	455
General and Administration	150	150	180	180	190
Total Employment Expenses	**$ 585**	**$ 935**	**$ 989**	**$ 1,207**	**$ 1,248**

Figure 5.13:   Example: Human Resources Budget

the information in the Organizational Chapter. The total employment costs may also be presented together in the financial summary, as described in Section 5.10 of this book, however, we recommend presenting the costs for human resources within the functional area. For example, production workers will appear in the COGS (as in Figure 5.12), and the sales force will appear under sales and marketing (as in Figure 5.8), etc. This provides a more complete picture of the costs by function in the pro forma reports.

5.10   The Financial Projections Chapter

By this time, you have created a detailed blueprint for your business. The Financial Projections Chapter now presents all of the elements of your business proposal in financial terms. This is an extremely important chapter, and it will be closely scrutinized by a serious entrepreneur or investor. If it is prepared well, it provides the best test of feasibility available for the company and its investors. Beyond serving investors who seek assurance of a high return on capital for their investment, it provides a framework for the entire company.

Over the life of the company, the financial projections will change, together with the rest of the business plan, as the company meets fresh opportunities and faces new obstacles. The projections should be reviewed periodically, and the plans should be analyzed compared to the actual results. Doing so keeps the company focused and well informed, as almost all of the company's activities have financial consequences.

The Financial Chapter should be clear, objective and based on hard data. Overly optimistic projections will not impress the readers; in fact, they are more likely to look suspicious to investors. A good financial analysis that factors in all of the specific budgets and includes an examination of the risks involved inspires confidence and establishes a benchmark for the future.

The level of detail and the presentation form of the financial projections depends on your goals. For example:

- If you are seeking a business partner for marketing, the Financial Chapter can be relatively simple, with the main focus on the forecasted income and the costs for setting up the marketing facilities. In addition, provide a brief profit and loss statement showing the business rationale, and including pricing and costs.
- If you are seeking capital investment, you will need to prepare a very detailed Financial Chapter. Describe the planned capital structure and the various financing options available to the company. The details of your income, projections and expected costs should be well-founded and should withstand careful scrutiny. Potential investors will want to know when the company will break even, and what levels of profits are projected.
- When your business plan has been prepared for internal purposes, for example, for strategic planning, it is often helpful to evaluate two or more alternative plans. This is a valuable way of assessing the company's options and their effect on the company's financial results.

- Some new companies focus on developing a completely innovative product or service, different from anything else on the market. In these cases, there may be very little foundation for revenue projections. It is still very important to present a credible business plan. The company should focus on the costs side and the burn rate, or the rate at which the venture expects to spend money. Investors who believe in the company will invest only if they have a reasonable idea of how much cash will be spent before the product or service is launched. It is a good idea to prepare a pro forma profit and loss statement (P&L), with revenue projections. Be sure to differentiate between the costs, which can be estimated with reasonable accuracy, and the revenues, which are as yet impossible to determine, even if there is an expectation that there will be a high profit margin.

The Financial Chapter should cover three main areas:

1. The planned investments and capital requirements over a given period, usually two to five years.
2. The available sources of capital and planned capital structure.
3. The financial projections and return on investment.

5.10.1 *The Planned Investments and Capital Requirements*

Having done all of the necessary work to prepare the previous chapters, you should now have a fairly accurate picture of the resources you will need: offices, equipment, materials and human resources. This will allow you to prepare a clear schedule of costs expected until your sales take off and the company can finance its own activities. The most difficult parameter to estimate is the duration of this period, which is affected by hard to quantify factors, such as the actual time it will take to develop the product, build the business relationships and ramp up sales. However, the length of this period is highly significant, as it will determine how much cash you will burn before reaching profitability. Companies are often overly optimistic and plan for the minimal time frames without allowing for delays. We recommend that you build in extra time for the various contingencies you may encounter. If you are overly optimistic, you may raise insufficient funding and you could run out of cash due to the slightest delays in schedule.

There are two main elements to consider when presenting your capital requirements: the money that you need to invest and how the investment is distributed over time.

The Investment

The main components requiring capital are shown in Figures 5.14 and 5.15 and include:

• Land
• Buildings
• Equipment
• Working capital, as described in Section 4.5.1

You will have provided some detail about these components within the budgets in the previous chapters, and there is no need to do so again here. The Financial Chapter is the place to present a summarized picture, which can be broken down into more detail in an appendix.

The Investment Schedule

Not all of the money you will need will be spent at once. Timing is a significant factor, as we discussed in Section 4.5.1

	Year 1	Year 2	Year 3	Year 4	Year 5
	(in $K)	(in $K)	(in $K)	(in $K)	(in $K)
Land	60,000				
Buildings	85,000				
Machinery	60,000	20,000	15,000	15,000	15,000
Laboratory equipment	70,000	70,000	10,000	10,000	10,000
Vehicles	45,000		45,000		
Offices (including overseas branches and subsidiaries)	-	-	-	-	-
Furniture	35,000	20,000	10,000	5,000	5,000
Computers and electronic equipment	45,000	10,000	5,000	5,000	5,000
Total fixed assets	**400,000**	**120,000**	**85,000**	**35,000**	**35,000**

Figure 5.14:   Example: Investment in Assets

	Year 1	Year 2	Year 3	Year 4	Year 5
	(in $K)	(in $K)	(in $K)	(in $K)	(in $K)
Working Capital					
Change in inventories	7	8	9	10	11
Change in accounts receiveable	14	15	15	16	17
Change in accounts payable	25	27	29	31	34
Total working capital	$ 46	$ 50	$ 54	$ 58	$ 62

Figure 5.15: Example: Working Capital Forecast

on capital. One company may need to have full financing for two, three or more years before even beginning to see revenues, while another might have revenues ramping up within a few months, with the incoming funds reducing the company's financing needs.

Plan your financing needs using investment schedules, such as in Figures 5.14 and 5.15. The schedule can be prepared on a monthly, quarterly or annual basis, depending on the length of the investment period. Use monthly or quarterly periods for the short term, and half year or full year periods for the long term.

The following points are important when preparing the forecast of your financing needs:

- Currency Translation
  Many companies work with multiple currencies. You may be buying your equipment from several different countries, or paying subcontractors in different currencies. Be sure to use a consistent method of converting everything into one single currency which is used in your business plan. Take into account inflation and currency fluctuations. Describe your methodology briefly within this chapter, particularly if you are working with an unstable currency rate.

- Differentiate between Expenses and Investments
  From a cash flow perspective, there is no immediate difference between $10,000 paid for equipment and $10,000 paid for current expenses, such as payroll. However, the investment in equipment will be treated differently from

the payroll expense in the company's income statements, and they will have different tax implications, which will affect the cash flow over time. An item is considered an expense when the asset has been used up within the accounting period. An investment is that portion of an asset that continues to have future economic value beyond the accounting period. From the accounting perspective, only the assets which have been used up within the accounting period appear on the profit and loss statement. The remaining assets which are available to the company for future use remain on the balance sheet, including net depreciation, which reflects the usage of the assets. Two examples:

o Your company spent $20,000 on merchandise items at the start of the year. At the end of the year, most of the merchandise was sold, but you still have $7,000 in merchandise to sell during the following year. Your financial reports at the end of the year would show $13,000 as cost of goods sold (COGS) in your profit and loss statement (P&L), and $7,000 remaining as an asset on your balance sheet, under inventory. So, although you paid out $20,000 in total from a cash flow perspective, only $13,000 of it was expensed in accounting terms, or used up in the generation of sales, in that year, and $7,000 remains on the books as an asset (under inventory as shown later in Figure 5.17). From a tax perspective, only $13,000 is subtracted from the revenue to calculate the profit. The portion which remains on the balance sheet as an asset to be used in the following years has the effect of increasing your profitable income, as the expenses are $7,000 lower. This results in higher taxes in the short run in a profitable company.

o Your company invested $50,000 in equipment which has a five-year life span. From a cash flow perspective, you spent $50,000. From an accounting perspective, this equipment will depreciate over five years, so that every year for five years, twenty percent will appear as a depreciation expense in the profit and loss statement. From a tax perspective, only $10,000 is subtracted annually from the gross profit to calculate the net profit (under depreciation as shown in Figure 5.16). By entering the net value of the equipment on the balance sheet as an asset to be used in the following years, as opposed to fully expensing the entire cost at once at the time of the investment, the expenses are lower and the net

	P&L					
		(in $K)	*(in $K)*	*(in $K)*	*(in $K)*	*(in $K)*
No.		Year 1	Year 2	Year 3	Year 4	Year 5
	Revenue					
1	Product sales	640	2,297	4,275	4,418	4,912
2	License revenues	8	39	308	1,040	1,373
3	Service revenues	24	117	923	2,121	3,119
4	Subtotal Revenue (1-3)	673	2,453	5,505	7,579	9,404
	Cost of Goods Sold					
5	Cost of goods sold	331	1,418	2,445	2,081	2,544
6	Gross Profit (4 minus 5)	$ 341	$ 1,035	$ 3,060	$ 5,498	$ 6,860
	Expenses					
7	Research and development	135	337	526	639	702
8	Sales and marketing	67	245	551	798	940
9	General and administration	218	482	516	442	539
10	Subtotal Expenses (7-9)	420	1,064	1,593	1,879	2,182
11	EBITDA* (6 minus 10)	$ (79)	$ (30)	$ 1,467	$ 3,619	$ 4,677
12	Net financial expenses	-	-	-	-	-
13	Depreciation	13	10	22	8	15
14	Taxes (less accrued benefit)	-	-	-	1,605	1,865
15	Net Profit (11 minus (12-14))	$ (92)	$ (40)	$ 1,445	$ 2,007	$ 2,798

* Earnings before Interest, Depreciation and Taxes

Figure 5.16:   Example: Profit and Loss Statement

profit is higher. This results in higher taxes in the short term in a profitable company.

Although R&D usually has long-term benefits, it is typically expensed during the tax year in which the expenses were incurred.

- Equipment Replacement
  Consider the life span of your equipment when you prepare your capital requirements. Some equipment needs to be renewed regularly, particularly computer equipment and vehicles. Your projections should account for the necessary replacement over time.

- How Accurate Should Your Projections Be?
  Use your judgment when preparing your projections. Some parts of the business plan need to be quantified as accurately as possible, either because of their importance to the project or because they are material expenses. In other cases, it may be sufficient to prepare an estimate based on data from similar companies or as a percentage of revenue.

  For example, if manufacturing costs are a fairly small component of your overall budget, and can be expected to grow proportionally to the units sold without major jumps, there is no need to include detailed schedules of costs at different manufacturing volumes. It is enough to calculate the cost as a percentage of revenue. However, if, for example, your company relies heavily on R&D and it is a substantial component in your overall budget, include a more detailed breakdown.

- Uncertainty
  Describe the main areas of uncertainty in the capital investment plan, and try to quantify them. One option is to add a "miscellaneous" line item and reserve a portion of the capital to cover these uncertainties. The exact amount to reserve

depends heavily on the project. Ten to twenty percent of the total capital is a common buffer.

• Working Capital
Working capital measures the difference between cash out-flows and inflows during a given period, usually a year. Net working capital is calculated as the current assets minus the current liabilities. Your current assets include:

○ Cash and short-term investments, including all types of cash equivalents
○ Inventories of raw materials as well as of semi-finished and finished products
○ Accounts receivable (amounts due for payment by your customers)
○ Prepaid liabilities

Your current liabilities include:

• Accounts payable: Amounts due for payment over this time period.
• Payments due over the short term for financing

Despite its importance, working capital is often underes-timated, miscalculated and even ignored, partly because the need to finance customer credit and inventory is less obvious than the need to pay for equipment ordered. However, work-ing capital funds are usually needed for the ongoing company activity, particularly in early days when building inventories, before significant sales. Neglecting your working capital is bound to lead to cash shortages, especially for a startup com-pany or a company growing at a fast pace. Section 4.5.1 pro-vides a more detailed explanation of working capital.

5.10.2   *Capital Structure and Sources of Financing*

The business plan should always provide details of its capital structure and financing resources. If the primary goal of the business plan is raising capital, this section should be comprehensive and include the following information:

- Primary Sources of Funding
  - o Equity
  - o Preferred stocks
  - o Loans from owners
  - o Short-term bank credit
  - o Long-term bank loans
  - o Supplier credit
  - o Corporate bonds
  - o Grants or loans through government or other incentive programs

- The Cost of Capital
  The Financial Chapter should provide details on the cost of the loans and credit that the company has taken, or the effective interest rates. The effective interest rate takes into account whether the debt was issued at a discount or at a premium. In the former case, the effective interest rate is above the coupon rate. Provide a table detailing each material loan separately and including the loan amount, the loan provider, the interest rate, the loan period, the payment amount and the number of outstanding payments. If there are early repayment options, detail them. It is quite complicated to calculate the company's weighted average cost of capital (WACC) and it isn't necessary to do so in most business plans. WACC is the average of the costs of all of the company's sources of financing, including both debt and equity. A firm's WACC is the overall required return on the firm as a whole. It is the appropriate discount rate to use for cash flows with risk that is similar to that of the overall firm. Many books on corporate finance provide comprehensive information on

WACC[2]. If the firm has a solid basis for estimating its cost of capital, the estimate should be included. Discounting and cost of capital are explained further in Appendix I.

- The Planned Capital Structure
  The capital structure is described at a specific point in time, and is subject to change. If there are any planned changes, describe the target capital structure in this chapter, and any significant changes which are expected to take place.

  Any intention the company may have to raise capital through a public offering, as part of the immediate plan or in the future, should be stated.

When your primary goal is not financing, it is not necessary to provide a high level of detail on the sources of financing. For example, if your main goal is to build a partnership with a distributor, it is sufficient to describe the capital structure in a few sentences. You may choose to describe your primary shareholders, particularly if they have a strong reputation.

5.10.3   *The Financial Forecast*

The third section of the Financial Chapter presents the projected financial results. In this section, all the estimated forecasts previously described in the business plan are quantified and reflected in the company's profitability forecast for the coming years. This financial data can be described in summary, or explained in complete detail, depending on how much information the company chooses to share, among other considerations. For example,

---

[2] For example, R. Brealey, S. Myers, and F. Allen, *Fundamentals of Corporate Finance* (2013, 11th edition), McGraw-Hill. For estimations of cost of capital for firms and industries in the United States and other countries, see Aswath Damodaran's web site: http://people.stern.nyu.edu/adamodar/, under "data page".

providing the total revenue without giving a breakdown by product or geographic location may be sufficient in some cases. It may even be necessary, if the company does not want to reveal information which could harm its competitive advantage. On the other hand, too little detail can create the impression that there is no serious basis for the projections. It is important to find the right balance. The same can be said on the expense side; the company can provide the total only, or a detailed schedule corresponding with the work plans outlined in the plan. Again, provide the information needed to demonstrate the feasibility of your plan without compromising your operational interests.

Consider what level of information is material and interesting for the reader. Don't provide tiresome details of immaterial income or cost items. These should be summed up and presented briefly. But do not skip over the important items which have a material impact on the company's financial results. Describe the main assumptions upon which you have based your projections.

Accounting Reports
The financial results are most commonly presented in the form of a pro forma profit and loss statement (P&L, see Figure 5.16), with or without a balance sheet (see Figure 5.17). Alternatively, or in addition, some companies present their financial results in a cash flow report (see Figure 5.20), which is a valuable tool to plan the company's funding needs. These reports present the forecasted accounting results, providing a basis for comparison with similar companies in the industry or field.

It is a good idea to become familiar with the industry standards and to check them against your projected results. Benchmarking in this manner is a good way to test the reasonableness of your forecasts.

The profit and loss statement should resemble that found in Figure 5.16, which shows a P&L for a five-year

No.		(in $K) Year 1	(in $K) Year 2	(in $K) Year 3	(in $K) Year 4	(in $K) Year 5
	Current Assets					
1	Cash and cash equivalents	(91)	114	2,243	3,723	6,209
2	Accounts receivable	53	338	808	3,192	3,762
3	Inventory	453	930	36	0	21
4	Subtotal Current Assets (1-3)	415	1,382	3,087	6,915	9,991
	Fixed Assets (net of depreciation)					
5	Land and Buildings	-	-	-	-	-
6	Equipment	16	38	58	81	106
7	Other	-	5	19	65	117
8	Subtotal Fixed Assets (5-7)	16	43	77	146	224
9	**Total Assets** (4+8)	$ 431	$ 1,426	$ 3,164	$ 7,061	$ 10,215
	Current Liabilities					
10	Accounts payable	27	169	404	1,596	1,881
11	Short term bank loans	-	42	101	399	470
12	Subtotal current liabilites (10-11)	27	211	505	1,995	2,351
	Long Term Liabilities					
13	Long term bank loans	-	-	-	-	-
14	Corporate bonds	-	-	-	-	-
15	Shareholders loans	-	-	-	-	-
16	Subtotal long term liabilites (13-15)	-	-	-	-	-
	Equity					
17	Share capital	523	1,373	1,373	1,373	1,373
18	Retained earnings	(119)	(159)	1,286	3,693	6,491
19	**Total Liabilities and Equity** (12+16+17+18)	$ 431	$ 1,426	$ 3,164	$ 7,061	$ 10,215

Figure 5.17:   Example: Balance Sheet

period. The chosen forecast period can vary, depending on the type of business. An example of a long-term project is a manufacturing plant, whereas a smartphone app or a computer-based social game may have a significantly shorter forecast period.

Specify the main assumptions used in your P&L calculations. Assumptions are frequently used in forecasting revenues and costs, or when revenues and costs correspond with other factors. For example, if you estimate your marketing costs as a percentage of the total revenue, be sure to report that. Or, if you assume that your overhead will have a constant growth rate, this should be clearly stated. Give a brief explanation of any assumptions that were used and the reasoning behind them. This will add credibility to your forecast.

Your pro forma P&L statement incorporates information from other financial forecasts which appeared throughout your business plan, including:

1. The revenues (shown in Figure 5.6 in Section 5.6)
2. The cost of goods sold (COGS, shown in Figure 5.12 in Section 5.8)
3. R&D expenses (shown in Figure 5.11 in Section 5.7)
4. Sales and marketing expenses (shown in Figure 5.8 in Section 5.6)
5. Salary and benefits (shown in Figure 5.13 in Section 5.9), usually incorporated within other tables. For example, R&D salaries are incorporated in the R&D table, etc.
6. General and administrative (G&A) costs

Taxation

When preparing the financial plan, you will need to consider the different applicable taxes, including federal taxes, municipal taxes, value added tax (VAT) and sales tax, all of which will influence your bottom line. Sometimes the taxation is straightforward, and you need only provide a table of the applicable tax rates with a brief explanation. However, tax considerations are often complex, with different rates and tax incentives applying in different countries or even localities. The applicable tax rate also depends on the capital structure of the company. Some business plans provide detailed tax calculations. While this information may be material to the business, it can also be complicated and distract the reader from the main issues. In most cases, it is best to explain the assumptions for the tax calculations in general terms within the business plan. If taxation is major consideration for potential investors, or if your profitability depends on specific tax considerations, prepare a backup document illustrating the different tax scenarios and referring to the main applicable tax laws which can be presented upon request. This document can also be included as an appendix to the business plan.

7. The investment in fixed assets (shown in Figure 5.14 in Section 5.10)
8. Financing costs

Some business plans go beyond the pro forma statements and present different accounting ratios which can be helpful indicators in analyzing the business. For example, the ratio between the operational or pre-tax profit to sales, or between the total profit and the total investment, help analyze the profitability of the company in relative terms.

Pro forma financial statements present the anticipated financial results of the company, with particular emphasis on projected cash flows and net profits.

For a complete picture, include:

1. A pro forma profit and loss report for the forecast period (as shown in Figure 5.16)

Figure 5.18:   Example: Graph of Revenue Growth

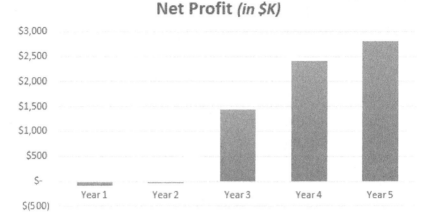

Figure 5.19:   Example: Graph of Profit Growth

2. A balance sheet for the end of the forecast period (optional, as shown in Figure 5.17)
3. A graphic depiction of your expectation for the growth of sales and profits and other major indicators over time (examples are shown in Figures 5.18 and 5.19).
4. A cash flow report (as shown in Figure 5.20)

Following are a few more guidelines on the accounting reports:

a. Include all of the material assumptions used in the calculations.
b. Provide a good level of detail in the breakdown. Consider what information you can provide without compromising confidentiality. Avoid detailing immaterial items.
c. If your reports yield results which are very different from the industry norm, such as a much higher profit margin or lower COGS, etc., be sure to provide convincing explanations for these disparities.

	(in $K)	(in $K)	(in $K)	(in $K)	(in $K)
	Year 1	Year 2	Year 3	Year 4	Year 5
Cash flows from operating activities					
Net Income	(92)	(40)	1,445	2,407	2,798
add back non-cash elements (depreciation)	13	10	22	8	15
Changes in assets and liabilities					
Accounts receivable	(48)	(285)	(470)	(2,384)	(570)
Inventories	(459)	(477)	894	35	(20)
Accounts payable	27	142	235	1,192	285
Accruals and long term liabilities	-	42	59	298	71
Net cash from operating activities	(559)	(606)	2,185	1,556	2,578
Cash flows used in investing activities					
Purchase of fixed assets	(20)	(38)	(56)	(77)	(92)
Cash flows (used in) provided by financing					
Issuance (Redemption) of stock	499	850	-	-	-
Change in cash and cash equivalents					
Net cash increase in cash and equivalents	(79)	206	2,129	1,479	2,486
Cash and equivalents at beginning of period	(12)	(91)	114	2,243	3,723
Cash and equivalents at end of period	$ (91)	$ 114	$ 2,243	$ 3,723	$ 6,209

Figure 5.20:   Example: Statement of Cash Flows

Notes:

1. The items in parentheses are negative cash flows.
2. The cash flow reports at the company level do not include interest income or expense. These cash flow reports show the results of the company's business activity.

To calculate the net cash flow which will be available to the company's shareholders, deduct the net interest expense (the interest expense minus the interest income) from the cash flow.

d. Mention the main tax laws which apply to your business and their effect on profitability. Have your accountant review the assumptions that you made regarding taxation.
e. Use a consistent currency throughout the business plan, so that data can be compared from one section to another.

New Indicators for Reporting Results

Pro forma accounting reports and cash flow reports have been the primary way to present the company's financial results. At times, and particularly during the high tech bubble which ended with the NASDAQ crash in 2000, there were attempts to find other valuation criteria. These included number of subscribers, subscription values and multiples of sales, for example. Following the bankruptcies of many companies which raised money using these indicators, there has been, to some extent, a return to the more conventional methodologies. Nevertheless, these parameters should be used when they are the industry's accepted methodology, together with other indicators.

Consider using a widely used currency, such as the American dollar or the euro. Some business plans use both a local currency together with American dollars or euros. If you choose to use two currencies, be consistent throughout the business plan.

f. When inflation is a significant factor, the accounting reports should be adjusted according to the forecasted impact.

Cash Flow Reports

Many business plans present the financial results in terms of forecasted cash flow to the investors in the company, either in addition to the pro forma accounting reports or instead of them.

Figure 5.20 shows an example of a cash flow report. Cash flow reports are valuable because the profit shown on the P&L report is usually very different from the amount of cash that the company has available to reinvest or to distribute to shareholders. A company can be profitable and still go bankrupt, due to lack of liquidity. Even with large sales volumes, many companies need a large amount of interim financing.

Cash flow reports show at what stage the company will have a healthy cash balance in the bank. They also show how the company intends to resolve problems of cash shortages which arise at different stages.

The cash flow can be used to calculate the net present value (NPV), as described in Appendix I, and the internal rate of return (IRR) of the project. These are the leading financial criteria in making investment decisions. However, because setting the cost of capital for calculating NPV is very complicated, many business plans provide only the cash flow details. This gives investors the information they need to make the investment decision based on whatever cost of capital they estimate should be used for the project. Another methodology is to provide a sensitivity analysis using different costs of capital.

Estimations of the cost of capital for firms and industries in the United States and other countries can be found on Aswath Damodaran's data page on his website: http://people.stern.nyu.edu/adamodar/.

Some general ranges are:

- Six to ten percent for low risk projects
- Ten to fifteen percent for medium risk projects
- Sixteen percent or more for higher risk projects

Some considerations when preparing cash flow reports include:

1. Use Consistent Financial Terms
When preparing your cash flow reports, you need to decide whether the amounts will be reported in nominal terms or in real, such as inflation adjusted, terms. Specify the basis for your calculations. For example, if you are expecting a 15 percent growth in sales, specify if this is a real total increase of 15 percent, or only a partial real increase, such as 10 percent, with the remaining amount due to an increase in price, which, in this example, is five percent. See Figure 5.21.

Nominal cash flow is a product of the real cash flow and the cumulative inflation over the period T:

$$CF_N = (CF_R) \times \{(1 + I)\}^T$$

To adjust nominal cashflow (CF_N) to real cashflow, we discount it:

$$CF_R = \frac{(CF_N)}{(\{1 + I\})^T}$$

Where:
- CF_R is the cash flow in real terms
- CF_N is the cash flow in nominal terms
- T is the number of time periods
- I is the inflation rate

Figure 5.21:   Real Cash Flow vs. Nominal Cash Flow

2. The Cost of Capital and the Rate of Return in Nominal vs. Real Terms

The cost of capital and the rate of return depend on whether your cash flow reports are in nominal terms or real terms. Nominal rates measure the rate at which money invested grows. If you invest $100,000 in your project and expect $110,000 at the end of your project, you are expecting a nominal return of 10 percent. However, even though you expect to have $110,000 at the end of the period, there is no guarantee what that amount will buy. This is due to inflation, which causes the prices of goods and services to change during a given period, changing the purchasing power of $110,000 relative to the invested $100,000. For example, if prices increase by five percent, the purchasing power will be $110,000/1.05, which equals $104,762 in current terms.

3. Forecasted Return for Investors

By subtracting your outgoing cash flows from your incoming cash flows, you can calculate the net amount that will remain for investors.

4. **Credit Policy**

The credit terms that you extend to your customers are an important consideration and will affect the company's cash flows. Describe this policy in the cash flow report. If your policy differs from the typical industry policy, explain why. The credit terms that you receive from your suppliers should also be described, and your cash flow should be adjusted accordingly.

5. **Reasonability**

Your project should be tested for reasonability. Examine your cash flows and see if there are any problems which stand out. You will be expected to provide explanations for any unusual elements in your forecast.

6. **Uncertainty**

When preparing forecasts, there is obviously a great deal of uncertainty. The actual income can be very different from what was originally expected, and there may be surprises in the costs, too. Cost factors may have been overlooked, or the project schedule may be extended due to setbacks. The level of detail that you provide in the cash flow reports depends to some degree on the level of uncertainty. At very early stages, there is so much uncertainty that it is not necessary to go into high levels of detail on the income and cost components. Instead, provide an estimated forecast and illustrate a few different possible scenarios using sensitivity analysis (see Appendix II).

When forecasting for established firms, indicate any major changes relative to previous years, in addition to the above.

5.11   The Appendices

The body of the business plan should include only the most compelling and important information about your business or project. Because it is best to keep the plan concise, interesting and informative, don't weigh it down with detailed schedules and information which are not critical for your readers. If you have additional material which is valuable for completing the profile of the project or which adds credibility to the plan, you can include it in the appendices. Material in the appendices is usually provided for the benefit of the reader seeking specific details about certain issues. Give references to the appendices throughout the text, so that the interested reader will know that there is more information available. Don't go overboard with details in the appendices, either. If you need to provide a lot of additional material in a specific area, it might be best to prepare a separate document which can be presented upon request.

The topics covered in the appendices vary greatly. Some examples:

- **Resumés**
  Strategic alliances are often entered into because of the people leading the company. In this appendix, provide a brief resumé (curriculum vitae) of the key people in the organization, highlighting the aspects relevant to your company or project.
- **Detailed Plans**
  Provide more details about the key information provided in the business plan as needed. You may want to add information on your marketing plans, or on the technology, or present additional data for the various forecasts appearing in the business plan. Sometimes the technological plans are quite complex, running to many pages. In such cases, consider preparing a separate document to be offered as needed. In some cases, companies separate the technological details from the business plans for confidentiality purposes. If so, it may be prudent to draw up a non-disclosure agreement (NDA) to be signed by the reader before releasing the document. This will be discussed in more detail in Chapter 6 of this book.

- **References and Support Information**
  Providing objective evidence to support the different sources you used throughout the business plan, such as statistical reports, scientific articles, etc., lends a great deal of credibility to your presentation.
- **Previous Financial Reports**
  A company with a financial history should provide a summary of previous financial reports.
- **Professional Assessments**
  When possible, supply expert assessments which back up your claims. For example, if your company is relying on technological innovation, it is very valuable to have an expert's recommendation confirming that you indeed have the capabilities that you claim to have, or are able to attain those capabilities. Technological certifications are also often beneficial.
- **Letters of Recommendation**
  Letters of recommendation from satisfied customers or from other parties who are familiar with you, your company and/or your product can be very helpful, particularly when they are written by parties or companies considered good references by those reading your business plan. These may include well-known companies or opinion leaders, or professionals in your field. Don't include letters unless they really strengthen your presentation, and if the letters are from non-credible organizations, leave them out.
- **Market Surveys**
  Key tables and statistics from relevant market surveys can be included.
- **Letters of Intent**
  If you have already established working relationships with other parties or companies, and expect to work together as partners, or to sell to them as customers, ask for letters of intent and include them in the business plan. This offers assurance that your business plans are well-founded and

may reduce the level of risk readers estimate is involved in the project. However, don't include letters of intent that are too general or insignificant. These won't make a serious impression.

- **Rules and Regulations**
  If your company or project is strongly bounded by a particular law or regulation, or if your profitability is strongly affected by particular tax laws or other laws, consider including the relevant texts in the document.

- **Examples and/or Demonstrations of your Product or Service**
  There is nothing more powerful than a demonstration when introducing a new product or service. In these cases, the more graphic, the better. Be as explicit as possible without compromising confidentiality. Software companies often provide an appendix which includes a graphic description of the various interfaces and outputs. If you have a product prototype or an actual product or service already available, include pictures, a video demonstrating it or the product itself, when possible.

- **News Articles**
  If your company has received positive news coverage, you can include the articles in an appendix. This is particularly beneficial when the article has been published in a reputable newspaper, magazine or professional journal. Press releases initiated by the company are less helpful.

Choose the relevant items from the list above that you feel are compelling and helpful for the reader. Don't weigh the document down with too many appendices; stick to the minimum. Consider attaching a list of documents which are available upon request in place of some of the appendices. An overloaded document is very unappealing to decision makers who may have stacks of business plans to go through. Have your document stand out for its efficiency, using great graphics and concise wording to convey your message, rather than long and boring texts and attachments.

5.12   Risk and Uncertainty Factors

A business plan reflects your analysis of your company's potential in uncertain markets. As confident as you may be of your success, you are obviously facing many obstacles on the way to reaching your goals. Even assuming that you can overcome these obstacles, there are many factors which are beyond your control, including market factors, economic factors, technological changes and more. The risks and uncertainty that you face should be addressed in the business plan.

The most important thing to keep in mind is that minimizing or hiding the risk factors is always the worst strategy. Your reader is hardly likely to take a real interest in your business and become a partner or investor without analyzing the project's potential in depth. Your forecasts will be challenged and the risks will be evaluated. If you avoid mentioning risks and challenges, or underestimate their significance, you will look unprofessional, and possibly also naive. On the other hand, your readers' confidence in your project will increase if their concerns are addressed appropriately within the business plan.

There are different approaches to addressing risk factors and uncertainty within the document. One is to discuss them throughout the business plan, analyzing them as you go along. The technological risks would be addressed in the Technology Chapter, the market risks in the Market Chapter, etc. Another approach would be to analyze all of the risk and uncertainty factors in detail in a separate chapter.

There are two major risk categories, which should be addressed separately. First, there are general external market risks which affect all the companies in your market, including your company; however your company will not influence them. These risks are also called exogenous risks. The second category includes the internal business risks which are related directly to your business decisions and activities.

General market risks may include:

- Changes in supply levels and prices of raw materials, machinery and other supplies
- Changes in the available work force or terms of employment
- Economic changes which affect the demand for your product or service
- Changes in laws, regulations or taxes
- Political risks, such as changes of governments and policies, and, in some cases, even revolutions or wars
- Labor-related risks, such as industry-wide strikes
- Weather risks and the risks of natural disasters, such as earthquakes, floods, drought, etc.

Business Risks may include:

- Technological risks, such as poor R&D results
- Production risks
- Unsuccessful marketing
- Post-sales support risks
- Risks which result from a high level of dependency on certain suppliers; supply can be severely affected by a change in the business relationship or in the supplier's business
- Dependence on a small group of important customers; demand can be severely affected by a change in the business relationship or in the customer's business
- Dependence on specific key employees, who might leave the company or become incapacitated
- Geographic risks, which may lead to heavy reliance on transportation systems
- Changes in financial valuations, particularly if your company is using, or intends to use derivatives and financial instruments

Your business plan need not cover all of these risks. Here, as in the rest of the document, use common sense. There is no need to cover all possible natural disasters if you are not relying heavily on a particularly disaster prone area. You should, however, address risks which are relevant and prominent ones. For example:

- If you are relying heavily on one employee's expertise, discuss how you will build backup over time.
- If you are relying on supplies from one area where there are constant political struggles which may affect your supply levels, you should address this by building up a higher reserve and/or second sourcing, by pursuing other supply channels.
- If you rely heavily on sales to one customer, as is often the case with products for the military, for example, analyze the different scenarios if your customer fails to order your product at the levels that you are forecasting.
- Some risks may be covered or at least mitigated by insurance policies, but these are often quite expensive, so the decision on the risks to be covered by insurance should be made carefully.
- Many products must be covered by insurance for product safety and recalls. Some examples include medical products, foods, electronics and children's products, among other product categories. This insurance may be costly, but is often necessary.

5.13 Miscellaneous Words of Advice

In this section we present some tips and pointers which you should take into account when writing the business plan. These are items that may seem minor, but overlooking them can make the business plan look sloppy and reflect badly upon you and your company.

- Editing and Typos
  We have mentioned this point before, but it is worth stressing again here. Your choice of wording, grammar and spelling will reflect upon you. The business plan

represents the company and a sloppy document with typos and grammatical mistakes does not make a good impression.

- Numerical Consistency
Your numerical data will appear in different parts of the document. For example, your marketing costs will appear in the Marketing Chapter, and will also be summarized in the Financial Chapter. Because the numbers often go through many revisions, there is a high risk of making a sloppy mistake and not updating all the tables in the document. Make sure that you have all of your numbers right, and that they are consistent throughout the document.

- Currencies
When writing currency amounts, the placement of the sign varies by currency. For many currencies, especially in Latin America and the English-speaking world, the currency sign is placed to the left of the amount, e.g., $100,000 and not 100,000$, although the cent sign, ¢, appears to the right of the number. However, in other countries, the convention may be to place the sign to the right of the amount. The euro sign, €, is usually placed to the left of the amount in documents in English. However, this is not a strict rule and you are likely to encounter instances in some European countries where it is placed to the right of the amount. When using currency signs, check on the convention for the sign placement, and most importantly, be consistent throughout the document.

- Rounding
When dealing with forecasts, nobody expects precise numbers. Rounded numbers are easier on the eyes and look more sensible. Consider $1.2M vs. $1,225,678. Your spreadsheets may produce the detailed numbers down to the cents, but when presenting them in the business plan, round the numbers to thousands or hundreds of

thousands, or millions, depending on the size of your business.

- Table of Contents, Page Numbering and Tables
  Begin your document with a Table of Contents and number the pages for easy reference. Pages are most commonly numbered sequentially throughout the document. However, some documents use chapter numbering, where the pages are numbered for each chapter separately, and the first number refers to the chapter. Using this method, the pages in Chapter Two would be numbered 2-1, 2-2, 2-3, etc. Page numbering in either method is easily done automatically with word processing software. The chapter numbering method may be more convenient if your chapters are being prepared separately.

  Tables and diagrams should also be numbered. Consider providing a reference list of tables and diagrams. Include titles which give a brief description of the content of the table or diagram for easy reference.

  Make sure that the text within the tables is clear. This is particularly important when providing forecasts. The columns should clearly show what period the data relates to (2016, 2017, or quarterly, Q1/16, Q2/16, etc.). Be sure to include a summary column for numerical data.

  Within the tables, the text should be very brief. If you wish to add a long description, do so using footnotes, or with numbered comments which will appear immediately after the table. Diagrams should include labels and a key when applicable. A good way to check whether your tables or diagrams are clear enough is to ask a few people to look at them and provide feedback.

- Provide Summaries
  Throughout the document, use bulleted lists to summarize the main points you raised in the text. This helps stress the major areas of focus in each section, either for reinforcement or to help the reader who prefers to just skim through a particular section.

- Margins and Spacing
  Your business plan should be visually pleasing, and should leave room for notes and questions. Crowded text is hard to read. Use 1.5 line spacing, or even double spacing, and use a reasonable margin on the page.

- Product Catalogues
  If you have a product catalogue, we recommend that you send it with the business plan as a separate document, or refer the reader to your online catalogue.

- Assumptions
  Describe the assumptions you have made throughout the document. Your readers can take them into account when reading the document, regardless of whether or not they agree with them. If you feel that some of your assumptions are weak and need to be reevaluated over time, you should state this explicitly; it shows integrity and a serious attitude.

- Formal or Informal Language
  Try to maintain a conversational level in your wording of the document. Don't go to either extreme of overly formal language or language which is too casual and informal. Industry buzzwords are acceptable; slang is not.

- Protecting Your Intellectual Property
  Information that has been included in a business plan which has been widely distributed and read, or in presentations to wide audiences, tends to become public domain information. This may compromise your plans to file for patents. If you are planning to file for patents, seek advice from a patent lawyer before distributing the business plan, to make sure that it does not include information which must remain confidential.

5.14 The Presentation

Your business plan is not complete without a presentation. In fact, some investors will ask for some slides or an entire PowerPoint presentation before reviewing the business plan. The presentation has many visual advantages over the written document. It must be very concise and eye-catching. However, the minimalistic presentation of the content can be disadvantageous, which is why it is best to present the slide presentation personally and not just send it.

The presentation must be brief: usually up to 25 slides, which can be presented in 30 minutes to one hour. It can't possibly incorporate the full contents of the business plan. Aim for two to five slides per chapter. For example, the slides on marketing might include a slide on the market need, a slide on the market potential, broken down by the relevant segments, a slide on the marketing strategy and the sales projections.

The slides should summarize the main points of the business plan in a concise point format. The font should be large enough to be read easily from any position in a conference room or a lecture hall. Slides with too much text or crowded tables full of data do not get the message across as well as slides with concise bullet points. Overly wordy slides are difficult to read and will distract your audience from the verbal presentation.

Complete the presentation with a "thank you" slide, and a website and address for further information.

5.15   The Pitch Video

Pitch videos are a great way to communicate with your potential investors, partners and clients in a few short minutes. The goal of these videos is very different from that of the presentation and the business plan document. These videos are meant to spark interest, create engagement and convey the basics about your company or project. They can be used as an introduction sent over the web, or as an attention grabber at the beginning of your presentation to your audience. The great thing about pitch videos is that if they are good, they are fun to watch and easy to share, and the best of them go viral.

If you are preparing a pitch video, take the following guidelines into account:

1. Information:
   You have a few short minutes to convey the following:

   - The business idea
   - The problem you are solving
   - Who you are
   - What the money raised will be used for

   Get straight to the point in your video. Assume that your viewer is unfamiliar with your project, and make sure that the information conveyed in your video is complete. Use examples and testimonials, if possible.

2. Length
   Keep it short. This has the double advantage of fitting easily into your viewers' schedule, and holding the viewers' attention. A pitch video must run under five minutes.

3. Quality
   Don't compromise on quality. Make sure that your video is visually interesting. It is easy enough to produce a video with clear pictures and good audio. Eliminate static and background noise. Use subtitles if needed.

Chapter 6

Confidentiality and Disclosure

6.1 Confidentiality and Disclosure

Holding a competitive advantage is an important key to your new enterprise's success. The stronger your advantage, the more attractive your venture is to your competitors. When writing the business plan, you always face the dilemma of how to protect your ideas and plans while still providing essential information to readers. Many questions arise:

- How much should you disclose?
- What is the optimal level of detail? How much is needed to gain your readers' confidence without compromising your propriety information?
- Can you rely on non-disclosure agreements?
- Can confidential information in the business plan fall into the wrong hands and harm the company's prospects?

These are serious questions. Unfortunately, even if you clearly write "Limited Distribution" or "Confidential" on your document, and you have your readers sign non-disclosure agreements, you will have very little control over where your document goes once it is circulated outside your company. Your reader may want to get other viewpoints and your plan may be passed around from reader to reader, with the best of intentions. Attitudes to confidentiality may differ from one reader to another, and some readers may have conflicting interests. Some readers may even deliberately pass on the information in your business plan to competitors who can benefit from it, thus threatening your potential for success. Even if you don't suspect any of your readers of willful disclosure, sometimes things slip out unintentionally during a casual conversation. That is why when you have any worthwhile propriety information and/or ideas, your safest assumption is that the information disclosed in your business plan is likely to reach the public domain, including your potential competitors.

On the other hand, you can't set up a business without disclosing information. Your readers need to gain a thorough understanding of your business and obtain enough information to build their confidence in your potential for success. If you don't disclose enough information, you will not be able to gain the trust of your prospective investors and partners. They will not appreciate an exaggerated and unjustified cloak and dagger attitude. If you show signs of paranoia and are overly suspicious of potential partners, they will not be eager to cooperate with you. But if you disclose too much information too easily, your readers may view you as reckless and irresponsible, or naive. Either extreme will undermine your readers' confidence in you and your project.

There is no set formula for the right amount of information to disclose, and in the end, you will have to use your common sense to figure out what is right for your company. It is important to take into account all of the considerations above. Put yourself in your readers' shoes and try to see things from their perspectives. Your goal is to find the middle ground between disclosing information which is helpful for your readers' decision-making process and disclosing intellectual property which may harm your prospects.

Your business plan should include enough information to enable your reader to seriously evaluate your prospects. For example, if you are developing a new product, you should describe the product's uses and the costs involved in producing it. In many cases, it won't be necessary to provide detailed technological specifications, and it will be enough to supply basic information on how the product works. For example, if your product is a new medical lotion, you can discuss the major ingredient and its efficacy, without disclosing the details of the production process and the formulation of all of the active ingredients.

Your initial readers are often business people who lack the expertise to ask more than basic questions on the technology. However, if they become more seriously interested, they may bring in an expert to scrutinize the technology more thoroughly. At this point, you may need to disclose more information, but this can be done directly with the expert, and you can confine the disclosure more carefully. For example, you may have the expert sign a non-disclosure agreement, then give them a tour of your facility, show some diagrams or give a verbal presentation. This is less risky than having all of your confidential information available to all of your business plan readers. When an expert is called in, he or she will usually express an opinion on the feasibility of your project, including the technology and development schedule, and possibly your estimated costs. Having an expert involved is an opportunity for you to learn, so listen carefully so that you can both implement any changes necessary and improve your presentation going forward.

6.2 Credibility

While the decisions on confidentiality are complicated, when it comes to credibility, your goal is clear. The information in your business plan must be completely credible. Sometimes, even one suspicious assumption or detail can seriously harm your credibility and raise doubts about the business plan and the project.

Your business plan is written for serious investors and business partners, and they may evaluate it in depth, at times with expert help. The business plan's value is not only the information it contains. It also represents an important step towards establishing trust and mutual respect. The more serious the potential partner is, the more serious the evaluation is likely to be. Anything that looks suspicious may be perceived as a deliberate fabrication or evasion, which can lead to very negative outcomes. Even if the flaw is excused as an oversight or a mistake due to lack of experience or knowledge, and the partner continues to negotiate with you, your position has been harmed and you may lose some leverage.

To ensure credibility, make sure that all of the information in your business plan is well-founded, tested and realistic. For example, if you assume that your product will sell for a given price, make sure that the price makes sense. For example, at a $120 retail price, when the ex-factory or production cost is $80, you are likely to lose money. Products are often sold for three or four times their production cost, if not more, in order to cover the many cost factors along the way, including packaging, logistics, marketing, wholesalers' discounts, retailers' markups, and, most important, your profit margin. In addition, you need to take into account discounts, sales and price deflation. Make credible estimates on how much market share you will capture. If you assume that within three years your innovative product will capture 50 percent of the market share, you will have to prove that this is a credible estimate. Very few products have achieved that high a market share within three years of being introduced.

Credibility is a serious issue. In extreme cases, you may be legally challenged for luring in investors based on false assumptions, if they are convinced that you deliberately misled them or were criminally negligent.

6.3   Full Disclosure

Public companies are strictly bound to fully disclose to the public all information that is pertinent to the company's stability and prospects. There are detailed legal and accounting rules which apply to ensure that the public has all of the relevant information at its disposal. For example, if the company has extended loans or credit, and there is any doubt about the debt repayment, the company must make accounting allowances for doubtful debt, also known as a bad debt reserve, on its public financial statements.

When it comes to business plans, there are no formal regulations on the level of disclosure required. However, we recommend that you practice full disclosure in your business plan and pro forma financial statements. Full disclosure is critical for honestly evaluating your business prospects and establishing trust with your potential business partners.

Your business plan should include any information which is material and significant for the evaluation of your company, whether it appears in the financial statements or not. For example, contractual obligations, such as employment contracts or exclusivity clauses in your distribution agreements which bind the company to certain commitments, will not appear in the financial statements, but they will affect the company's operations. Senior executive contracts often have expensive commitments for options, bonuses and severance payments which should be disclosed.

If your business plan is for a public company, or one division of a public company, be sure that it is reviewed by legal counsel to ensure that full disclosure is made to the public as required.

The status of patent filings should be revealed, including specific patent details once they are approved, since they are then in the public domain in any case. You should also provide a general description of patents which are pending. In these cases, wait for patent approval before releasing more details in order to protect the patents.

Disclosure is very important and you should review your business plan carefully, considering whether there are any obligations or problem areas which may affect your readers' decision to invest in or partner with your project. Any such information should be shared.

Part 4: Getting the Most Out of Your Business Plan

Chapter 7

Promoting Your Business Plan

7.1 Your Target Audience

We opened this book with a discussion of the goals you want to achieve with your business plan, keeping in mind your potential readers. Throughout the preparation of the business plan, consider your target readers. Who are they? What they are seeking? What information is most important to them? What level of detail is appropriate for them? And most important, what kind of partnership or other cooperation do you want with them? If you have answered these questions successfully, you will be better prepared for the next steps after the document has been written and bound.

Prioritize and determine the order of distribution to the different parties or companies you are interested in establishing business relations with, taking into account the following factors:

- Finding the best partner for your business
- The probability of successfully interesting them in your proposal
- The timeframe needed for:
  - o An initial response
  - o Clarifications and providing supplementing information
  - o Entering negotiations
  - o A final decision

<u>Companies Seeking Equity Investments:</u>

If you are seeking funding, the stage your company is in will determine the nature or identity of your potential business partners. In Section 4.5.2.2, we reviewed the different funding stages:

- <u>Pre-seed funding</u>: Your first funding is often raised from friends and family, enabling you to work on your idea and reach a workable plan.
- <u>Seed Money</u>: This early funding is provided to help entrepreneurs prove the validity of their new ideas. Seed money is often initially provided by angel investors.
- <u>Startup</u>: Companies with a proven concept need funding for developing their product and for other functions of a new company, such as marketing and initial production.
- <u>First Round</u> (Series A round): This round is targeted towards production expansion, working according to a working sales model.
- <u>Second Round</u>: This funding is typically targeted towards increasing the existing revenue level and becoming profitable.
- <u>Third Round</u>: Funding for expansion in a profitable company, also called mezzanine financing.
- <u>Fourth Round</u>: This round of funding is made to finance a public offering.

At the stage of developing an idea, preparing patent filings and setting up a small start-up team, many entrepreneurs turn to friends and family for their initial funding, in the range of $100,000 to $500,000.

At the next stage, once you already have a plan and perhaps even a prototype, funding can be sought from angel investors, usually for up to $500,000 from a single investor or several million dollars from a group of angels. There are some capital funds that are also active at this stage, but most are interested in companies that are further along in development.

Once the idea is feasible, many companies will need to raise R&D capital, usually in the range of $2 million to $5 million. During the Internet bubble, much larger amounts were raised, even at this relatively early stage. The money for R&D is usually raised from venture capital funds, and is used to complete a final developed product ready for production and to begin marketing activity.

Venture capital funds should be evaluated based on their portfolios and experts. The best match is a venture capital fund which can offer the company a lot of added value in the specific market in which the company will be active, or with the specific product category on which the company is working.

If the company has successfully produced products and has demonstrated sales potential, it will need more capital to launch the product in a broader market. This time, the company will need a larger amount, of $5 million to $20 million, for expanding production and developing sales. These funds may be provided by the same venture capital fund which provided the R&D capital, or by new venture capital funds which may join the project.

Some of the well-established venture capital firms look for opportunities to make large investments of $10 million or more in a single venture. While these firms have sizeable funds, their capacities for managing their portfolios are finite. As a result, they may prefer not to work with many smaller investments.

Eventually, a successful company will be ready to raise capital from the public through an IPO. Companies that have raised money through venture capital funds are often headed in this direction, whereas successful privately-held companies may choose to continue to maintain private ownership. There is often an additional funding stage prior to the IPO.

The IPO terms can vary among the different stock exchanges. Some exchanges require that companies raise a minimum of $50 million, with a pre-IPO evaluation of over $100 million. Although other exchanges encourage smaller issues of new equity, smaller issues raise the risk that the

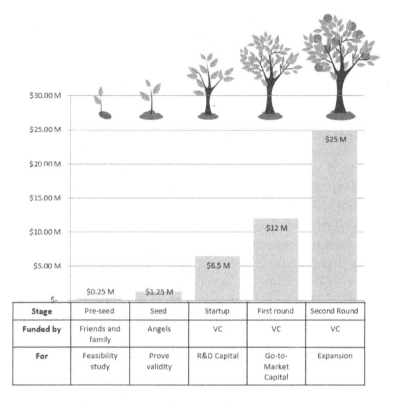

Stage	Pre-seed	Seed	Startup	First round	Second Round
Funded by	Friends and family	Angels	VC	VC	VC
For	Feasibility study	Prove validity	R&D Capital	Go-to-Market Capital	Expansion

Figure 7.1:   An Example of Funding Stages

In Figure 7.1 above, we see an example of different funding stages within a company. Funding differs greatly from one company to another, depending on the company's needs and the resources that become available to it.

shares will not be liquid enough after the IPO and investors will be unable to liquidate their holdings.

Other Target Audiences

Your business plan may be addressed to many other target audiences for purposes other than raising equity. A few examples include:

- Potential strategic partners will use your business plan to evaluate your potential contribution to an alliance, whether for technology, distribution or other purposes.

- Future senior recruits: As the company expands, it will want to attract top-level management. Successful managers will want to understand the company well before deciding to join, and the business plan is a great way to present the company to them.
- Existing management and employees are also target audiences, and they will refer to the business plan to align themselves with the company's strategy and objectives, and to communicate about the company to others.
- Bankers: When seeking banking services, credit lines and loans, you may be asked to provide a business plan.
- Your business plan will often be needed for grant applications submitted to public funds.
- Customers and suppliers may scrutinize your business plan when they are contemplating whether to enter a long-term relationship with you.

7.2 Distributing the Business Plan

Once you have chosen your target recipients, begin by approaching those who are your highest priority. Sending your business plan out to too many recipients can make a bad impression. If you want the business plan to be evaluated seriously, make the recipient understand that you are very interested in them specifically. Expect the evaluation period to take some time: anywhere between a few weeks to a few months. This delay might not be a bad thing for you, as projects that are rejected usually receive responses more quickly.

You may be asked to send the Executive Summary only, or you may be invited to come in and make a brief presentation. This helps save time and allows everyone involved to determine right away if there is a partnership potential. It is also recommended to send out only the Executive Summary in the following cases:

- If you don't really know the best party or company to which to address your business plan

- If you want to get a speedy initial reaction
- If you are interested in spreading the word quickly in the market, both to potential allies and to your competitors

The party or group receiving your business plan may seek expert evaluation, whether on the plan's feasibility, the assumptions that were made, or on the team itself. This takes time and can be expensive.

7.3 Timing

The ideal timing is perhaps the trickiest question when you are raising capital. At the early stages, you will need capital, but have little assurance of success to offer. Because of the high risk involved, investors expect a higher return in the event of success, and you will have to give up more equity in return for the investment. When you know that you have some important events or milestones coming up, it may be wise to wait, if you can. Reaching an important development milestone, such as finalizing a product or closing a big sales contract, are all factors which will increase your valuation and earn your company better investment terms. If your product is on the market and you can demonstrate enthusiastic customer response, or a healthy growth in sales, your company will look much more attractive and less risky.

7.4 Finding the Right Contact Person

Once you have determined to which companies or funds you want to send your business plan, and the timing is right, you should try to make the right contact within the company. The following are some of the factors to bear in mind when approaching the company:

Aiming High

In some cases, it is helpful to go straight to the CEO or other senior official. The CEO is often the most influential person, and if you can get the CEO interested, you may have a more successful and shorter decision-making process. On the other hand, the CEO is usually extremely busy and preoccupied with other issues, and may not give you the full attention that you would like to get. In large organizations, the CEO may not even deal with business plans and new businesses, and will not appreciate being bothered with yours. Or, in other cases, the CEO may not be the most knowledgeable person in the organization when it comes to your particular field.

Find a Champion

Sometimes a lower ranking individual with the right area of expertise will understand the potential benefits quickly and become an enthusiastic champion for your project. Such individuals may be much more accessible than higher ranking managers. Make sure that this person has the right amount of influence and can get things moving for you. Otherwise, you may spend a lot of time and end up with nothing more than a well-meaning enthusiast who can't actually further your goals.

However you choose to establish a relationship with potential contacts, try and find out more about them before approaching them. Learn about the internal politics and the decision-making processes in the organization. You can do so by reading about the company or fund, talking to people from the organization informally, or speaking to other companies which have working experience with them, who are often willing to help. Gathering such background can prove invaluable when working with the organization. You may discover that there are internal conflicts and organizational politics which could weigh heavily in the decision-making process. For example, if you are trying to market a skin care product under a private label, you may find that the marketing department in the target company is interested in going ahead, but the R&D department is raising opposition because they want to develop the product in-house. Having this information can help you choose the right approach to secure the right partner.

7.5   The Business Proposition

When sending out the business plan, state clearly what kind of business proposition you are making. A few examples:

- Capital investment: outline the terms that you are seeking, such as what percentage of equity is being offered, at what target price.
- An R&D investment in return for royalties.
- A marketing partnership.

Some business plans outline the business proposition within the document. However, it may be preferable to send the business proposition separately as an attached letter. In this way, you will be able to use the business plan for several different purposes without having to alter the text. For example, you might use it for raising capital, marketing, or obtaining government grants for R&D.

The terms you outline in the business proposition can range from very detailed to quite broad, depending on a number of factors:

- The level of confidence you have in the terms that you can get
- Whether the recipient has the experience and knowledge to lead the process of setting the terms
- The possibility that setting the terms from the outset might harm the potential for negotiations

Some examples:

- You are seeking a distributor to develop markets for your products. If you are a new company trying to establish a business relationship with a leading distributor, your objective is to interest them in your products. Your business proposition should state in broad terms that you are seeking a distribution agreement for the relevant markets. The distributor will likely have their own standard terms, and may not be willing to negotiate them at the early stages.

- You are raising a loan for your company. In this case, your business proposal should state very clearly the size of the loan you are requesting and what repayment plan you are interested in.

- You have developed products and are seeking a private label agreement with a large multinational company, such as Unilever or Proctor & Gamble. These companies will have experienced experts who will evaluate the proposals and offer terms.

- You are trying to raise seed money and have a few potential private investors whom you know are interested in your company. Outline clearly the amount you expect to raise and what share of equity you are offering.

- You want to raise capital from a venture capital fund. If this a major fund, they will have experts who will evaluate your proposal and make you an offer. You might outline your expectations in the business proposal, but expect them to come up with a counterproposal which can be very different from yours.

7.6 Statement of Confidentiality and Non-Disclosure Agreements

In Chapter 6, we discussed the subject of confidentiality and the risks of distributing confidential information. We recommend that you limit the amount of confidential information in the business plan, which can be expected to reach a wider distribution than you originally planned.

If you want to clearly state that the information in the business plan should be kept confidential, you should write, "Strictly Private and Confidential" on the document and open the document with a brief paragraph stating that the information inside is confidential. Two examples of confidentiality statements:

- "Information, data and drawings embodied in this business plan are strictly confidential and are supplied on the understanding that they will be held confidentially and not disclosed to third parties without the prior written consent of [INSERT YOUR NAME]."
- "The Business Plan is confidential and may not be quoted in full or in part without the explicit permission in writing from [INSERT YOUR NAME]. This document constitutes a trade secret and its confidentiality should be strictly maintained. Unauthorized use of this document constitutes a violation of property rights that relates to the trade secret."

We don't recommend the use of Non-Disclosure Agreement (NDAs) at the initial stages of sending out the business plan. When you are turning to different potential business partners for the purpose of interesting them in your plan, it's unwise to start by raising barriers and setting terms. NDA terms can be quite restrictive, and many potential partners will refuse to sign an NDA just for the sake of seeing your business plan. The best policy is to simply exclude information from the business plan which might put you at risk, and let the recipient know that further details will be disclosed as needed.

Once you have entered negotiations and are being asked to reveal higher level confidential information, you can and should have your business partners sign NDAs. Find the middle ground between giving away information which can harm your business solely on the basis of trust, and becoming so cautious that your partners might sense unjustified paranoia. Always use a good NDA document, even if your partner seems decent and trustworthy, but avoid using an NDA with impossible terms.

7.7 Agents and Intermediaries

Companies seeking to contact investors, distributors or other business partners sometimes choose to work with a middleman to make the introductions and help smooth the way towards establishing a business relationship. These intermediaries are sometimes professionals, such as investment bankers, but they may be business contacts with the right connections or even friends or family members. One of the prominent social networks, LinkedIn, positions itself as a professional connection network and is one way of finding contacts in other companies through people you know.

There are advantages and disadvantages to using an intermediary. One obvious consideration is that doing so can be very costly. Investment bankers or other agents that help companies raise capital are typically paid an upfront or monthly retainer, a cash fee paid upon closing a deal, and additional equity compensation which can amount to three to ten percent of the total capital raised. Intermediaries that facilitate distribution agreements or large sales also charge a fee or demand a percentage of the sales. As a result, some companies are understandably hesitant before undertaking these considerable costs.

In addition, in some cases, an intermediary may not be as fervent a representative as someone from within your company. Intermediaries may have other loyalties, and they may not exhibit the level of enthusiasm that one of the founders might show.

However, intermediaries can have considerable advantages. Look for the following qualities when considering working with an intermediary:

- Market experts who have valuable information to use to your advantage
- Skilled negotiators
- The ability to provide information on your prospective counterparties, before and during negotiations

- The ability to create new opportunities and to spark interest among parties which may not otherwise have been considered as partners

An intermediary can be particularly valuable to young and inexperienced entrepreneurs and save them from costly mistakes. More mature entrepreneurs and managers with experience and contacts may require less help. Even so, it is fairly common for large corporations to contract the services of professional advisors and investment bankers to explore investment opportunities or to act as negotiators in mergers or acquisitions.

An important advantage with intermediaries is that they can propose deals without actually committing the company to any position; both sides are always free to say no. This can be an effective way to ascertain what your counterparty is willing to consider without stating your terms at the outset. It is also advantageous to use intermediaries when your company doesn't have the right people and expertise for this function in-house, and does not want to hire them permanently.

When working with more than one intermediary, be sure that each has a clear plan and that you know which investors and companies are being approached and in what order. These are very important decisions in which your company must be involved. Make sure that no potential investor or business partner is approached by more than one party, or it will reflect poorly both on the representatives themselves and on your company.

When contracting the services of an investment banker or any other intermediary, do your homework ahead of time. Determine who has the right experience and expertise for your company and with whom you can have a trustworthy business relationship. Set the terms down clearly in a written contract before starting the process to avoid misunderstandings later. This can be especially important with people you know personally. You do not want to discover that they are expecting a high fee only after you are in negotiations with an investor or business partner. At best, this will create an awkward situation, but it can also be a deal breaker. Worst of all is becoming unwittingly obligated to pay fees to a broker who doesn't provide adequate services and isn't instrumental in closing the deal.

Items to include in the terms of your contract:

1. The specific work that the intermediary will perform, such as introductions only, complete facilitation of the deal, etc.
2. What parties will be approached
3. A deadline for results
4. Terms of exclusivity. These can be limited by time, geographic location, such as American corporations, business sector, such as pharmaceutical companies, or other parameters.
5. Payment milestones, such as closing an investment deal, introductions to a potential distributor, etc.
6. Compensation, whether a retainer, a one-time payment, a percentage fee, equity, options, etc.
7. Termination of the agreement

Payment of the bulk of the sum should be based on a successful outcome, with specific targets required to be met. This will motivate the intermediary to identify the best potential partners and facilitate the negotiations. Don't structure the deal so that the intermediary will be tempted to rush through negotiations even if you aren't receiving the best terms.

7.8 Approaching Large Corporations

Many large companies have a business development or capital investment group which actively seeks opportunities for investing in or acquiring companies with assets that are potentially valuable to them. Such assets can include unique products, intellectual property, a customer base, a workforce with special skills, and other areas of interest. Often, companies also try to acquire companies that may become competitors.

In a major deal in 2013 the traffic tracking and mapping application, Waze, was bought by Google. This acquisition may have been motivated by the attractiveness of the Waze model which, unlike Google Maps, involves a lot of customer engagement, as well as Google's desire to block competitors from buying Waze. Both Facebook and Apple are thought to have been bidders for the company prior to Google's purchase.

Companies that are active in acquisitions and investments are also constantly looking for fresh opportunities for entering new markets, expanding their product lines and incorporating new technologies. Corporations such as Johnson & Johnson, Proctor & Gamble, Intel and many others have large departments that receive thousands of business proposals annually. Their departments can range in size from a few individuals to hundreds of employees who work on developing and expanding new partnerships and business opportunities. Eventually, they may choose one out of several hundred options to pursue and transform into a business relationship. Only the minority of business plans and proposals that have made it through these filtering processes will actually culminate in deals and contracts.

When working with these large companies, be prepared to accept their terms. Many companies have instruction manuals on how to examine outside proposals. The process may be very slow, and chances are that they will not be flexible in any way. Don't expect them to sign your NDAs; it is more likely that you will be required to waive their responsibility in case of a leak of your confidential information. These companies often state explicitly that they can't guarantee that each and every employee will secure your information properly. In addition, they may have proposals similar to yours being evaluated, in which case ownership of the information or ideas may become complex.

Consider these issues when approaching corporations with a business proposal. It is often helpful to try to approach someone more senior through a mutual contact or a professional representative, as discussed in the previous section, to help your proposal stand out from the other options the company is evaluating and reach more advanced stages of the evaluation process. Having an insider champion your proposal is invaluable.

Another way to approach large corporations is by developing a business relationship with one of their local branches. Companies such as IBM, General Electric, Amazon, General Motors and many others have branches all over the world and you may be able to establish contacts locally that can help you access the right individuals in the corporation.

7.9   Negotiations

If you have been successful in finding a business partner to take an interest in your business plan, you then hold a series of meetings to get to know more about each other and discuss possible synergies. This may be a very lengthy process. If you are successful, you will begin to negotiate terms for a deal.

Many inexperienced managers feel uncomfortable about negotiating. They are reluctant to bargain and argue about the terms, or they may feel offended by the offers made. They may also have to face criticism of their projections, their management or different technical aspects of their proposal. Negotiations require steady nerves, a calm attitude, a lot of patience and keeping clear goals in mind.

Some pointers for preparing for negotiations:

- Familiarize yourself with similar projects in your market. What is the common method of evaluation? What terms did analogous companies close?

- Try to gain an understanding of your counterparty's goals. What are they trying to accomplish? For example, if a company is interested in investing only if it can buy at least 50 percent of the equity and you are not willing to lose a controlling share, there is no point in entering into negotiations, even if it otherwise seems like a good match. Be sure to calculate both your benefit and that of your counterparty so that you understand the full picture.
- Determine in advance what your goal is and what terms you can and cannot compromise on.

One way to prepare for tough negotiations is by simulation. Rehearse the negotiations and try to foresee the positions your counterparties might take. Consider how the dynamics of the negotiations might cause them to react. To keep the simulations as realistic as possible, try to work with experienced negotiators who are familiar with organizations and people similar to your counterparties. The simulations should be held in the same language in which the negotiations will take place so you can practice formulating your positions and responses verbally.

Another recommendation is not to start your negotiations with your most senior level personnel when possible, but send in other representatives to start the negotiations. These should be managers who can represent the company but are not authorized to make binding decisions for it. They can provide and acquire a lot of the information needed. The CEO should step in at a more advanced stage, when final decisions need to be made or if there is a major obstacle to overcome. The CEO then has the advantage of not having made any hasty commitments during the discussions that have taken place.

Legal counselors play an important role at the final stages of the negotiations, but do not have to be involved from the start. They will be needed to summarize the terms and write the contract which reflects everything agreed upon between the parties. They may also raise legal issues which must be considered and resolved.

The summary of negotiations is often summarized in a Memorandum of Understanding (MoU). The MoU is typically a short document of three to four pages which summarizes the principle points agreed upon, such as the type of financing and equity, unit prices, order levels, board of director rights or other important components of the agreement. The MoU will serve as the basis for a detailed contract which will then be prepared.

One of the advantages of preparing a MoU is that it formalizes the agreement over the principle terms under negotiation in a relatively brief document, before beginning the process of formulating all the legal wording that will be needed for the comprehensive contract. The understanding is that once these principle terms have been agreed upon, the parties will succeed in reaching agreement on the remaining details, although there will often be weighty discussions on other variables as well. However, if the principle terms are not agreed upon, there is no point in discussing the less critical contractual points.

Closing Words

Engaging in the full business plan process is a significant challenge for any company or project. It is our hope that, having read this book, you have come to regard the business plan process as much more than a means of communicating the essence of your business to external parties. The business plan is perhaps most important as an internal management practice, one which is critical in evaluating your business options, making decisions and actively advancing your organization.

Any organization or project operates within a complex and continually-changing ecosystem. The business plan will integrate the tools needed for data collection and analysis, decision-making and business promotion on an on-going, dynamic basis. With these tools in hand, your team can aspire to leverage the business, associate with the right partners, grow and create more value.

Your business plan may start out as an excel model, with sales and cost projections; that may be sufficient for a small group of entrepreneurs sketching out initial plans for a new company. Eventually, it will become imperative to add a clear outline of your company's business environment (with the risks and the opportunities), its line of offerings and its specific business objectives — short-term through long-term.

Ideally, your business plan will continually evolve and grow with the company, as you incorporate a broader and deeper understanding of the business into it. As your company develops, and there are more team members, it will serve as an important aid in assuring consistency and collaboration within the company. It will also contribute to planning the wisest and most productive use of resources.

Building a comprehensive model and plan is an acquired skill. Over time it will be integrated into your mindset and is certain to enhance your current and future projects.

Appendix I

Profitability Analysis: A Primer

Throughout the book we have used various terms relating to financial valuations. In this appendix we will explain a few of these terms and provide an example. For a more complete understanding, there are several excellent textbooks which teach these topics in depth. We recommend "Principles of Corporate Finance" by Richard A. Brealey, Stewart C. Myers, Franklin Allen, published by McGraw Hill/Irwin.

We calculate the current or present value of a stream of payments to be received in the future using a method called **discounting**, by establishing a **discount rate** and applying it to all incoming and outgoing cash flows.

1. **The time value of money: calculating the present value of a stream of payments to be received in the future:**

   Before we explain about discounting, we will demonstrate that a sum of money that will be received at some point in the future is worth less than having the same amount now. To give a simple example, given an annual interest rate of 5%, 100 euros that will be paid in 1 year is worth only 95.24 euros today. This can be calculated in the following manner:

$$\frac{100}{1+ interest\, rate} = \frac{100}{1.05} = 95.2381$$

This is easily understood if you consider that 95.2381 euros that are deposited in the bank today at 5% annual interest will yield 100 euros in one year:

$$95.2381 \ x \ (1 + interest \ rate) = 95.2381 \ x \ 1.05 = 100$$

In a similar manner, we can conclude that 100 euros to be paid in 2 years is worth only 90.70 euros today, if we assume the same annual interest rate of 5%. This is calculated in almost the same way. However, we will now assume that there are two interest periods, and that the sum earns **compound interest,** i.e. that the first 5% interest payment which is accrued at the end of the first year is added to the 90.70 euros we started out with, and will also earn the same rate of interest in the second year.

In this example, at the end of the first year we have the following sum in our account:

$$90.70295 \ x \ (1 + 0.05) = 95.2381$$

And at the end of the second year we have:

$$95.2381 \ x \ (1 + 0.05) = 100$$

We can also calculate the two years together:

$$90.70295 \ x \ (1 + 0.05) \ x \ (1 + 0.05) = 100$$

Which is: $\quad 90.70295 \ x \ (1 + 0.05)^2 = 100$

When calculating compound interest with annual interest compounding, we take the original amount and multiply it by (1+ interest rate) to the power of the number of years until the payment of the principal and interest.

Similarly, we can generalize for periodic compounding, where the period may be a day, a week, a quarter or any other period after which the interest is accrued. The general formula for periodic compounding is:

$$A = P\left(1 + \tfrac{r}{n}\right)^{nt}$$

In this formula:

A = the amount of money accumulated after t years (principal and interest)

P = the principal, i.e. the initial amount that you borrow or deposit

r = the annual interest rate

t = the number of years the amount is deposited or borrowed for

n = the number of times the interest is compounded per year

The interest rate has a very significant impact on the outcome of these calculations. Consider the difference between a 10 year deposit of 100 euros with annual interest of 6% compounded monthly, versus the same deposit with annual interest of 3%, also compounded monthly:

$$100x(1+\tfrac{0.06}{12})^{12x10} = 181.94$$

versus

$$100x(1+\tfrac{0.03}{12})^{12x10} = 134.94$$

In these calculations, we have shown the future value (FV) of $100 deposited at different interest rates.

In a similar way we can calculate the present value (PV) of a stream of payments to be received in the future.

Since the future value (FV) of a single amount may be calculated using the formula above as:

$$FV = PV\left(1+\tfrac{r}{n}\right)^{nt}$$

We can calculate the present value of a single future amount to be received after t years by extracting PV from the formula above.

$$PV = \frac{FV}{\left(1+\tfrac{r}{n}\right)^{nt}}$$

In these formulas:

FV = the amount of money accumulated, or to be received after t years

PV = the principal, i.e. the initial amount that you borrow or deposit, or the present value of a future cash flow

r = the annual interest rate

t = the number of years the amount is deposited or borrowed for

n = the number of times the interest is compounded per year

When forecasting, we generally need to calculate more complicated streams of multiple incoming and outgoing cashflows. The next two sections will explain how to do this, and will explain two important terms:

- The discount rate
- Net cash flows

2. The Discount Rate

The discount rate is the cost of raising money and it reflects both the time value and the level of risk. Sometimes the discount rate is clear, for example, when we know the interest rate for a given loan. However, it is often more complicated to figure out the appropriate discount rate. In many companies, the riskiness of the business changes over time. This may be due to changes in the capital structure, due to changes in the riskiness of the company's activities or for other reasons. The riskier the business, the higher the discount rate will be, to reflect the higher return investors will expect for their investment in a risky project. The discount rate should be calculated considering:

a. The cost of equity. This can be estimated according to the stockholders' expectations, i.e., what they expect to earn on their investment in the equity of the company.

b. The cost of debt. This is easier to determine, and can be derived from the cost of bonds or loans.

The cost of raising equity and debt will determine the company's discount rate, which is defined as:

Discount rate = risk free rate + risk premium

In a new and risky venture, the risk premium may have a very significant impact on the discount rate.

Consider an example of a 15-year-old company with a capital structure comprised of 40% equity and 60% debt. Let us assume that investors in this type of company currently expect a return of 20% on their equity investment. We will therefore place 20% as the first value, the cost of equity. Let us assume that the cost of debt, i.e., the cost to borrow money from banks and other lenders, is 8%. In this example we can calculate the current cost of capital using a weighted average as follows:

$$40\% \times 20\% + 60\% \times 8\% = 12.8\%$$

If we are raising capital for a new project in the company, the investors will revise the calculation of the risk premium to reflect the new risk arising from the proposed line of business. If the new project is similar to the company's ongoing activities, the additional risk premium may be quite low. However, if the new project is very different, the effect on the riskiness of the company may be an increase or a decrease of risk, depending on the project and how it correlates to the existing business. If it is hard to predict the company's success in the new project, the risk premium will be higher, and might be 13–14%, for example.

Now let us consider a completely new company, which does not have a proven track record. The risk premium in this case will be higher, and can be 6-10% on a low risk project, for example, and much higher on a high risk project.

So we can see that it is rather challenging to set the cost of capital in a new project. This is one of the reasons that many companies perform sensitivity analyses, in which the discounting uses a range of values for the cost of capital, so that potential investors can see the different scenarios that are within a reasonable range. We will explain sensitivity analysis in Appendix 2.

3. <u>Calculating Net Cash flows</u>

During the course of business, a company will have both cash inflows and outflows.

Inflows include any funds transferred to the company, including payments to the company by customers as well as money from the sale of property. Other types of inflows are funds from bank financing, equity investments and even funds from legal settlements.

Outflows include any funds transferred from the company to another party, including employees' salaries, payments to suppliers, dividends paid to equity owners or money spent on any long term acquisitions. Depreciation expenses are not included in the outflows, as this is not a cash payment, only an accounting book entry.

The company's inflows minus the outflows in a given period (e.g. a quarter or a year) is the net cash flow for that period. Once we have the net cash flow, we can proceed to calculate the present value of the net cash flows to be received at a later date.

When calculating the present value of the firm to all of its claimholders (i.e., equity and debt holders), the net cash flows include only inflows and outflows from operations and exclude financial flows such as getting a loan or paying out interest payments or payments to settle old debts, etc.

4. Net Present Value

Net present value is the current worth of a future stream of net cash flows, using the appropriate discount rate to value future cash flows in terms of today's value.

To calculate the net present value, we calculate the discounted value of each period's net cash flow, and add up the discounted cash flows for all of the periods.

The formula for NPV is:

$$NPV = -I_0 + \frac{NCF_1 - I_1}{(1+r)^1} + \frac{NCF_2 - I_2}{(1+r)^2} + \frac{NCF_3 - I_3}{(1+r)^3} + \cdots\cdots + \frac{NCF_n - I_n}{(1+r)^n}$$

This can also be written in the form:

$$NPV = -I_0 + \sum_{t=1}^{n} \frac{NCF_n - I_n}{(1+r)^t}$$

In this formula, NPV is calculated by measuring the investments (denoted by I_t, t = 0, 1,...n) required in the project against the total value of the future net cash flows from operations (denoted by NCF_t, t = 1, 2....,n). I_0 is the required investment at the start of the project, and because it is an outflow it is negative. NCF_1 is the net cash flow at the end of year 1 and so forth until year n which is the final year calculated in evaluating the project. I_t is the additional investment in each period t. r is the discount rate used. NPV therefore reflects the economic value of the project, or its added value.

For the sake of simplicity, the NPV formula assumes that all of the cash inflows and outflows in a given period t happen at the same point in time. This may not always be the case, and sometimes this assumption can cause problems. To resolve these problems, adjust the period t to be quarters or even months, to get a clear picture.

Here is an example, for a company with the cash flows in the table below, and a discount rate of 12%, compounded annually:

Period	Outflows (salaries, rent, materials etc.) In USD	Inflows (revenue and other positive inflows) In USD	Total cash flow In USD
Initial Investment	–550,000	0	–550,000
Year 1	–460,000	255,000	–205,000
Year 2	–655,000	1,300,000	645,000
Year 3	–825,000	2,050,000	1,225,000

We will calculate the net present value of all of the net cash flows for each period separately, as shown below:

	Project start	Year 1	Year 2	Year 3
Outgoing cash flow	-550,000	-460,000	-655,000	-825,000
Incoming cash flow		255,000	1,300,000	2,050,000
Net cash flow	-550,000	-205,000	+645,000	+1,225,000
Net present value:				
-550,000				
$\dfrac{-205,000}{1+12\%}$				
$\dfrac{645,000}{(1+12\%)^2}$				
$\dfrac{1,225,000}{(1+12\%)^3}$				

Here is the same calculation, using the NPV formula:

$$NPV = -550,000 + \frac{-460,000 + 255,000}{(1+0.12)^1} + \frac{-655,000 + 1,300,000}{(1+0.12)^2}$$
$$+ \frac{-825,000 + 2,050,000}{(1+0.12)^3}$$

This will give us the following result:

$$NPV = -550,000 + \frac{-205,000}{1.12} + \frac{645,000}{1.25} + \frac{1,225,000}{1.40} = 653,085$$

A positive NPV is a sign that the project is worthwhile and should be accepted. A negative NPV is a sign that there are better alternatives for the money invested, and the project should be rejected. The NPV is the value of the entire project today, i.e., the price which would be worthwhile to pay today for the future cash flows. In our example above, the NPV is positive, and amounts to $653,085. This is a simplified calculation, since in fact the annual outflows would not occur at one point only during the year, and the interest would probably be compounded monthly and not annually, but it gives an approximation of the value of the project which can be compared against alternative investments. The same methodology can be applied to a much more detailed cash flow, with more details in the periods for the inflows and outflows (e.g. monthly) and shorter interest compounding periods.

Appendix II

A Brief Introduction to Sensitivity Analysis

In planning the future activities of a company and quantifying them in economic terms, there is so much uncertainty that some give up on planning altogether. After all, you know in advance that the numbers that will be calculated on the spreadsheet will almost certainly be different in reality.

However, as we have stressed throughout the book, our approach is certainly not to forfeit planning. Planning is always worthwhile, since the planning process itself is so beneficial, and since not planning altogether is certain to lead to gross misjudgments and errors. To deal with uncertainty, different scenarios should be incorporated into the plan, and the plan should be evaluated with varied assumptions.

Scenario Analysis

In scenario analysis we consider possible future outcomes to our plan under alternative scenarios, also called "alternative worlds". This is particularly important in companies with great uncertainty and in particularly volatile markets.

For example, some possible scenarios for a company that is working on the research and development of a pioneering medical treatment, at the end of a given period, are:

- A true breakthrough, in which the product surpasses existing treatments by far, in efficacy, safety and cost.
- A disappointing outcome, in which the product's efficacy cannot be proven, or the product has too many safety issues or is too expensive.
- The product is a moderate improvement in comparison to the existing alternatives.

In the first scenario, our company will have valuable knowledge, which can attract the leading companies in the pharmaceuticals market and lead to very lucrative licensing or distribution agreements. If the knowledge is protected by patents, or there is a significant lead time for other companies to catch up and introduce competing products, the premium our company can demand will be even higher.

In the second scenario, the project will either need more funding to overcome the problems which have come up, or perhaps the project will be abandoned altogether, and the money spent on R&D will be lost. Or perhaps the company will be able to find a partner that is interested in the knowledge accumulated, despite the imperfect outcome, but with far less lucrative terms then in the first outcome.

And in the last scenario, the company can expect that the project will yield some value, and may be able to partner with another interested company, but at a much lower premium than in the first scenario.

Let's look at a another example of a company called GreatApp that has a smartphone app with a freemium business model, where it offers a basic suite of functions that are completely free, and plans to offer premium functions for a small charge after six months, in addition to the free functions. Let's assume that GreatApp has 700,000 users for the freemium functions, and will charge $5 monthly for the paid functions. Here are a few possible scenarios:

- The company is successful in converting a percentage of their user base. A 5% conversion rate from freemium to premium subscriptions will create annual revenues of $2.1M. A 15% conversion rate from freemium to premium subscriptions will create annual revenues of $6.3M.
- New competitors appear offering similar functions similar to our company's premium functions for free and GreatApp does not succeed in converting free users to paid users.
- GreatApp's free user base increases drastically, and the company needs to invest in more resources to continue to provide good service to all of the subscribers.
- GreatApp receives an acquisition offer from a leading internet company.

Sensitivity Analysis

When performing sensitivity analysis we test how changes in important quantitative assumptions will affect the company results over a period of time. Sensitivity analysis is performed by choosing the critical parameters upon which we based our pro forma computations, and systematically changing them to assess how the changes will affect the overall outcome.

Some of these factors are external, and change according to the market and economy. This analysis is important towards understanding how the company will withstand external changes, for example:

- Market demand
- Market price changes
- Exchange rates

Other factors are typically internal, and in these cases sensitivity analysis is valuable in making important decisions within the company. For example:

• Initial investment
• Investment in R&D
• Production costs
• Marketing costs
• Launch dates
• Product prices

Sensitivity analysis is very important in making pricing decisions, and striking the right balance in which the price is attractive enough to generate enough sales, yet is also profitable for the company. It is also an important aid in determining how much can be spent on development or on marketing, etc.

Factors which relate to the sales forecast include:

• Market size — analyze what would happen if the market expands or shrinks
• Market share — analyze the company's performance at varying rates of penetration into the market
• Product prices — analyze the overall sales performance as a function of the company's pricing

The sales forecast will also directly affect all of the variable costs, i.e., those costs that vary depending on a company's sales (and production) volume.

Analyzing how changes in the timing of cash flows affect your business is very important. For example, if you are projecting to launch a product in January 2018 and expect to have revenues from that point on, analyze what would happen if you have to delay the launch for three months, or if the sales build up only after three months. Will you have enough cash to cover the additional three months of costs without revenues? This analysis will help you plan to have the necessary reserves for these contingencies.

Another parameter which is often tested using sensitivity analysis is the cost of capital, which is often an important factor in negotiating with investors and determining the valuation of the company.

The best way to perform sensitivity analysis is on a spreadsheet, using a simplified pro forma report. It is very simple to do by listing the parameters which will be analyzed in a specified area of the spreadsheet, and using cell references for the calculations.

In the example below created on an Excel spreadsheet, we look at various scenarios for the app company Great-App. The parameters are in rows 2-12, and the calculations in the pro forma in rows 15-30 refer to those cells. For example, the COGS per user is calculated for the first year with the formula = C9*C5*(1 − C6) + C10*C5*C6.

	A	B	C	D	E	F
1						
2		**Parameters - in annual terms, USD**				
3						
4			Year 1	Year 2	Year 3	
5		No. of users	700,000	1,100,000	1,400,000	
6		% of paid users	3%	6%	10%	
7						
8		Revenue - per paid user	$60	$60	$60	
9		COGS per free user	$1	$1	$1	
10		COGS per paid user	$3	$3	$3	
11		sales support for free user	$0.50	$0.50	$0.50	
12		sales support for paid user	$2.50	$2.50	$2.50	
13						
14						
15						
16		**Pro Forma P&L - in USD**				
17						
18		Revenues	1,260,000	3,960,000	8,400,000	
19		COGS - Fixed	250,000	325,000	450,000	
20		COGS - per user	742,000	1,232,000	1,680,000	
21		Gross Profit	268,000	2,403,000	6,270,000	
22						
23		Expenses				
24		Research and Development	150,000	180,000	210,000	
25		Sales and Marketing - Fixed	255,000	330,000	380,000	
26		Sales Support - per user	392,000	682,000	980,000	
27		General and Administrative	220,000	250,000	280,000	
28		Total Expenses	1,017,000	1,442,000	1,850,000	
29						
30		Net Profit (Loss)	(749,000)	961,000	4,420,000	
31						
32						

When the parameters are specified in designated cells on the spreadsheet, and not hidden within the cells of the pro forma report it is very simple to analyze different outcomes. In our example above, the parameters are in rows 4-12, and the pro forma report is in rows 18-30. In this example, we can analyze the impact of the conversion rate to paid users, simply by changing the percentage of paid users in row 6. This is what it will look like:

Parameters - in annual terms, USD			
	Year 1	Year 2	Year 3
No. of users	700,000	1,100,000	1,400,000
% of paid users	5%	10%	15%
Revenue - per paid user	$60	$60	$60
COGS per free user	$1	$1	$1
COGS per paid user	$3	$3	$3
sales support for free user	$0.50	$0.50	$0.50
sales support for paid user	$2.50	$2.50	$2.50

Parameters - in annual terms, USD			
	Year 1	Year 2	Year 3
No. of users	700,000	1,100,000	1,400,000
% of paid users	1%	3%	5%
Revenue - per paid user	$60	$60	$60
COGS per free user	$1	$1	$1
COGS per paid user	$3	$3	$3
sales support for free user	$0.50	$0.50	$0.50
sales support for paid user	$2.50	$2.50	$2.50

Pro Forma P&L - in USD - Higher conversion rate			
Revenues	2,100,000	6,600,000	12,600,000
COGS - Fixed	250,000	325,000	450,000
COGS - per user	770,000	1,320,000	1,820,000
Gross Profit	1,080,000	4,955,000	10,330,000
Expenses			
Research and Development	150,000	180,000	210,000
Sales and Marketing - Fixed	255,000	330,000	380,000
Sales Support - per user	420,000	770,000	1,120,000
General and Administrative	220,000	250,000	280,000
Total Expenses	1,045,000	1,530,000	1,990,000
Net Profit (Loss)	35,000	3,425,000	8,340,000

Pro Forma P&L - in USD - Lower conversion rate			
Revenues	420,000	1,980,000	4,200,000
COGS - Fixed	250,000	325,000	450,000
COGS - per user	714,000	1,166,000	1,540,000
Gross Profit	(544,000)	489,000	2,210,000
Expenses			
Research and Development	150,000	180,000	210,000
Sales and Marketing - Fixed	255,000	330,000	380,000
Sales Support - per user	364,000	616,000	840,000
General and Administrative	220,000	250,000	280,000
Total Expenses	989,000	1,376,000	1,710,000
Net Profit (Loss)	(1,533,000)	(887,000)	500,000

And the analysis can be summarized in the following chart:

GreatApp 3-year results: changed conversion rate

	Revenues	Net Profit (Loss)
Paid users — base estimate	13,620,000	4,632,000
Paid users — Higher conversion rate	21,300,000	11,800,000
Paid users — Lower conversion rate	6,600,000	1,920,000

Note that the table above and the other tables used for this example show simple sums of the revenues and profits over three years. To discount these amounts, use the method described in Appendix I. Now we will use the same spreadsheet, but now look at pricing, seeing how a $5 change in the price (without changing any other parameters) will affect GreatApp's results.

Parameters - in annual terms, USD			
	Year 1	Year 2	Year 3
No. of users	700,000	1,100,000	1,400,000
% of paid users	3%	6%	10%
Revenue - per paid user	$65	$65	$65
COGS per free user	$1	$1	$1
COGS per paid user	$3	$3	$3
sales support for free user	$0.50	$0.50	$0.50
sales support for paid user	$2.50	$2.50	$2.50

Parameters - in annual terms, USD			
	Year 1	Year 2	Year 3
No. of users	700,000	1,100,000	1,400,000
% of paid users	3%	6%	10%
Revenue - per paid user	$55	$55	$55
COGS per free user	$1	$1	$1
COGS per paid user	$3	$3	$3
sales support for free user	$0.50	$0.50	$0.50
sales support for paid user	$2.50	$2.50	$2.50

Pro Forma P&L - in USD - Higher price			
Revenues	1,365,000	4,290,000	9,100,000
COGS - Fixed	250,000	325,000	450,000
COGS - per user	742,000	1,232,000	1,680,000
Gross Profit	373,000	2,733,000	6,970,000
Expenses			
Research and Development	150,000	180,000	210,000
Sales and Marketing - Fixed	255,000	330,000	380,000
Sales Support - per user	392,000	682,000	980,000
General and Administrative	220,000	250,000	280,000
Total Expenses	1,017,000	1,442,000	1,850,000
Net Profit (Loss)	(644,000)	1,291,000	5,120,000

Pro Forma P&L - in USD - Lower price			
Revenues	1,155,000	3,630,000	7,700,000
COGS - Fixed	250,000	325,000	450,000
COGS - per user	742,000	1,232,000	1,680,000
Gross Profit	163,000	2,073,000	5,570,000
Expenses			
Research and Development	150,000	180,000	210,000
Sales and Marketing - Fixed	255,000	330,000	380,000
Sales Support - per user	392,000	682,000	980,000
General and Administrative	220,000	250,000	280,000
Total Expenses	1,017,000	1,442,000	1,850,000
Net Profit (Loss)	(854,000)	631,000	3,720,000

The analysis can be summarized in the following chart:

GreatApp 3-year results: changed price

	Revenues	Net Profit (Loss)
Price — base estimate	13,620,000	4,632,000
Price — $ 5 higher	14,755,000	5,767,000
Price — $ 5 lower	12,485,000	3,497,000

Once again, the table shows simple sums of the revenues and profits.

This is of course a very simple example. In fact, the price is very likely to affect the conversion rate, so we should create a scenario in which the higher price leads to a lower conversion rate, and the lower price to a higher conversion rate.

We can merge the assumptions that we made before, and see what the results look like:

Parameters - in annual terms, USD	Year 1	Year 2	Year 3
No. of users	700,000	1,100,000	1,400,000
% of paid users	5%	10%	15%
Revenue - per paid user	$55	$55	$55
COGS per free user	$1	$1	$1
COGS per paid user	$3	$3	$3
sales support for free user	$0.50	$0.50	$0.50
sales support for paid user	$2.50	$2.50	$2.50

Parameters - in annual terms, USD	Year 1	Year 2	Year 3
No. of users	700,000	1,100,000	1,400,000
% of paid users	1%	3%	5%
Revenue - per paid user	$65	$65	$65
COGS per free user	$1	$1	$1
COGS per paid user	$3	$3	$3
sales support for free user	$0.50	$0.50	$0.50
sales support for paid user	$2.50	$2.50	$2.50

Pro Forma P&L - in USD - Higher conversion rate			
Revenues	1,925,000	6,050,000	11,550,000
COGS - Fixed	250,000	325,000	450,000
COGS - per user	770,000	1,320,000	1,820,000
Gross Profit	905,000	4,405,000	9,280,000
Expenses			
Research and Development	150,000	180,000	210,000
Sales and Marketing - Fixed	255,000	330,000	380,000
Sales Support - per user	420,000	770,000	1,120,000
General and Administrative	220,000	250,000	280,000
Total Expenses	1,045,000	1,530,000	1,990,000
Net Profit (Loss)	(140,000)	2,875,000	7,290,000

Pro Forma P&L - in USD - Lower conversion rate			
Revenues	455,000	2,145,000	4,550,000
COGS - Fixed	250,000	325,000	450,000
COGS - per user	714,000	1,166,000	1,540,000
Gross Profit	(509,000)	654,000	2,560,000
Expenses			
Research and Development	150,000	180,000	210,000
Sales and Marketing - Fixed	255,000	330,000	380,000
Sales Support - per user	364,000	616,000	840,000
General and Administrative	220,000	250,000	280,000
Total Expenses	989,000	1,376,000	1,710,000
Net Profit (Loss)	(1,498,000)	(722,000)	850,000

The following chart is the summary of our results:

GreatApp 3-year results: changed price and conversion rate

	Revenues	Net Profit (Loss)
Paid users — base estimate	13,620,000	4,632,000
Paid users — Lower Price, higher conversion rate	19,525,000	10,025,000
Paid users — Higher Price, lower conversion rate	7,150,000	(1,370,000)

As before, these three-year sums of the revenues and the profits may be discounted using the method described in Appendix I.

The important principles in performing sensitivity analysis are:

1. Make meaningful assumptions. In the example above, we tested different prices and conversion rates, but didn't

provide any justification for our assumptions. In reality, assumptions should be based on market data or what is known about similar products. Some products are very price sensitive, and a small change in price can change the sales figures drastically (particularly freemium products). Others are less price sensitive.

2. Change the correlated parameters together: some parameters directly influence others. For example, the number of users directly affects the COGS and the number of sales support personnel. The date of the launch of a product directly affects the timing of the revenues. Consider what parameters will create a chain reaction, and change your assumptions accordingly.

3. Create clear spreadsheets: Begin with a simplified base assumption, after considering all of the revenue and cost components. The details behind the numbers are important for other parts of your business plan, but for the sensitivity analysis try to present condensed data.

4. Create a parameter section on your spreadsheet: Remember to separate the parameters and to refer to them within the pro forma reports as shown above, so that changes made to the parameters will quickly drill down into all of the pro forma data.

5. Summarize your findings: A simple table with your base assumptions, a more pessimistic scenario and a more optimistic scenario can make it very easy to understand your results.

Appendix III

Tables of Contents — Examples

In Section 5.3 of this book we suggested that you look through several examples of Tables of Contents to help you decide on the structure of your business plan. We will provide a few examples in this appendix. The table of contents will be determined by the importance of the presentation of the most relevant topics of your business plan, as well as by your style preference. Get ideas and inspirations for your particular business plan from the numerous examples to be found on the Internet. Take elements from different options and customize the table of contents to your needs. We will provide four examples here.

Sample Business Plan Structure

Chapter	Description
Title page/s	• The name of the company or product
	• The date
	• Confidentiality, disclaimers
	• Optional: instructions to return the document
	• Optional: the author
TOC	• Table of contents
Executive Summary	• 1–3 pages long
	• A summary of the document's highlights
	• A summary of the business strategy
	• Goals of the document
	• A summary pitch
The opportunity: The proposed product/ service	• Description of the problem
	• The unique solution through the proposed product/service

(Continued)

Chapter	Description
The Technology	• Description of the technological environment • Description of technology, unique advantages • Lead time, brief patents description
The Market Environment and Strategy	• The market environment • Description of target markets • Marketing and competitive strategy • Sales projections • Marketing budget
R&D	• Goals • Milestones and schedules • R&D budget
Production and Operations	• The production plan • The logistics plan • Production and operations budget
The Company	• The organizational structure • Personnel forecast • Budget for personnel

The Financial Chapter	• Investment plan
	• Financing plan
	• Summary budget and pro forma financial reports:
	  ○ Profit and loss statements
	  ○ Cash flow
	  ○ Sensitivity analysis
	• Risk analysis

Appendices	• CVs of key personnel
	• Clinical data
	• Technical data
	• Research
	• Case studies
	• More detailed financial pro forma reports, including a balance sheet
	• References
	• Others:
	  ○ Description of agreements
	  ○ Patents summary
	  ○ Certificates and licenses
	• Previous financial statements

Example 1 - Table of Contents for Orange DSP Inc, a company that develops software tools for CPU design engineers:

1. Executive Summary
2. Investment Highlights

   2.1 Our Software Solution
   2.2 Strategic Relationships
   2.3 Large and Growing Market
   2.4 Our Scalable and Profitable Business Model
   2.5 Management Team

3. Industry Overview

   3.1 DSP Overview
   3.2 DSP Market
   3.3 DSP Software Development Tool Market

4. Business Overview

   4.1 Business Description
   4.2 The Orange Solution

5. Business Strategy

   5.1 Strategic Relationships
   5.2 Technology

6. Marketing and Sales

   6.1 Marketing Strategy
   6.2 Customer Service
   6.3 Competition

7. Intellectual Property
8. Facilities
9. Financial Projections

   9.1 Revenue Forecast
   9.2 Product Pricing
   9.3 Pro forma Reports

Appendix 1: Financial Data
Appendix 2: Detailed Budget
Appendix 3: Capitalization and Ownership
Appendix 4: Competitive Analysis

Example 2 - Table of Contents for K. Industries Ltd., a company that developed a unique methodology for gas analysis:

1. Executive Summary
2. Gas Analysis

    2.1 The Applications for Gas Analyzers
    2.2 Existing Gas Analysis Techniques
    2.3 K. Industries Analyzers

3. Marketing

    3.1 Market Characteristics, Competition, Clients and Channels
    3.2 Market Potential
    3.3 Market Penetration and Sales

4. Financial Plan

    4.1 Financial Plan Summary
    4.2 Research and Development
    4.3 Production
    4.4 Employees
    4.5 Marketing
    4.5 Taxes
    4.6 Investment

5. Organization

    5.1 The Company
    5.2 Development Stages

6. Intellectual Property

Appendix 1: Market Data:

    a. Information sources
    b. Preliminary report on the market

    c. A sample of competing manufacturers and prices
    d. Market survey in Europe
    e. Clinical applications

Appendix 2: Financial Data:

    a. Sales Forecast
    b. Cost of Sales
    c. Human Resources
    d. Marketing expense detail
    e. General and Administration detail
    f. Investment in Assets
    g. Investment in R&D
    h. Financing Expenses

Appendix 3: Capitalization and Ownership
Appendix 4: Competitive Analysis

Example 3 - Table of Contents for Bright Idea Inc., a company that developed solar lighting products:

    1. Executive Summary
    2. Product Description
    3. Market Analysis
    4. Summarized Business Strategy
    5. Financial Summary
    6. The Competition
    7. Risks and Contingent Strategies
    8. Team

Appendix 1: Case Studies
Appendix 2: Technical Data
Appendix 3: Testimonials and News items

Example 4 - Table of Contents for Your Choice Inc., a retail business.

    1. Executive Summary

    1.1 Mission
    1.2 Objectives

2. Products

   2.1 Sourcing

   2.2 Unique Technologies

   2.3 Future Plans

3. Competitive Analysis

   3.1 Market Overview

   3.2 Positioning

   3.3 Main Competitors

4. Implementation Strategy

   4.1 Distribution

   4.2 Pricing

   4.3 Marketing

   4.4 Strategic Partnerships

   4.5 Sales Strategy

5. Financial Projections

   5.1 Revenue Forecast

   5.2 Pro forma Reports

7. Human Resources

8. Facilities

Appendix I: Detailed Sales Forecast

Appendix II: Sensitivity Analysis

Index

Boldfaced page numbers indicate primary references.